OPC

RAIL ATLAS
Great Britain
& Ireland

S. K. Baker

10th Edition

An imprint of
Ian Allan Publishing

Glossary of Abbreviations

ABP	Associated British Ports		H.L.	High Level
ARC	Amey Roadstone Co		IE	Iarnrod Eireann (Irish Rail)
ASW	Allied Steel & Wire		Junc.	Junction
BnM	Bord na Mona (Peat Board)		L.L.	Low Level
BSL	Bord Solathair an Leactreachais (Electricity Board)		LUL	London Underground Ltd
			MDHC	Mersey Docks & Harbour Co
BP	British Petroleum		MoD	Ministry of Defence
BPC	Bristol Port Company		MSC	Manchester Ship Canal
C. & W.	Carriage & Wagon		NR	Network Rail
Cal-Mac	Caledonian MacBrayne		OLE	Overhead Line Equipment
C.C.	County Council		P.S.	Power Station
CE	Civil Engineer		PTE	Passenger Transport Executive
C.S.	Carriage Sidings		P.W.	Permanent Way
D.C.	District Council		RPS	Railway Preservation Society
Dist.	Distribution		RPSI	Railway Preservation Society of Ireland
D.P.	Disposal Point (Opencast Coal)		S. & T.	Signal & telegraph
ECC	Imerys (formerly English China Clays International)		SAI	Scottish Agricultural Industries
			T. or Term.	Terminal
EMU	Electric Multiple Unit		Tun.	Tunnel
FLT	Freightliner Terminal			

Publisher's Note

Although situations are constantly changing on the railways of Britain, every effort has been made by the author to ensure complete accuracy of the maps in the book at the time of going to press.

First published 1977
2nd Edition 1978
3rd Edition 1980
4th Edition 1984, Reprinted 1985
5th Edition 1988, Reprinted 1988 and 1989
6th Edition 1990
7th Edition 1992, Reprinted 1995
8th Edition 1996, Reprinted 1998
9th Edition 2001, Reprinted 2001
10th Edition 2004, Reprinted 2005

ISBN (10) 0 86093 576 0
ISBN (13) 978 0 86093 576 6

Published by Oxford Publishing Co

an imprint of Ian Allan Publishing Ltd, Hersham, Surrey KT12 4RG.
Printed by Ian Allan Printing Ltd, Hersham, Surrey KT12 4RG.

Code: 0511/B

Cartography by Maidenhead Cartographics, Berks

Visit the Ian Allan Publishing website at:
www.ianallanpublishing.com

Cover illustrations

Front: No at 334006 Glasgow Central, 11 April 2002.
Back, top: No 37418 at Cardiff Central, 17 January 2002.
Back, centre: Siemens Desiro EMU No 450030.
Back, bottom: 11 August 2003 sees DART EMUs 8309 and 8614 at Dublin Connolly.
All photographs Stuart Baker

Contents

Preface to First Edition

The inspiration for this atlas was two-fold; firstly a feeling of total bewilderment by 'Llans' and 'Abers' on first visiting South Wales four years ago, and secondly a wall railway map drawn by a friend, Martin Bristow. Since then, at university, there has been steady progress in drawing the rail network throughout Great Britain. The author feels sure that this atlas as it has finally evolved will be useful to all with an interest in railways, whether professional or enthusiast. The emphasis is on the current network since it is felt that this information is not published elsewhere.

Throughout, the main aim has been to show clearly, using expanded sheets as necessary, the railways of this country, including the whole of London Transport and the light railways. Passenger lines are distinguished by colour according to the operating company and all freight-only lines are depicted in red. The criterion for a British Rail passenger line has been takes as at least one advertised train per day in each direction. On passenger routes, to assist the traveller, single and multiple track sections with crossing loops on single lines have been shown. Symbols are used to identify both major centres of rail freight, such as collieries and power stations and railway installations such as locomotive depots and works. Secondary information, for example junction names and tunnels over 100 yards long, with lengths if over one mile has been shown

The author would like to express his thanks to members of the Oxford University Railway Society and to Nigel Bird, Chris Hammond and Richard Warson in particular for help in compiling and correcting the maps. His cousin, Dr Tony McCann deserves special thanks for removing much of the tedium by computer sorting the index, as do Oxford City Libraries for providing excellent reference facilities.

June 1977

Preface to Tenth Edition

With this tenth edition and a period of 30 years since the author drew his first railway maps, this popular Rail Atlas can be said to have reached maturity! Over this period, there has been a number of major changes to the publishing arrangements, production methods, style and quality and more detail has been included.

Many external contributions have been received and the author would like to thank everyone who has helped, particular the individual who painstakingly cross checked every index entry against the maps. Further information and comments are always welcome. Please contact me through the publisher: Ian Allan Publishing Ltd, Riverdene Business Park, Molsey Road, Hersham, Surrey KT12 4RG.

It is also an appropriate time to consider what has happened to the network since the first edition in 1977. Most encouragingly, each edition has shown an expanding rail passenger network as well as the implementation of new light rail schemes. This latest edition shows new routes or the reopening of lines in England, Ireland, Scotland and Wales. Conversely, the number of freight terminals has fallen markedly, particularly with the sharp decline in the coal industry. Indeed, if it had not been for the author wanting to understand the complex South Wales freight network serving the many local collieries in the 1970s, this Atlas may never have been published. More recently, there have been some encouraging signs of the rebirth of freight, with several new facilities being brought into service.

Stuart Baker
York
April 2004

KEY TO ATLAS

		Surface	Tunnel	Tube
Passenger Rail Network *(With gauge where other than standard gauge: i.e. 4' 8½" Britain/5' 3" Ireland)*	Multiple Track	————	)----(	———————
	Single Track	+++++++++	++++)+++++(++++	+ + + + + + + +
Municipal/Urban Railways or Irish Peat Railways *(London Underground Ltd lines indicated by code, Irish Peat lines are 3' gauge unless shown)*	Multiple Track	—— C ——	)C—(	— — C — —
	Single Track	——C++++++++	++++)C++++(++++	+ + +C+ + + +
Preserved & Minor Passenger Railways *(With name, and gauge where other than standard gauge)*	Multiple Track	————	)----(	
	Single Track	+++++++++++	++++)+++++(++++	
Freight only lines	No Single/ Multiple Distinction	————	)----(	

Advertised Passenger Station: Saltburn ————•————

Crossing Loop at Passenger Station: Newtown +++++++++✱++++++++++

Crossing Loop on Single Line: *Kincraig* +++++++++✗+++++++++

Unadvertised/Excursion Station: Dunleer* ————•————

Major Power Signal Boxes	PRESTON	Line Ownership Boundaries	NR | LUL
Carriage Sidings	———| C.S.	Power Station	————△
Freight Marshalling Yard	▬▬◣█◢▬▬	Oil Refinery	————●
Freightliner Terminal	———| FLT	Oil Terminal	————○
Locomotive Depot/Stabling Point	▬ BS	Cement Works or Terminal	————■
Railway Works	▨	Quarry	————□
Junction Names	*Haughley Junc.*	Other Freight Terminal	————|
Country Border	▬ ▬ ▬ ▬	Proposed Railway	==========
County Boundary *(PTE Areas, London & Ireland only)*	— · — · —	Colliery (incl. Washery & Opencast site)- UK Coal unless otherwise specified	————▲
Shipping Service	- - - - - - -		

IV

DIAGRAM OF MAPS

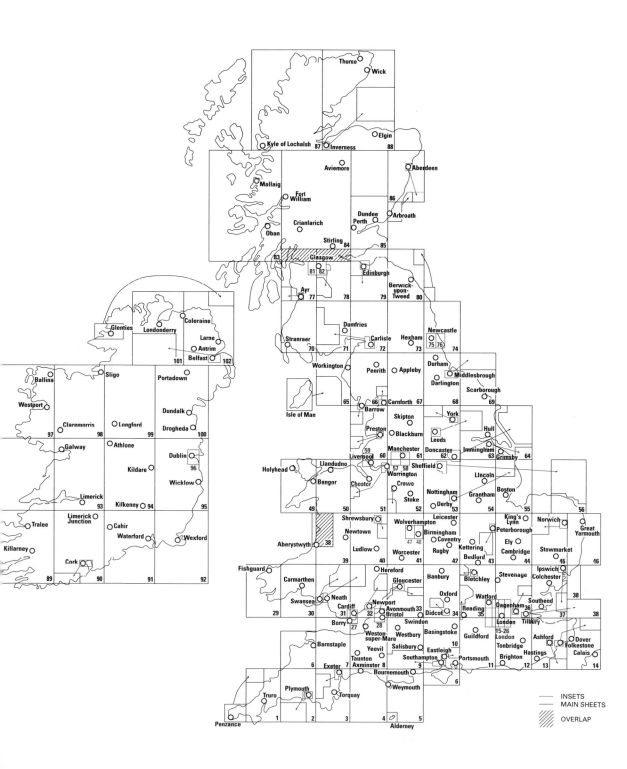

INSETS
MAIN SHEETS
OVERLAP

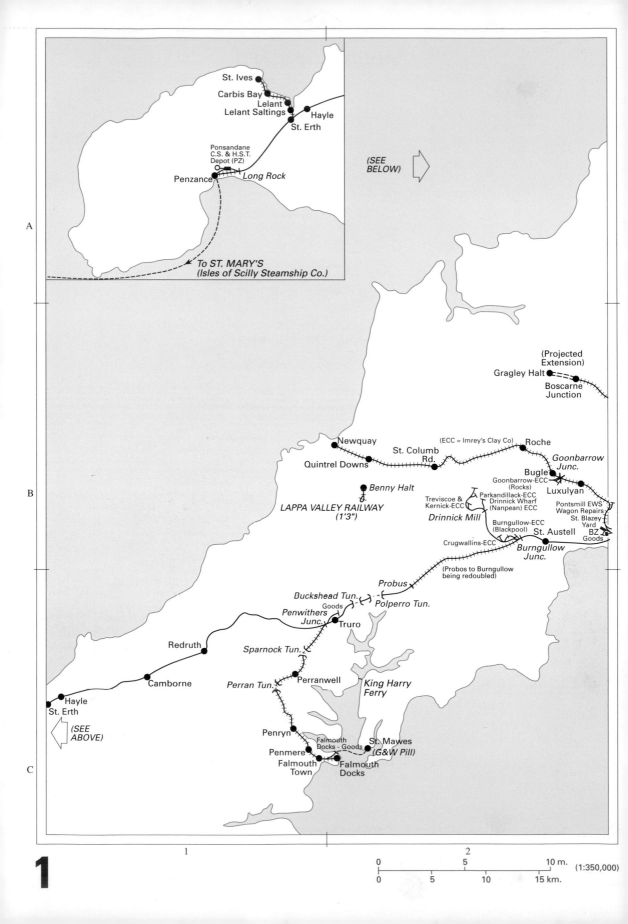

A

St. Ives
Carbis Bay
Lelant
Lelant Saltings
Hayle
St. Erth

Ponsandane
C.S. & H.S.T.
Depot (PZ)
Penzance   Long Rock

(SEE BELOW)

To ST. MARY'S
(Isles of Scilly Steamship Co.)

(Projected
Extension)
Gragley Halt
Boscarne
Junction

(ECC = Imrey's Clay Co)
Newquay   Roche
St. Columb
Quintrel Downs   Rd.   *Goonbarrow*
                                          Junc.
                                         Bugle
• *Benny Halt*   Goonbarrow-ECC
                         (Rocks)
LAPPA VALLEY RAILWAY   Luxulyan
(1'3")   Treviscoe &   Parkandillack-ECC
                   Kernick-ECC   Drinnick Wharf
                                 (Nanpean) ECC   Pontsmill EWS
                   Drinnick Mill   Wagon Repairs
                                 Burngullow-ECC   St. Blazey
                                 (Blackpool)   Yard
                   Crugwallins-ECC   St. Austell BZ
B   Goods
                                      Burngullow
                                      Junc.
                              (Probos to Burngullow
                   Probus   being redoubled)

                   Buckshead Tun.
                              Polperro Tun.
         Penwithers Goods
         Junc.   Truro

         Redruth   *Sparnock Tun.*

                   Perran Tun.
         Camborne   Perranwell   *King Harry*
                                          Ferry
         Hayle
         St. Erth
         (SEE   Penryn
         ABOVE)   Falmouth   St. Mawes
                         Penmere Docks - Goods *(G&W Pill)*
                         Falmouth
C   Town   Falmouth
                                 Docks

1

0   5   10 m.
0   5   10   15 km.
(1:350,000)

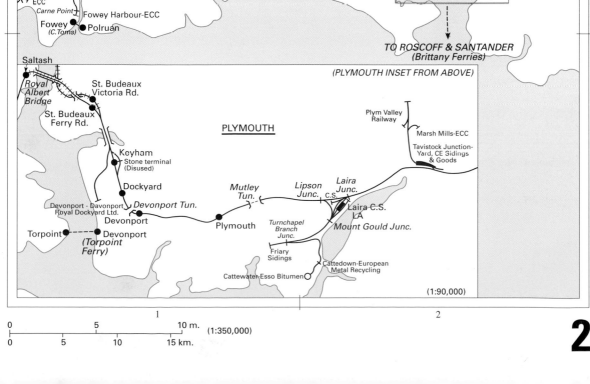

DARTMOOR
RAILWAY

Meldon
Quarry

Meldon Quarry-
Aggregate Industries

A

LAUNCESTON STEAM RAILWAY
(1' 11½")
Newmills   Newchurches
Deer
Park   Launceston

Gunnislake

Calstock

Bere Alston

BODMIN & WENFORD RAILWAY
Bodmin
General
Fitzgerald Lighting (Disused)
Coleslogett Halt   St. Pinnock
Largin Viaduct E.   Moorswater- Blue Circle
Cement Terminal
Liskeard
Bodmin Parkway
Brownqueen Tun.   Coombe
Bere Ferrers

St. Keyne   Menheniot

Lostwithiel
Sidings   Causeland
Ernesettle - MoD
Wivelscombe   Saltash   St. Budeaux
Treverrin   Sandplace   Tun.   Keyham
Tun.   St. Germans   Plymouth
Par   Looe
Par Harbour-
ECC   Dockyard   Devonport
Carne Point   Fowey Harbour-ECC   (SEE INSET BELOW)   B
Fowey   Polruan
(C.Toms)

TO ROSCOFF & SANTANDER
(Brittany Ferries)

Saltash   (PLYMOUTH INSET FROM ABOVE)

Royal   St. Budeaux
Albert   Victoria Rd.
Bridge   Plym Valley
Railway
St. Budeaux   Marsh Mills-ECC
Ferry Rd.   PLYMOUTH   Tavistock Junction-
Yard, CE Sidings
& Goods
Keyham
Stone terminal
(Disused)   Laira Junc.
Dockyard   Mutley   Lipson   C.S.
Devonport - Davonport   Tun.   Junc.
Royal Dockyard Ltd.   Devonport Tun.   Laira C.S.
LA
Devonport   Plymouth   Mount Gould Junc.
Torpoint   Devonport   Turnchapel
(Torpoint   Branch
Ferry)   Junc.
Friary   Cattedown-European
Sidings   Metal Recycling
Cattewater-Esso Bitumen   (1:90,000)   C

3

1   2

0   5   10 m.
0   5   10   15 km.   (1:350,000)   **2**

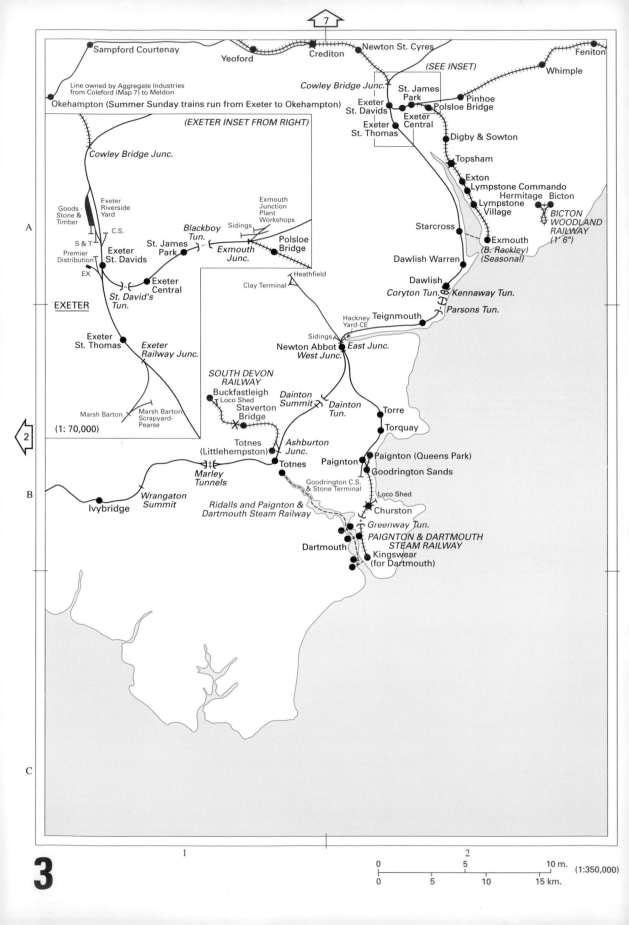

Sampford Courtenay

Yeoford

Crediton

Newton St. Cyres

(SEE INSET)

Feniton

Whimple

Line owned by Aggregate Industries from Coleford (Map 7) to Meldon

Cowley Bridge Junc.

St. James Park

Pinhoe

Okehampton (Summer Sunday trains run from Exeter to Okehampton)

Exeter St. Davids

Polsloe Bridge

Exeter Central

Exeter St. Thomas

Digby & Sowton

(EXETER INSET FROM RIGHT)

Cowley Bridge Junc.

Topsham

Exton

Lympstone Commando

Exmouth Junction Plant Workshops

Hermitage Bicton

Goods - Stone & Timber

Exeter Riverside Yard

Sidings

Lympstone Village

Blackboy Tun.

Polsloe Bridge

BICTON WOODLAND RAILWAY *(1' 6")*

C.S.

St. James Park

Exmouth Junc.

Starcross

Exeter St. Davids

S & T

A

Premier Distribution

Exmouth *(B. Rackley) (Seasonal)*

EX

Exeter Central

Dawlish Warren

St. David's Tun.

Heathfield

Dawlish

EXETER

Clay Terminal

Coryton Tun. *Kennaway Tun.*

Parsons Tun.

Exeter St. Thomas

Exeter Railway Junc.

Hackney Yard-CE

Teignmouth

Sidings

SOUTH DEVON RAILWAY

Newton Abbot *East Junc.*

West Junc.

Buckfastleigh

Loco Shed

Staverton Bridge

Dainton Summit

Dainton Tun.

Torre

Marsh Barton

Marsh Barton Scrapyard-Pearse

(1: 70,000)

Torquay

Totnes (Littlehempston)

Ashburton Junc.

Paignton

Paignton (Queens Park)

Totnes

Goodrington Sands

Marley Tunnels

Goodrington C.S. & Stone Terminal

Loco Shed

Ivybridge

Wrangaton Summit

B

Ridalls and Paignton & Dartmouth Steam Railway

Churston

Greenway Tun.

PAIGNTON & DARTMOUTH STEAM RAILWAY

Dartmouth

Kingswear (for Dartmouth)

C

1

2

0   5   10 m.

(1:350,000)

0   5   10   15 km.

2

8

Axminster

Maiden Newton

SEATON TRAMWAY
(2'9")

Colyton

Cownhayne
Tye Lane

Swan's Nest

Colyford
Axmouth

Riverside

Seaton

Depot

A

5

B

C

1

2

0   5   10 m.
0   5   10   15 km.   (1:350,000)

4

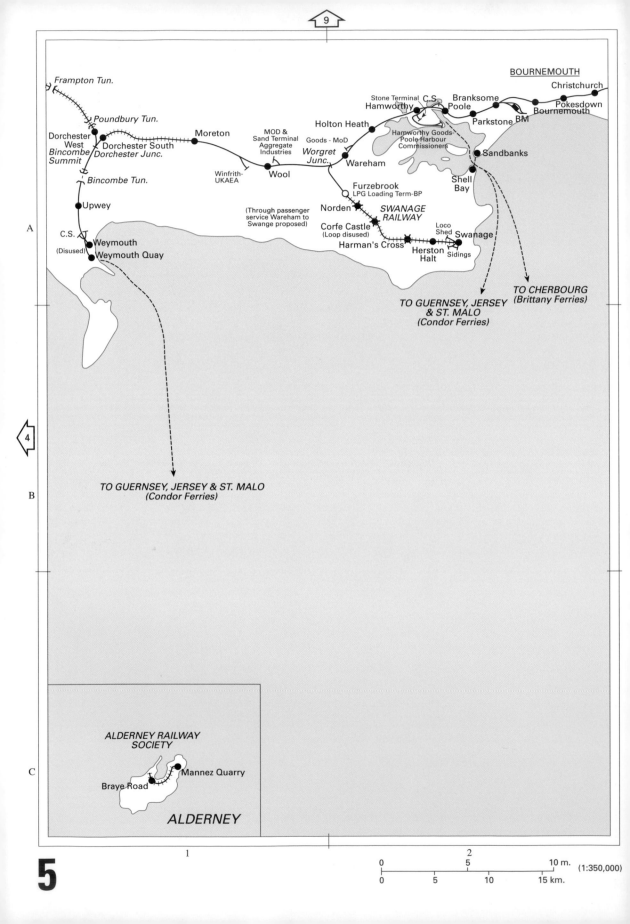

Frampton Tun.

Poundbury Tun.

Moreton

BOURNEMOUTH

Christchurch

Stone Terminal C.S.
Hamworthy

Branksome
Poole

Pokesdown

Bournemouth

Parkstone

BM

Dorchester
West

*Bincombe
Summit*

Dorchester South

Dorchester Junc.

MOD &
Sand Terminal
Aggregate
Industries

Holton Heath

Goods - MoD

Hamworthy Goods
Poole Harbour
Commissioners

Bincombe Tun.

Winfrith-
UKAEA

Wool

*Worgret
Junc.*

Wareham

Sandbanks

Upwey

Furzebrook
LPG Loading Term-BP

Shell
Bay

C.S.

(Disused)

Weymouth

Weymouth Quay

(Through passenger
service Wareham to
Swange proposed)

Norden

*SWANAGE
RAILWAY*

Corfe Castle
(Loop disused)

Loco
Shed

Swanage

Harman's Cross

Herston
Halt

Sidings

**TO GUERNSEY, JERSEY
& ST. MALO**
(Condor Ferries)

TO CHERBOURG
(Brittany Ferries)

A

4

B

TO GUERNSEY, JERSEY & ST. MALO
(Condor Ferries)

C

*ALDERNEY RAILWAY
SOCIETY*

Mannez Quarry

Braye Road

ALDERNEY

5

1

0
0

2
5

5

10

10 m.

15 km.

(1:350,000)

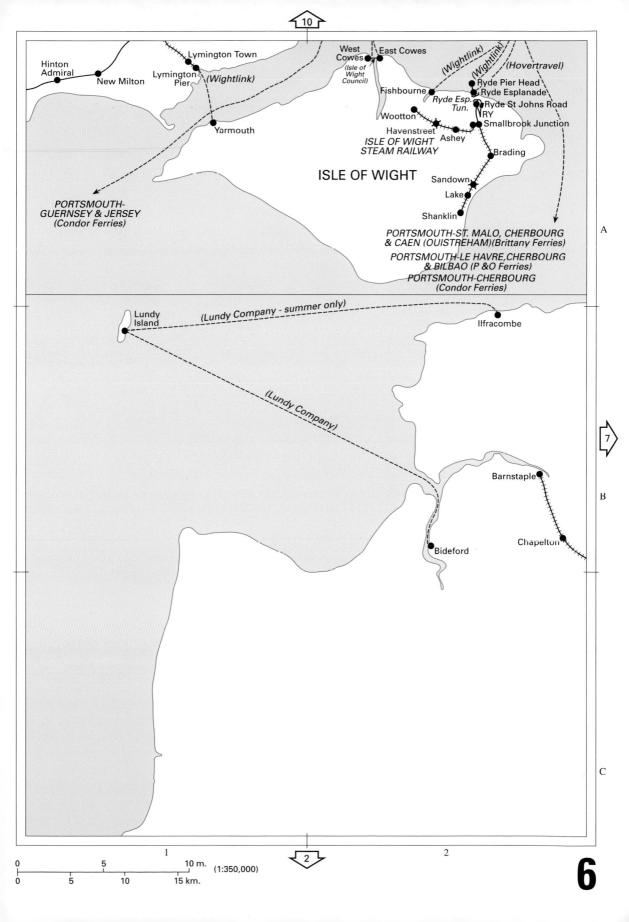

Hinton Admiral

New Milton

Lymington Town

Lymington Pier

(Wightlink)

Yarmouth

West Cowes
(Isle of Wight Council)

East Cowes

(Wightlink)

(Wightlink)

(Hovertravel)

Fishbourne

Ryde Pier Head

Ryde Esplanade

Ryde Esp. Tun.

Ryde St Johns Road

RY

Wootton

Smallbrook Junction

Havenstreet

Ashey

ISLE OF WIGHT STEAM RAILWAY

Brading

ISLE OF WIGHT

Sandown

Lake

Shanklin

PORTSMOUTH- GUERNSEY & JERSEY (Condor Ferries)

PORTSMOUTH-ST. MALO, CHERBOURG & CAEN (OUISTREHAM)(Brittany Ferries)

PORTSMOUTH-LE HAVRE, CHERBOURG & BILBAO (P &O Ferries)

PORTSMOUTH-CHERBOURG (Condor Ferries)

A

(Lundy Company - summer only)

Lundy Island

Ilfracombe

(Lundy Company)

Barnstaple

7

B

Bideford

Chapelton

C

0   5   10 m.

0   5   10   15 km.

(1:350,000)

1

2

2

6

Llantwit Major
(Proposed)

Aberthaw
Sidings

Barry

(Barry-Rhoose-Llantwit Major-
Bridgend to reopen to passengers)

Aberthaw-
National Power

Rhoose
(Proposed)

Barry Island

Lynton 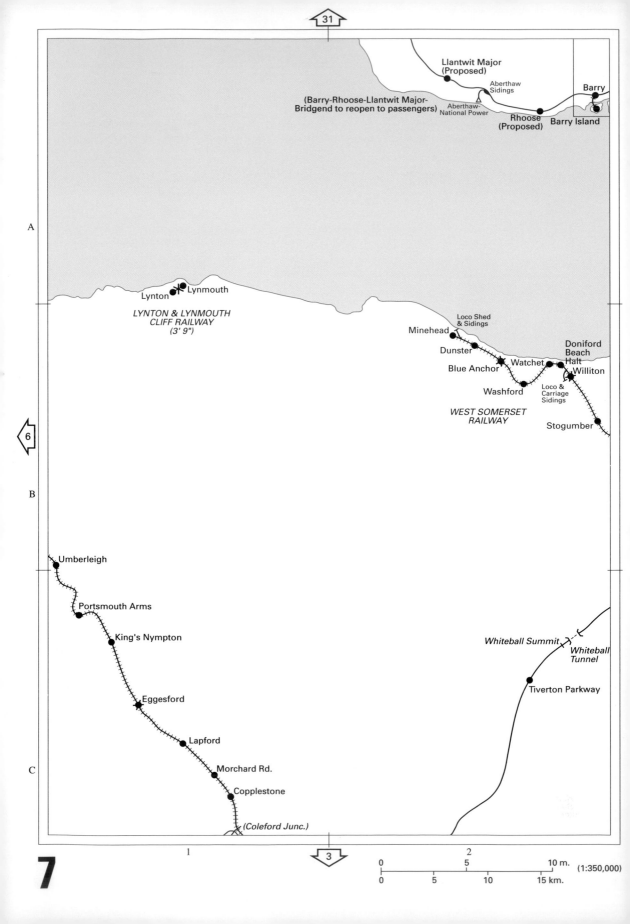 Lynmouth

LYNTON & LYNMOUTH
CLIFF RAILWAY
(3' 9")

Loco Shed
& Sidings

Minehead

Dunster

Doniford
Beach
Halt

Blue Anchor

Watchet

Williton

Washford

Loco &
Carriage
Sidings

WEST SOMERSET
RAILWAY

Stogumber

6

B

Umberleigh

Portsmouth Arms

King's Nympton

Whiteball Summit

Whiteball
Tunnel

Tiverton Parkway

Eggesford

Lapford

Morchard Rd.

C

Copplestone

(Coleford Junc.)

7

1

3

2

0   5   10 m.

0   5   10   15 km.

(1:350,000)

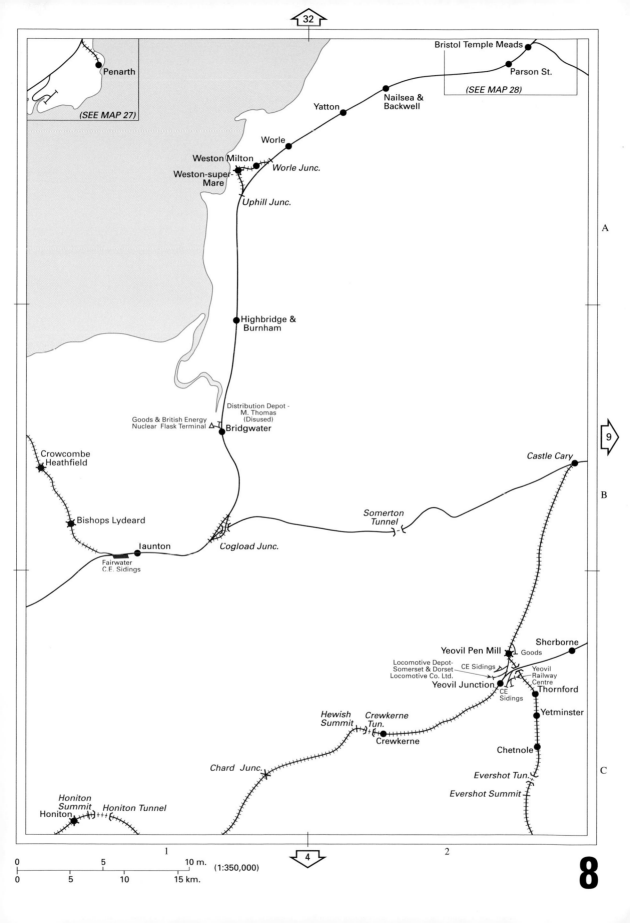

Penarth

(SEE MAP 27)

Bristol Temple Meads

Parson St.

(SEE MAP 28)

Nailsea &
Backwell

Yatton

Worle

Weston Milton

Worle Junc.

Weston-super-
Mare

Uphill Junc.

A

Highbridge &
Burnham

Distribution Depot -
M. Thomas
(Disused)

Goods & British Energy
Nuclear Flask Terminal

Bridgwater

9

Crowcombe
Heathfield

Castle Cary

B

Bishops Lydeard

Somerton
Tunnel

Taunton

Cogload Junc.

Fairwater
C.E. Sidings

Sherborne

Yeovil Pen Mill

Goods

Locomotive Depot-
Somerset & Dorset
Locomotive Co. Ltd.

CE Sidings

Yeovil
Railway
Centre

Yeovil Junction

Thornford

CE
Sidings

Hewish
Summit

Crewkerne
Tun.

Yetminster

Crewkerne

Chetnole

Chard Junc.

Evershot Tun.

C

Evershot Summit

Honiton
Summit

Honiton Tunnel

Honiton

	1			10 m.
0	5			

0   5   10   15 km.

(1:350,000)

AVON VALLEY RAILWAY (BITTON RAILWAY COMPANY)

Oldland Common

Bitton

Avon Riverside

Saltford Tun.

Keynsham

Twerton Long Tun.

Middle Hill Tun.

Box Tun. (1m. 1452yds.)

Bathampton Junc.

Oldfield Park

Thingley-CE Sidings

Thingley Junc.

Melksham

Bath Spa

Waste Term.

Bradford-on-Avon

Freshford

Avoncliff

Bradford Tun.

Bradford South Junc.

Trowbridge

WESTBURY

Pewsey

Radstock (Disused)

(Hapsford to Radstock is proposed for preservation by Somerset & Avon Railway Co.)

Mells Road (Projected)

(disused)

Hapsford (Somerset Quarry Junc.)

Hawkeridge Junc.

Westbury

La farge Cement Wks.

Westbury Yard & CE Yard

Fairwood Junc.

Heywood Road Junc.

Westbury East Loop Junc.

Bedlam Tun.
Great Elm Tun.

Loco & Wagon Depot (WH) Whatley Quarry (West Somerset) -Hanson Aggregates

Frome North Junc.

Frome

Clink Road Junc.

Dilton Marsh

Merryfield

Mendip Lane Vale

Whites Crossing

Merehead-Foster Yeoman

Mendip Rail Depot - (MD)

Blatchbridge Junc.

Warminster

Cranmore

West Cranmore

Merehead Quarry Junc

Witham East Somerset Junc.

EAST SOMERSET RAILWAY

Bruton

Fisherton Sidings

SALISBURY

Quidhampton-ECC

Fisherton SA Tun.

Wilton Junc.

Salisbury

Tunnel Junc.

a
b

Tisbury

a) Laverstock North Junc.
b) Laverstock South Junc.

Gillingham

Buckhorn Weston Tun.

Templecombe

GARTELL LIGHT RAILWAY (2' 0")

St. Denys

Bitterne

Totton

Redbridge

Freightliner Wagon Shops

Sidings

Millbrook FLT

Millbrook Car Terminal

Millbrook

Northam Junc.

Maritime FLT

Stone Loading Terminal-NR

Southampton Central Goods

Southampton Tunnel

Northam EMU Depot-Siemens

Woolston

Southampton Western Docks*

Town Quay

Sholing

Jetty Halt*

Jetties

Mulberry Halt*

Loco Depot

Marchwood-MoD

TO HYTHE (White Horse Ferries)

Car Terminal-STVA

Southampton Eastern Docks*

TO COWES

Ashurst New Forest

(SOUTHAMPTON INSET FROM MAP 10) (1:90,000)

9

1

2

0   5   10 m.
0   5   10   15 km.

(1:350,000)

A

B

C

8

10

Hungerford

Savernake Summit

Bedwyn

Kintbury

Newbury

Thatcham

Aldermaston

Midgham

Newbury Racecourse

Stone Terminal-Foster Yeoman & ARC

Murco

Theale

CE

Padworth- Goodwin Coal Depot & Stone Terminal (Disused)

Mortimer

Bramley

Barton Mill C.S.

Basingstoke Sidings

Basingstoke G.W.R. Junc.

BASINGSTOKE

Worting Junc.

Ludgershall*

Ludgershall (Tidworth)-MoD

Overton

Whitchurch

Litchfield Tun.

Popham No.1 Tun.

Popham No.2 Tun.

(Disused)

Goods

Andover

(Red Post Junc.)

Micheldever

Grateley

Medstead & Four Marks

Wallers Ash Tun.

MID-HANTS RAILWAY

Loco Shed

Alresford

Ropley

(1:90,000)

Allbrook Junc.

Dean

East Grimstead (Dean)-ECC (Disused)

Dunbridge

East Yard

Eastleigh CE Depot

Rail Welding Depot

EASTLEIGH

CE Plant Depot

Shawford

Eastleigh Field Sidings

Eastleigh Works-Alstom (ZG)

Foster Yeoman Stone Terminal

Romsey

Chandlers Ford

Eastleigh

Allbrook Junc.

Sidings

EH

Winchester

Southampton Airport Parkway

Southampton Airport Parkway

(SEE INSET TO RIGHT)

Foster Yeoman Stone Terminal

Botley

Swaythling

St. Denys

Hedge End

1) Southampton Central
2) Millbrook
a) Portcreek Junc.
b) Farlington Junc.
c) Blackfriars Junc.
d) Cosham Junc.

(SEE INSET P. 9)

Totton

Redbridge

2

1

Bitterne

Woolston

Sholling

Bursledon

Swanwick

Tapnage Tun.

PORTSMOUTH

Dks

Ashurst New Forest

Hythe

Netley

Hamble

Fareham No. 2 Tun.

Fareham

Stone Terminal-ARC

Portchester

Cosham

HYTHE PIER RAILWAY (2')

Hamble

Warsash

(Blue Star Boats)

South Hampshire Rapid Transit (Proposed)

Paulsgrove (Proposed)

d

a

b

Beaulieu Road

Fawley-Esso

Gosport Ferry

Hilsea

Brockenhurst

Portsmouth & Southsea

(Lymington Junc.)

Gosport

Portsmouth Hbr.

c

FR

Sway

TO COWES (Red Funnel Ferries)

C.S.Fratton

(Edwards)

Southsea

0   5   10 m.

0   5   10   15 km.

(1:350,000)

1

2

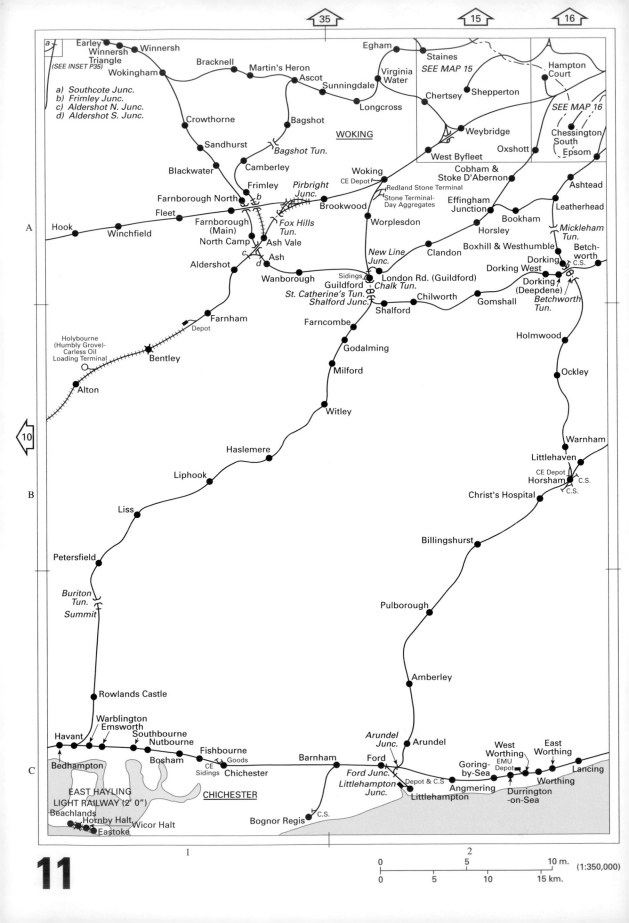

a)
Earley
Winnersh
Triangle
(SEE INSET P35)
Winnersh
Winnersh
Wokingham
Bracknell
Martin's Heron
Ascot
Sunningdale
Egham
Virginia
Water
Longcross
Staines
SEE MAP 15
Chertsey
Shepperton
Weybridge
West Byfleet
Oxshott
Hampton
Court
SEE MAP 16
Chessington
South
Epsom

a) *Southcote Junc.*
b) *Frimley Junc.*
c) *Aldershot N. Junc.*
d) *Aldershot S. Junc.*

Crowthorne
Sandhurst
Bagshot
Bagshot Tun.
WOKING
Blackwater
Camberley
Frimley
Pirbright Junc.
Woking
CE Depot
Cobham &
Stoke D'Abernon
Ashtead
Farnborough North
b
Brookwood
Redland Stone Terminal
Stone Terminal-
Day Aggregates
Effingham
Junction
Leatherhead
Bookham
Mickleham Tun.
Betch-
worth
C.S.
Hook
Winchfield
Fleet
Farnborough
(Main)
North Camp
Ash Vale
Fox Hills Tun.
c
d
Ash
Worplesdon
Horsley
Boxhill & Westhumble
Clandon
New Line Junc.
Dorking
Dorking West
Dorking
(Deepdene)
Betchworth Tun.
A
Aldershot
Wanborough
Sidings
Guildford
Chalk Tun.
London Rd. (Guildford)
Farnham
Depot
St. Catherine's Tun.
Shalford Junc.
Farncombe
Shalford
Chilworth
Gomshall
Holywell
Holmwood
Holybourne
(Humbly Grove)-
Carless Oil
Loading Terminal
Bentley
Godalming
Milford
Ockley
Alton
Witley
Warnham
Littlehaven
CE Depot
Horsham
C.S.
C.S.
Haslemere
Liphook
Christ's Hospital
B
Liss
Billingshurst
Petersfield
Buriton Tun.
Summit
Pulborough
Amberley
Rowlands Castle
Warblington
Emsworth
Southbourne
Nutbourne
Arundel Junc.
Arundel
West
Worthing
East
Worthing
Havant
Bedhampton
Bosham
Fishbourne
Goods
CE
Sidings
Chichester
Barnham
Ford
Ford Junc.
Littlehampton Junc.
Depot & C.S
Littlehampton
Goring-
by-Sea
Angmering
EMU
Depot
Durrington
-on-Sea
Worthing
Lancing
C
CHICHESTER
EAST HAYLING
LIGHT RAILWAY (2' 0")
Beachlands
Hornby Halt
Wicor Halt
Eastoke
Bognor Regis
C.S.

10

1   2   10 m.
0   5   10   (1:350,000)
0   5   10   15 km.

11

Wimbledon
Bromley North
St. Mary Cray
Longfield
Strood Tun.
(1m. 569 yds.)
Bromley South
Bickley
Swanley
Farningham Road
Fawkham Junc. Meopham
Sole Street
Cuxton
West Croydon
Petts Wood
Orpington
C.S.
Eynsford Tun.
Halling
Hayes
Chelsfield
Eynsford
North Downs Tun. (3 km.)
Snodland
East Croydon
Chelsfield Tun.
Shoreham
SEE MAP 17
GREATER LONDON
Knockholt
Otford
Brookgate-Aylesford Newsprint
New Hythe
Sutton
Purley
Riddlesdown
Polhill Tun. (1m. 851yds.)
Otford Junc.
Kemsing
West Malling
East Malling
Aylesford
Banstead
Reedham
SEE MAP 18
Dunton Green
Bat & Ball
Borough Green & Wrotham
2 1 5 c
Upper Warlingham
Sevenoaks
6
Epsom Downs
Kingswood Tun.
3
Coulsdon South
4
Woldingham
Sevenoaks Tun. (1m. 1693yds.)
Wateringbury
8
Tadworth
Caterham
Oxted Tun. (1m. 501yds.)
OXTED
Yalding
Merstham Old Tun. (1m. 71 yds.) *Quarry Tun. (1m. 353 yds.)*
Oxted
Hurst Green Junc. Earlswood
East Peckham CE Tip
Beltring
Merstham
Limpsfield Tun.
Hurst Green
Edenbridge Tun.
Hildenborough
Philips & Whirlpool & Transfesa
Redhill C.S.
Redhill Tun.
Bletchingley Tun.
Godstone
Edenbridge
Leigh West Yard
C.S.
Royal Mail Terminal
Keylands Sidings
Reigate
C.S.
Redhill
Sidings
Nutfield
Godstone Landfill Site
Edenbridge Town
Penshurst
Tonbridge
C.S.
Somerhill Tun.
Paddock Wood
Sidings
Stone Terminal Day Aggregates
Salfords
Lingfield
Hever
Mark Beech Tun.
High Brooms
North Terminal 'Peoplemover'
Horley
Dormans
Cowden
Tunbridge Wells
Wells Tun.
Gatwick Airport
RMC Sand Terminal C.S.
High Rocks Halt Loco Shed
Grove Hill Tun.
Strawberry Hill Tun.
Foster Yeoman Stone Terminal Tarmac Stone Terminal
Crawley New Yard
East Grinstead (PROPOSED EXTENSION)
Blackham Ashurst
Frant
Plant & Voyager Depots
Three Bridges
Kingscote
Groombridge
Tunbridge Wells West (PROPOSED EXTENSION)
Ifield
Crawley
Sidings
Wadhurst
Faygate
Three Bridges CE Depot
Eridge
TUNBRIDGE WELLS & ERIDGE R.P.S. (Spa Valley Railway)
Wadhurst Tun.
Balcombe Tun.
Sharpthorne Tun. (West Hoathy)
BLUEBELL RAILWAY
THREE BRIDGES
Balcombe
Sidings
Horsted Keynes
Crowborough
Crowborough Tun.
Stonegate
Etchingham
Ardingly ARC Stone Terminal
Carriage Shed
Greenhurst
Copyhold Junc.
Haywards Heath
Haywards Heath Tun.
Sheffield Park Loco Shed
Buxted
Mountfield-British Gypsum
Wivelsfield
Uckfield
1) Smitham
Keymer Junc.
Burgess Hill
LAVENDER LINE
Plumpton
Dingley Dell
2) Woodmansterne
3) Chipstead
4) Whyteleafe South
Hassocks
Isfield
5) Kenley
6) Whyteleafe
Clayton Tun. (1m. 499yds.)
Cooksbridge
7) Kingswood
8) Tattenham Corner
Kingston Tun. ↓ *Lewes Tun.*
9) Southwick
Falmer Tun.
Lewes
10) Fishersgate
Patcham Tun.
Preston Park C.S.
Falmer Moulsecoomb
Southerham Junc.
Glynde
Berwick
11) Portslade
12) Aldrington
9 11 12 a BI
London Road (Brighton)
Southease
Polegate
a) Cliftonville Tunnel
10
Hove b
Brighton
Normans Bay
Pevensey Bay
Cooden Beach
Collington
b) Hove Tunnel
c) Stoats Nest Junc.
Shoreham-by-Sea
Aquarium
Marina
Aggregate Loading Term.-Hall Aggregates
Newhaven Town
Newhaven Harbour
Hampden Park
Pevensey & Westham
Peter Pan's Playground & Depot
VOLK'S ELECTRIC RAILWAY (2' 8½")
Newhaven Marine
Bishopstone
Willingdon Junc.
C.S.
TO DIEPPE (Hoverspeed SeaCat - seasonal & Transmanche Ferries)
Seaford
Eastbourne

A

13

B

C

0   5   10 m.
0   5   10   15 km.
(1:350,000)

1   2

12

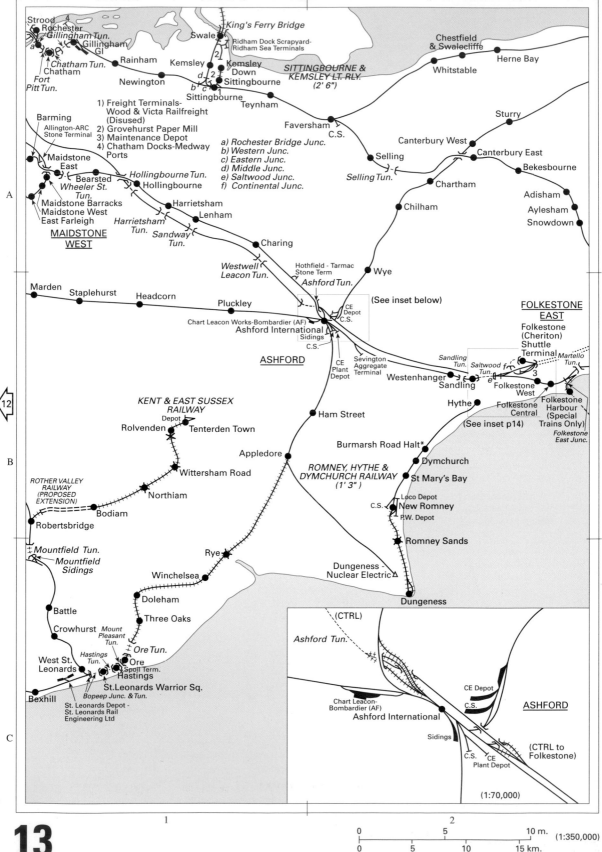

Strood
Rochester
Gillingham Tun.
Gillingham
Gl.
a
Chatham Tun.
Chatham
Fort
Pitt Tun.

Rainham
Newington

Swale
King's Ferry Bridge
Ridham Dock Scrapyard-
Ridham Sea Terminals

Kemsley
d
Kemsley
Down
Sittingbourne
b *c*
Sittingbourne
Teynham

**SITTINGBOURNE &
KEMSLEY LT. RLY.**
(2' 6")

Chestfield
& Swalecliffe
Herne Bay
Whitstable

Sturry

Faversham
C.S.

Canterbury West
Canterbury East
Bekesbourne

Selling
Selling Tun.

Chartham

Adisham
Aylesham
Snowdown

Barming
Allington-ARC
Stone Terminal

Maidstone
East
Bearsted
*Wheeler St.
Tun.*
Hollingbourne Tun.
Hollingbourne

Harrietsham
Lenham

Chilham

Maidstone Barracks
Maidstone West
East Farleigh

**MAIDSTONE
WEST**

*Harrietsham
Tun.*
*Sandway
Tun.*

Charing

1) Freight Terminals-
Wood & Victa Railfreight
(Disused)
2) Grovehurst Paper Mill
3) Maintenance Depot
4) Chatham Docks-Medway
Ports

a) Rochester Bridge Junc.
b) Western Junc.
c) Eastern Junc.
d) Middle Junc.
e) Saltwood Junc.
f) Continental Junc.

A

Marden
Staplehurst
Headcorn
Pluckley

*Westwell
Leacon Tun.*

Hothfield - Tarmac
Stone Term
Ashford Tun.

Wye

(See inset below)

CE
Depot
C.S.

**FOLKESTONE
EAST**
Folkestone
(Cheriton)
Shuttle
Terminal
*Martello
Tun.*

Chart Leacon Works-Bombardier (AF)
Ashford International
Sidings

ASHFORD

CE
Plant
Depot

Sevington
Aggregate
Terminal
Westenhanger

*Sandling
Tun.*
*Saltwood
Tun.*
e
f
3

Sandling

Folkestone
West
Folkestone
Central

Folkestone
Harbour
(Special
Trains Only)

*Folkestone
East Junc.*

C.S.

Hythe

(See inset p14)

**KENT & EAST SUSSEX
RAILWAY**
Depot
Rolvenden
Tenterden Town

Ham Street

Burmarsh Road Halt*

Dymchurch
St Mary's Bay

12

B

Appledore

**ROMNEY, HYTHE &
DYMCHURCH RAILWAY**
(1' 3")

*ROTHER VALLEY
RAILWAY
(PROPOSED
EXTENSION)*

Wittersham Road

Northiam

Bodiam
Robertsbridge

Mountfield Tun.
*Mountfield
Sidings*

Rye

Loco Depot
C.S.
New Romney
P.W. Depot

Romney Sands

Dungeness -
Nuclear Electric

Winchelsea

Battle

Doleham

Three Oaks

Crowhurst
*Mount
Pleasant
Tun.*
Ore Tun.

Dungeness

West St.
Leonards
*Hastings
Tun.*
Ore
Spoil Term.
Hastings
St.Leonards Warrior Sq.

Bexhill
Bopeep Junc. & Tun.
St. Leonards Depot -
St. Leonards Rail
Engineering Ltd

C

(CTRL)

Ashford Tun.

CE Depot
C.S.

ASHFORD

Chart Leacon-
Bombardier (AF)
Ashford International

Sidings

C.S.
CE
Plant Depot

(CTRL to
Folkestone)

(1:70,000)

13

1

2

0   5   10 m.
0   5   10   15 km.

(1:350,000)

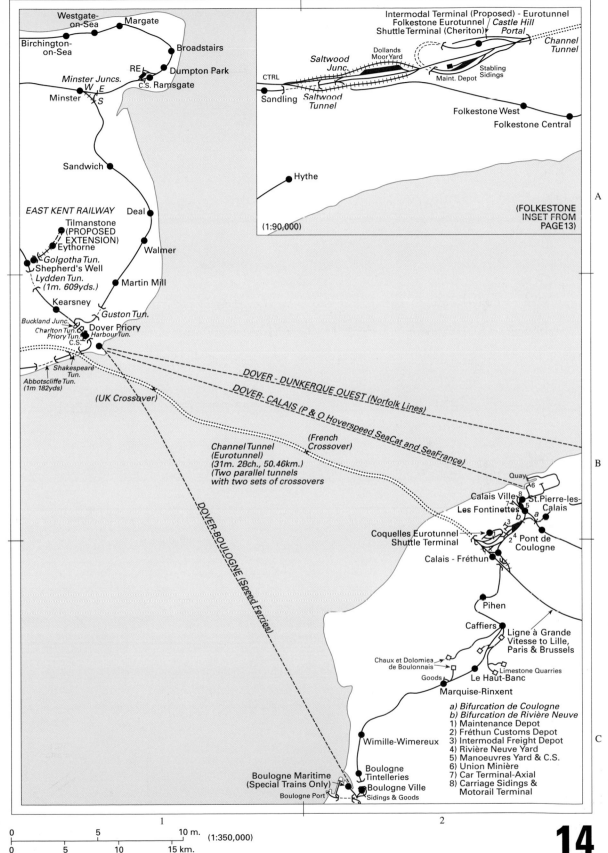

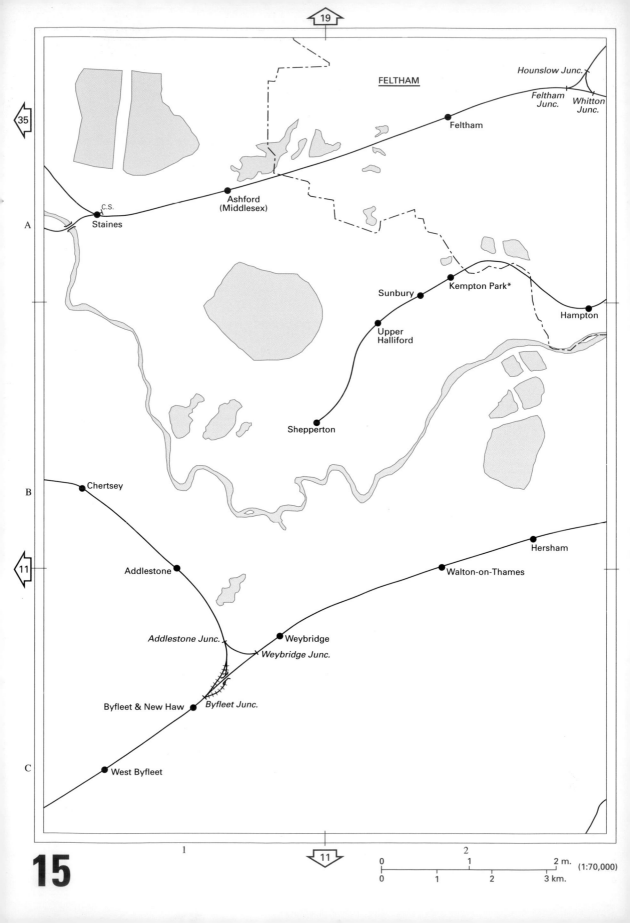

19

35

FELTHAM

Hounslow Junc.

Feltham Junc. *Whitton Junc.*

Feltham

A

C.S.

Staines

Ashford
(Middlesex)

Sunbury

Kempton Park*

Hampton

Upper
Halliford

Shepperton

B

Chertsey

Hersham

11

Addlestone

Walton-on-Thames

Addlestone Junc.

Weybridge

Weybridge Junc.

Byfleet & New Haw

Byfleet Junc.

C

West Byfleet

15

1

11

2

0   1   2 m.

0   1   2   3 km.

(1:70,000)

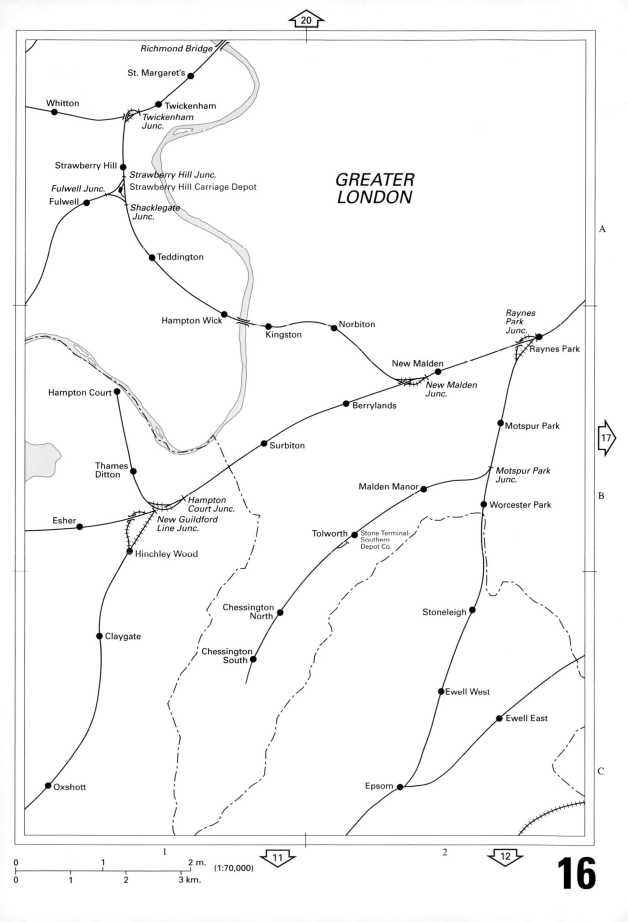

Richmond Bridge

St. Margaret's

Whitton

Twickenham
*Twickenham
Junc.*

Strawberry Hill

Strawberry Hill Junc.
Strawberry Hill Carriage Depot

Fulwell Junc.
Fulwell

*Shacklegate
Junc.*

Teddington

*GREATER
LONDON*

A

Hampton Wick

Kingston

Norbiton

*Raynes
Park
Junc.*

Raynes Park

New Malden

*New Malden
Junc.*

Hampton Court

Berrylands

Motspur Park

17

Surbiton

B

Thames
Ditton

Malden Manor

*Motspur Park
Junc.*

Esher

*Hampton
Court Junc.*
New Guildford
Line Junc.

Worcester Park

Tolworth
Stone Terminal-
Southern
Depot Co.

Hinchley Wood

Chessington
North

Stoneleigh

Claygate

Chessington
South

Ewell West

Ewell East

C

Oxshott

Epsom

0		1		2 m.	(1:70,000)
0	1	2	3 km.		

16

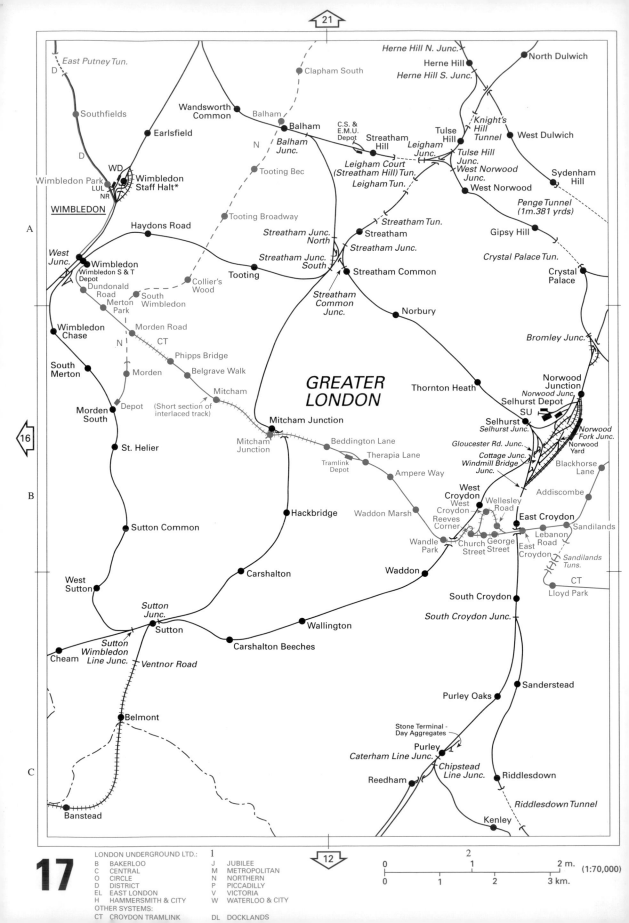

East Putney Tun.

D

Southfields

Wandsworth Common

Balham

Clapham South

Herne Hill N. Junc.

Herne Hill

North Dulwich

Herne Hill S. Junc.

Earlsfield

Balham

Balham Junc.

C.S. & E.M.U. Depot

Streatham Hill

Tulse Hill

Knight's Hill Tunnel

West Dulwich

N

Leigham Junc.

Tulse Hill Junc.

D

WD

Wimbledon Park

Wimbledon Staff Halt*

LUL

NR

WIMBLEDON

Tooting Bec

Leigham Court (Streatham Hill) Tun.

Leigham Tun.

West Norwood Junc.

West Norwood

Sydenham Hill

Tooting Broadway

Penge Tunnel (1m.381 yrds)

A

Haydons Road

Streatham Junc. North

Streatham

Streatham Tun.

Gipsy Hill

West Junc.

Wimbledon

Wimbledon S & T Depot

Streatham Junc. South

Tooting

Streatham Junc.

Crystal Palace Tun.

Crystal Palace

Collier's Wood

Dundonald Road

South Wimbledon

Merton Park

Streatham Common

Streatham Common Junc.

Wimbledon Chase

Morden Road

N

CT

Norbury

Bromley Junc.

South Merton

Phipps Bridge

Belgrave Walk

GREATER LONDON

Thornton Heath

Norwood Junction

Norwood Junc.

Selhurst Depot

Morden

Mitcham

Morden South

Depot

(Short section of interlaced track)

Mitcham Junction

Beddington Lane

Therapia Lane

SU

Selhurst

Selhurst Junc.

Norwood Fork Junc.

Norwood Yard

St. Helier

Mitcham Junction

Tramlink Depot

Ampere Way

Gloucester Rd. Junc.

Cottage Junc.

Windmill Bridge Junc.

Blackhorse Lane

B

Sutton Common

Hackbridge

Waddon Marsh

West Croydon

West Croydon

Wellesley Road

Addiscombe

Wandle Park

Reeves Corner

Church Street

George Street

East Croydon

East Croydon

Lebanon Road

Sandilands

West Sutton

Carshalton

Waddon

Sandilands Tuns.

CT

Lloyd Park

South Croydon

South Croydon Junc.

Wallington

Sutton Junc.

Sutton

Carshalton Beeches

Cheam

Sutton Wimbledon Line Junc.

Ventnor Road

Sanderstead

Purley Oaks

Belmont

Stone Terminal - Day Aggregates

Purley

Caterham Line Junc.

Chipstead Line Junc.

Riddlesdown

C

Reedham

Riddlesdown Tunnel

Banstead

Kenley

16

17

LONDON UNDERGROUND LTD.:

B	BAKERLOO	J	JUBILEE
C	CENTRAL	M	METROPOLITAN
O	CIRCLE	N	NORTHERN
D	DISTRICT	P	PICCADILLY
EL	EAST LONDON	V	VICTORIA
H	HAMMERSMITH & C'Y	W	WATERLOO & CITY

OTHER SYSTEMS:

CT CROYDON TRAMLINK

DL DOCKLANDS

0   1   2 m.

0   1   2   3 km.

(1:70,000)

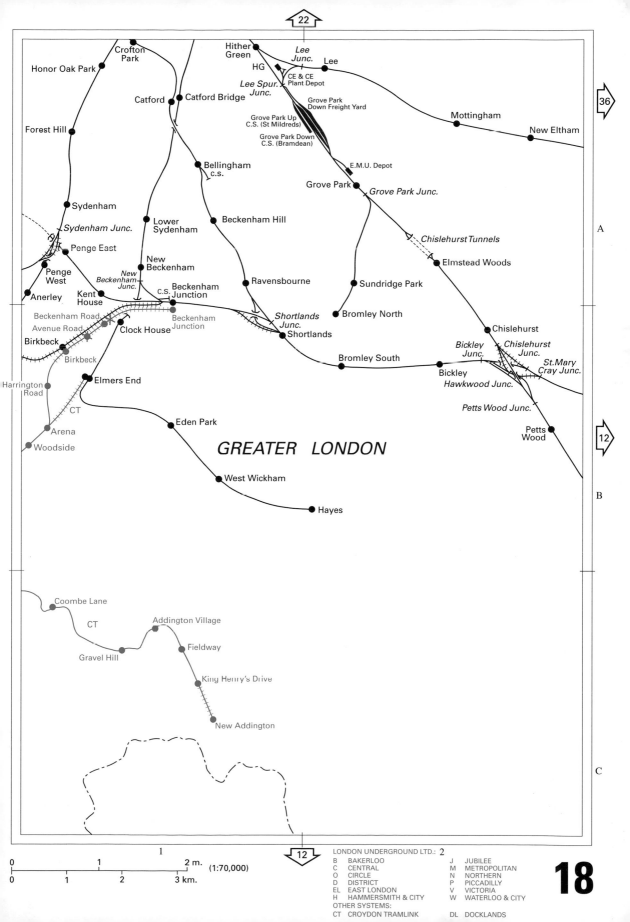

Hither
Green

*Lee
Junc.*

Lee

HG

CE & CE
Plant Depot

*Lee Spur.
Junc.*

Crofton
Park

Honor Oak Park

Catford

Catford Bridge

Grove Park
Down Freight Yard

Mottingham

New Eltham

Grove Park Up
C.S. (St Mildreds)

Grove Park Down
C.S. (Bramdean)

Forest Hill

E.M.U. Depot

Bellingham
c.s.

Grove Park

Grove Park Junc.

Sydenham

Sydenham Junc.

Lower
Sydenham

Beckenham Hill

Penge East

New
Beckenham

*New
Beckenham
Junc.*

C.S.

Beckenham
Junction

Ravensbourne

Chislehurst Tunnels

Elmstead Woods

Sundridge Park

Penge
West

Anerley

Kent
House

Beckenham Road

Avenue Road

Birkbeck

Clock House

*Beckenham
Junction*

*Shortlands
Junc.*

Shortlands

Bromley North

Chislehurst

*Bickley
Junc.*

*Chislehurst
Junc.*

Birkbeck

Harrington
Road

CT

Elmers End

Bromley South

Bickley

Hawkwood Junc.

*St.Mary
Cray Junc.*

Arena

Woodside

Eden Park

GREATER LONDON

Petts Wood Junc.

Petts
Wood

West Wickham

Hayes

Coombe Lane

CT

Addington Village

Fieldway

Gravel Hill

King Henry's Drive

New Addington

A

36

A

B

12

B

C

0   1   2 m.   (1:70,000)

0   1   2   3 km.

1

LONDON UNDERGROUND LTD.: 2
B   BAKERLOO   J   JUBILEE
C   CENTRAL   M   METROPOLITAN
O   CIRCLE   N   NORTHERN
D   DISTRICT   P   PICCADILLY
EL   EAST LONDON   V   VICTORIA
H   HAMMERSMITH & CITY   W   WATERLOO & CITY
OTHER SYSTEMS:
CT   CROYDON TRAMLINK   DL   DOCKLANDS

18

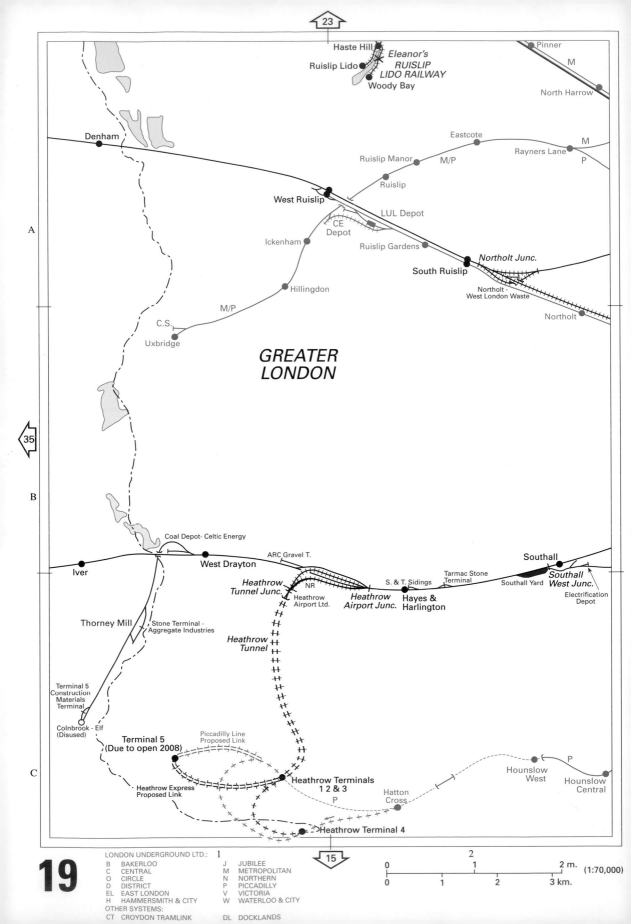

Haste Hill
Ruislip Lido
Eleanor's
RUISLIP
LIDO RAILWAY
Woody Bay

Pinner
M
North Harrow

Denham

Eastcote
Ruislip Manor
M/P
Rayners Lane
M
P

Ruislip

West Ruislip

LUL Depot

CE
Depot

Ickenham

Ruislip Gardens
South Ruislip
Northolt Junc.

Northolt -
West London Waste

Northolt

Hillingdon

A

M/P

C.S.
Uxbridge

**GREATER
LONDON**

35

B

Coal Depot- Celtic Energy

ARC Gravel T.

Southall

Iver
West Drayton

*Heathrow
Tunnel Junc.*
NR
Heathrow
Airport Ltd.
*Heathrow
Airport Junc.*
Hayes &
Harlington

S. & T. Sidings
Tarmac Stone
Terminal
Southall Yard
*Southall
West Junc.*

Electrification
Depot

Thorney Mill
Stone Terminal -
Aggregate Industries

*Heathrow
Tunnel*

Terminal 5
Construction
Materials
Terminal

Colnbrook - Elf
(Disused)

Terminal 5
(Due to open 2008)

Piccadilly Line
Proposed Link

Heathrow Terminals
1 2 & 3
P

Hatton
Cross
P

Hounslow
West
P
Hounslow
Central

C

Heathrow Express
Proposed Link

Heathrow Terminal 4

19

2
0   1   2 m.
0   1   2   3 km.
(1:70,000)

Harrow & Wealdstone

B

M

Harrow North Junc.

Harrow-on-the-Hill

West Harrow

LUL NR

Kenton

Northwick Park

M

Kingsbury

J

(Possible route for Crossrail to Aylesbury line trains shown at *)

a) Willesden H.L. Junc.
b) West London Junc.
c) Old Oak West Junc.
d) Cricklewood Curve Junc.
e) Mitre Bridge Junc.

1) Willesden S.W. Sidings - CE
2) Scrapyard - Mayer Parry Recycling
3) Brent Waste Terminal (Hendon) Shanks & McEwan
4) Acton - Foster Yeoman Stone Terminal
5) Willesden - FLT & Euroterminal
6) CE Yard
7) Heathrow Express Depot

Silkstream Junc.

Burroughs Tun.

Hendon Central

Hendon

Brent Cross

Cricklewood Freight Depot-Victoria Railfreight Sidings

Brent Curve Junc.

13

Cricklewood

d

A

Preston Road

M

Dudding Hill Junc.

South Kenton

J/M

Depot

Wembley Park

Neasden Depot

Neasden

Dollis Hill

Willesden Green

J/M

South Harrow Sidings

Sudbury Hill Harrow

North Wembley

Sudbury & Harrow Road

Wembley Stadium

Wembley DMU Depot

Neasden Freight Term. Tibbett & Britten

*

Neasden Junc.

Northolt Park

South Harrow Tun.

Sudbury Hill

Wembley Central

Sidings

Wembley Heavy Repair Shops

Neasden Junc. Stone Terminal-Aggregate Industries

Neasden Junc.

WILLESDEN JUNC. (WEMBLEY) (MAIN LINES)

Sudbury Town

P

B

LUL Depot

Stonebridge Park

WILLESDEN (LOCAL LINES)

Reversing Siding

Wembley InterCity Carriage Depot (WB)

Harlesden

Greenford W. Junc.

E. Junc.

Greenford

LTE Bay Junc. South Junc.

Wembley European Freight Yard

Willesden Royal Mail Terminal

Sudbury Junc.

Willesden 'F' Sidings- 'Virtual Quarry'

Willesden Brent Yard

MG Gas Products

Willesden Junc.

Kensal Green Junc.

WN

Kensal Rise

Kensal Green

South Greenford

Perivale

C

Hanger Lane

Park Royal-Guinness (Disused)

Stone Term.- Marcon Topmix

Acton Canal Wharf Junc.

North Acton Junc.

*

5

1

a

b

6

OC

e

Kensal Green Tuns.

Maintenance Depot

Castle Bar Park

Castle Bar Tunnel

Drayton Green Junc.

North Ealing

West Acton

Park Royal

Park Royal Branch Junc.

Acton Wells Junc.

North Acton

OO

7

c

North Pole Junc.

North Pole Servicing Depot (European Services) (NP)

White City (Proposed)

Latimer Road

B

Drayton Green

Hanwell

CE Sidings

Plasser Wks.

Ealing Broadway

D

Hanger Lane Junc.

C

Acton Yard

4

East Acton

Acton Main Line

Acton East Junc.

C

White City

H

White City LUL Depot

Shepherd's Bush

Hanwell Junc.

West Ealing Junc.

West Ealing

Ealing Common

P/D

LUL Depot

Acton Central

Shepherd's Bush

Goldhawk Road

Depot

South Ealing

P

Northfields

Depot

Boston Manor

Acton Town North Junc.

Acton Town

LUL Acton Works

South Acton

South Acton Junc.

Stamford Brook

H

Ravenscourt Park

P/D

P/D

Hammersmith

Osterley

Stone Term. - Aggregate Industries

Old Kew Junc.

Kew Bridge

New Kew Junc.

Gunnersbury Junc.

NR

LUL

Gunnersbury

Chiswick Park

Turnham Green

Bedford Park Junc.

Brentford Goods

Brentford

Waste Terminal West London Waste

Kew Bridge

D

Syon Lane

Chiswick

Kew Gardens

Hounslow East

P

Isleworth

Barnes Bridge

Barnes Bridge

C

Hounslow

Richmond

North Sheen

Mortlake

Barnes Junc.

Barnes

Putney

0   1   2 m.   (1:70,000)
0   1   2   3 km.

21

C

LONDON UNDERGROUND LTD.: 2

B   BAKERLOO
C   CENTRAL
O   CIRCLE
D   DISTRICT
EL EAST LONDON
H   HAMMERSMITH & CITY
OTHER SYSTEMS:
CT CROYDON TRAMLINK

J   JUBILEE
M   METROPOLITAN
N   NORTHERN
P   PICCADILLY
V   VICTORIA
W   WATERLOO & CITY
DL DOCKLANDS

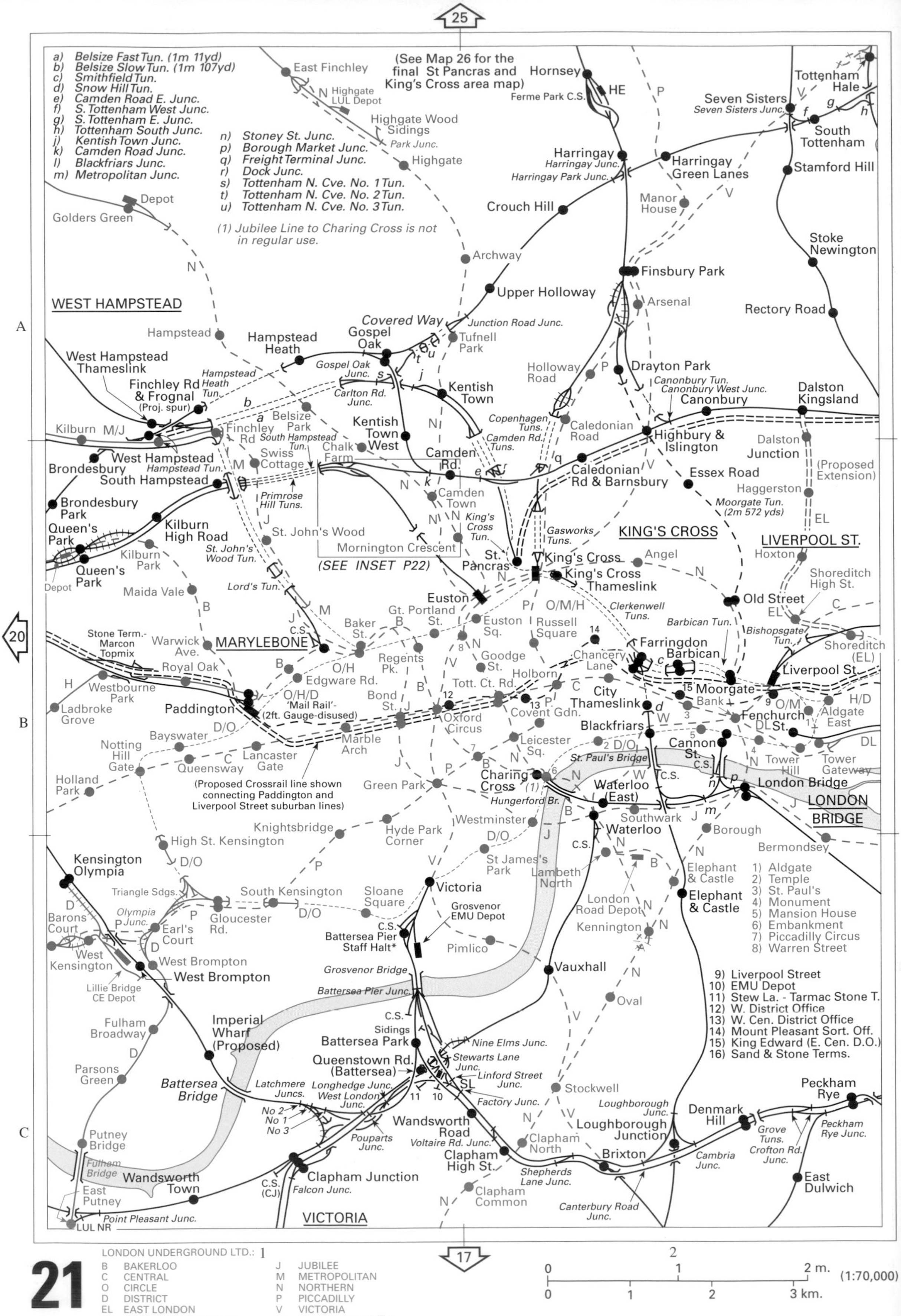

a) Belsize Fast Tun. (1m 11yd)
b) Belsize Slow Tun. (1m 107yd)
c) Smithfield Tun.
d) Snow Hill Tun.
e) Camden Road E. Junc.
f) S. Tottenham West Junc.
g) S. Tottenham E. Junc.
h) Tottenham South Junc.
j) Kentish Town Junc.
k) Camden Road Junc.
l) Blackfriars Junc.
m) Metropolitan Junc.

n) Stoney St. Junc.
p) Borough Market Junc.
q) Freight Terminal Junc.
r) Dock Junc.
s) Tottenham N. Cve. No. 1 Tun.
t) Tottenham N. Cve. No. 2 Tun.
u) Tottenham N. Cve. No. 3 Tun.

(1) Jubilee Line to Charing Cross is not
in regular use.

(See Map 26 for the
final St Pancras and
King's Cross area map)

Map labels (stations & junctions):

East Finchley, Highgate LUL Depot, Highgate Wood Sidings, Park Junc., Highgate, Hornsey, HE, Ferme Park C.S., Seven Sisters, Seven Sisters Junc., Tottenham Hale, South Tottenham, Stamford Hill, Harringay, Harringay Junc., Harringay Park Junc., Harringay Green Lanes, Crouch Hill, Manor House, Stoke Newington, Rectory Road, Archway, Finsbury Park, Upper Holloway, Arsenal, Drayton Park, Dalston Kingsland, Golders Green, Depot, WEST HAMPSTEAD, Hampstead, Hampstead Heath, Covered Way, Gospel Oak, Junction Road Junc., Tufnell Park, Holloway Road, Canonbury Tun., Canonbury West Junc., Canonbury, Highbury & Islington, Dalston Junction, (Proposed Extension), West Hampstead Thameslink, Finchley Rd & Frognal (Proj. spur), Hampstead Heath Tun., Gospel Oak Junc., Carlton Rd. Junc., Kentish Town, Kentish Town West, Copenhagen Tun., Camden Rd. Tuns., Caledonian Road, Caledonian Rd & Barnsbury, Essex Road, Haggerston, EL, Kilburn M/J, Belsize Park, South Hampstead Tun., Chalk Farm, Camden Rd., Brondesbury, West Hampstead, Hampstead Tun., Swiss Cottage, Primrose Hill Tuns., Camden Town, King's Cross Tun., Gasworks Tuns., KING'S CROSS, Moorgate Tun. (2m 572 yds), Dalston, LIVERPOOL ST., Hoxton, Brondesbury Park, Queen's Park, South Hampstead, Kilburn High Road, St. John's Wood Tun., St. John's Wood, Mornington Crescent, (SEE INSET P22), St. Pancras, King's Cross, King's Cross Thameslink, Angel, Shoreditch High St., Queen's Park, Depot, Kilburn Park, Maida Vale, Lord's Tun., Euston, Gt. Portland St., Euston Sq., Russell Square, Clerkenwell Tuns., Barbican Tun., Old Street, EL, Bishopsgate Tun., Shoreditch (EL), Stone Term.-Marcon Topmix, Warwick Ave., MARYLEBONE, C.S., Baker St., Regents Pk., Goodge St., Holborn, Chancery Lane, Farringdon, Barbican, Moorgate, Liverpool St., Royal Oak, Edgware Rd., Bond St., Tott. Ct. Rd., City Thameslink, Bank, Fenchurch St., Aldgate East, DL, Westbourne Park, O/H/D 'Mail Rail' (2ft. Gauge-disused), Oxford Circus, Covent Gdn., Blackfriars, Cannon St., Tower Hill, Tower Gateway, Ladbroke Grove, Paddington, Bayswater, Marble Arch, Leicester Sq., St. Paul's Bridge, Waterloo (East), London Bridge, LONDON BRIDGE, Notting Hill Gate, Lancaster Gate, Queensway, Green Park, Charing Cross (1), Hungerford Br., Southwark, Holland Park, High St. Kensington, Knightsbridge, Hyde Park Corner, Westminster, Waterloo, Borough, Bermondsey, (Proposed Crossrail line shown connecting Paddington and Liverpool Street suburban lines), St James's Park, Lambeth North, Kensington Olympia, Triangle Sdgs., South Kensington, Sloane Square, Victoria, Elephant & Castle, London Road Depot, Barons Court, Olympia Junc., Earl's Court, Gloucester Rd., Grosvenor EMU Depot, Pimlico, Kennington, West Kensington, West Brompton, Battersea Pier Staff Halt*, Vauxhall, Oval, Peckham Rye, Lillie Bridge CE Depot, Fulham Broadway, Grosvenor Bridge, Battersea Pier Junc., Imperial Wharf (Proposed), Battersea Park, Queenstown Rd. (Battersea), SL, Nine Elms Junc., Stewarts Lane Junc., Linford Street Junc., Stockwell, Loughborough Junc., Denmark Hill, Parsons Green, Battersea Bridge, Latchmere Juncs., No 2, No 1, No 3, Longhedge Junc., West London Junc., Pouparts Junc., Wandsworth Road, Voltaire Rd. Junc., Factory Junc., Clapham North, Loughborough Junction, Brixton, Cambria Junc., Grove Tuns., Crofton Rd. Junc., Peckham Rye Junc., Putney Bridge, Fulham Bridge, East Putney, Point Pleasant Junc., LUL NR, Wandsworth Town, C.S. (CJ), Falcon Junc., Clapham Junction, Clapham High St., Shepherds Lane Junc., VICTORIA, Clapham Common, Canterbury Road Junc., East Dulwich

Numbered list:

1) Aldgate
2) Temple
3) St. Paul's
4) Monument
5) Mansion House
6) Embankment
7) Piccadilly Circus
8) Warren Street
9) Liverpool Street
10) EMU Depot
11) Stew La. - Tarmac Stone T.
12) W. District Office
13) W. Cen. District Office
14) Mount Pleasant Sort. Off.
15) King Edward (E. Cen. D.O.)
16) Sand & Stone Terms.

21

LONDON UNDERGROUND LTD.:
B   BAKERLOO
C   CENTRAL
O   CIRCLE
D   DISTRICT
EL EAST LONDON
H   HAMMERSMITH & CITY
J   JUBILEE
M   METROPOLITAN
N   NORTHERN
P   PICCADILLY
V   VICTORIA
W   WATERLOO & CITY
OTHER SYSTEMS:
CT CROYDON TRAMLINK
DL DOCKLANDS

0   1   2 m.
0   1   2   3 km.
(1:70,000)

Blackhorse Rd.
Wood St.
Barkingside
St James Street
Walthamstow Central
Walthamstow Queens Road
C
Snaresbrook
Redbridge
Newbury Park
Copper Mill Junc.
Wanstead
Gants Hill
C
Leyton Midland Road
Clapton Junc.
Leytonstone

GREATER LONDON

Leytonstone High Road
ZI
IL
Clapton
(Eurostar Depot to be built on Temple Mills C E Sidings)
Ilford
Clapton Tun.
SF
Temple Mills C E Sidings
Leyton
Forest Gate Junc.
Aldersbrook C.S.
Queens Road Tun.
Hackney Downs N. Junc.
Wanstead Park
Manor Park
A
Hackney Downs   Homerton
Temple Mills E. Junc.
(Connection for empty stock)
Forest Gate
Woodgrange Park
High Meads Junc.
Maryland
Woodgrange Park Junc.
Barking Stn. Junc.
EM
Barking
b
Hackney Central
Reading Lane Junc.
Hackney Wick
Lea Junc.
Stratford
(Tunnel: 20km with open section for Stratford station under construction)
East Ham
H/D
C.S.
London Fields
Thornton Fields C.S.
c   g
a   d
h
J
Stratford Market Depot
Upton Park
Barking Tilbury Line Junc. West
Barking Tilbury Line Junc. East
Cambridge Heath
Bow Midland Waste
Bow Goods
Stone Terminal-Aggregate Industries
Bow Junc.
Pudding Mill Lane
Plaistow
(Under construction)
Bethnal Green
C
Bethnal Green E. Junc.
Bow Rd.
DL
West Ham
a) Carpenters Rd. N. Junc.
b) Navarino Rd. Junc.
c) Channelsea N. Junc.
d) Stratford Central Junc.
e) Charlton Junc.
f) South Bermondsey Junc.
g) Channelsea S. Junc.
h) Carpenters Road S. Junc.
H/D
Mile End
Bow Church
West Ham
Bethnal Green
Stepney Green
Gas Factory Junc.
Bromley-by-Bow
J
36
Whitechapel
Eastern District Office
Devons Road
DL
Langdon Park (Proposed)
DL
Canning Town
Beckton
DL
(Proposed Extension)
B
Limehouse
DL
Shadwell
All Saints
Siding
Poplar Maintenance Depot
East India
Custom House
Royal Victoria
Prince Regent
Royal Albert
Beckton Park
Beckton Depot
EL
Westferry
West India Quay
Poplar   Blackwall
Custom House
DL
Cyprus
Gallions Reach
Wapping
Canary Wharf
West Silvertown
Silvertown Tun.
London City Airport
Rotherhithe
J
Heron Quays
North Greenwich
J
Pontoon Dock
DL
King George V
South Quay
(Under construction to King George V)
Silvertown & City Airport
North Woolwich
Canada Water
DL
Crossharbour & London Arena
Angerstein Wharf
Marcon RMC Stone Loading Terminal
Dock St. Tun.
(Woolwich Free Ferry)
Pedestrian tunnel
(Proposed Extension)
EL
Surrey Quays
Siding
Bardon Stone Terminal
Coleman St. Tun.
George IV Tun.
Calderwood St. Tun.
Cross St. Tun.
S & T Depot
Southwark Park Junc.
Surrey Canal Junc.
Mudchute
Mount St. Tun.
Charlton Tun.
Woolwich Dockyard
Woolwich Arsenal
Plumstead
Goods
f
North Kent East Junc.
Island Gardens
Pedestrian tunnel
Westcombe Park
Charlton
e
Angerstein Junc.
Camden Road West Junc.
N
South Bermondsey
LUL Depot
Thames Tunnel
Maze Hill
Camden Road
Cutty Sark for Maritime Greenwich
Greenwich College Tun.
Primrose Hill Tuns.
Camden Carriage Sidings
N
Deptford
Greenwich
Deptford Bridge
DL
Camden Town
Morn. Cres.
New Cross
St John's
Blackheath Tunnel
Park St. Tuns.
N
Queens Road (Peckham)
New Cross Gate
Tanners Hill Junc.
Lewisham Vale Junc.
Elverson Road
Blackheath Junc.
(INSET FROM MAP 21)
(1:35,000)
Up empty Carriage Sidings
Nunhead
Nunhead Junc.
Brockley
Parks Bridge Junc.
Lewisham
Blackheath
Kidbrooke Tun.
Kidbrooke
EN
Down empty Carriage Shed
(TO EUSTON)
C
Falconwood
Courthill Loop Junc. North
Courthill Loop Junc. South
Ladywell Junc.
Ladywell
Eltham

1

0   1   2 m.   (1:70,000)
0   1   2   3 km.

LONDON UNDERGROUND LTD.:
B   BAKERLOO
C   CENTRAL
O   CIRCLE
D   DISTRICT
EL   EAST LONDON
H   HAMMERSMITH & CITY
OTHER SYSTEMS:
CT   CROYDON TRAMLINK

J   JUBILEE
M   METROPOLITAN
N   NORTHERN
P   PICCADILLY
V   VICTORIA
W   WATERLOO & CITY

DL   DOCKLANDS

22

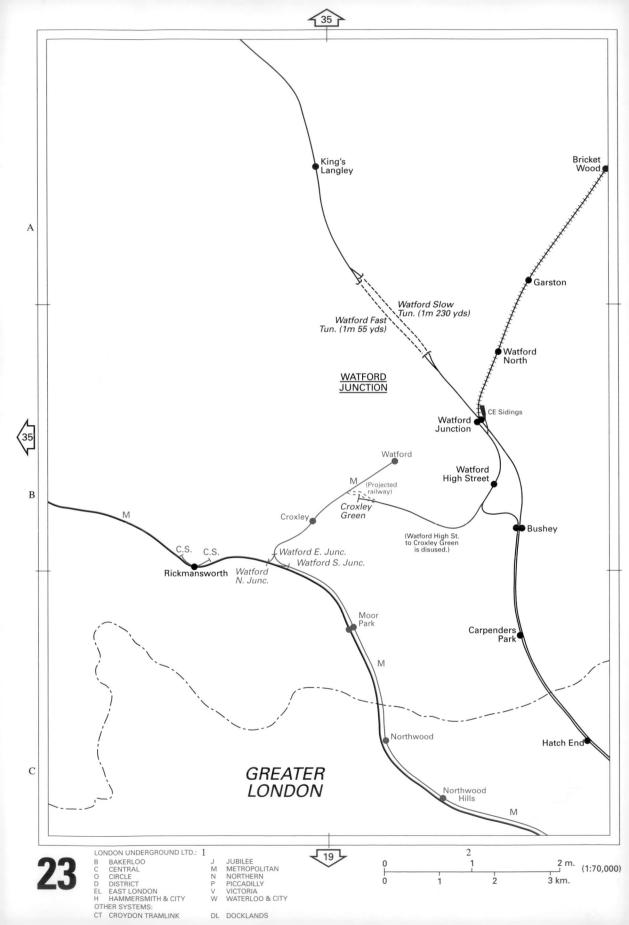

King's Langley

Bricket Wood

A

Garston

Watford Slow Tun. (1m 230 yds)

Watford Fast Tun. (1m 55 yds)

Watford North

WATFORD JUNCTION

CE Sidings

Watford Junction

Watford

Watford High Street

M

M (Projected railway)

B

M

Croxley Green

Croxley

Bushey

(Watford High St. to Croxley Green is disused.)

C.S.   C.S.

Watford E. Junc.

Watford S. Junc.

Rickmansworth

Watford N. Junc.

Carpenders Park

Moor Park

M

Northwood

Hatch End

C

GREATER LONDON

Northwood Hills

M

23

LONDON UNDERGROUND LTD.: 1
B   BAKERLOO
C   CENTRAL
O   CIRCLE
D   DISTRICT
EL   EAST LONDON
H   HAMMERSMITH & CITY
OTHER SYSTEMS:
CT   CROYDON TRAMLINK

J   JUBILEE
M   METROPOLITAN
N   NORTHERN
P   PICCADILLY
V   VICTORIA
W   WATERLOO & CITY

DL   DOCKLANDS

2
0   1   2 m.
0   1   2   3 km.
(1:70,000)

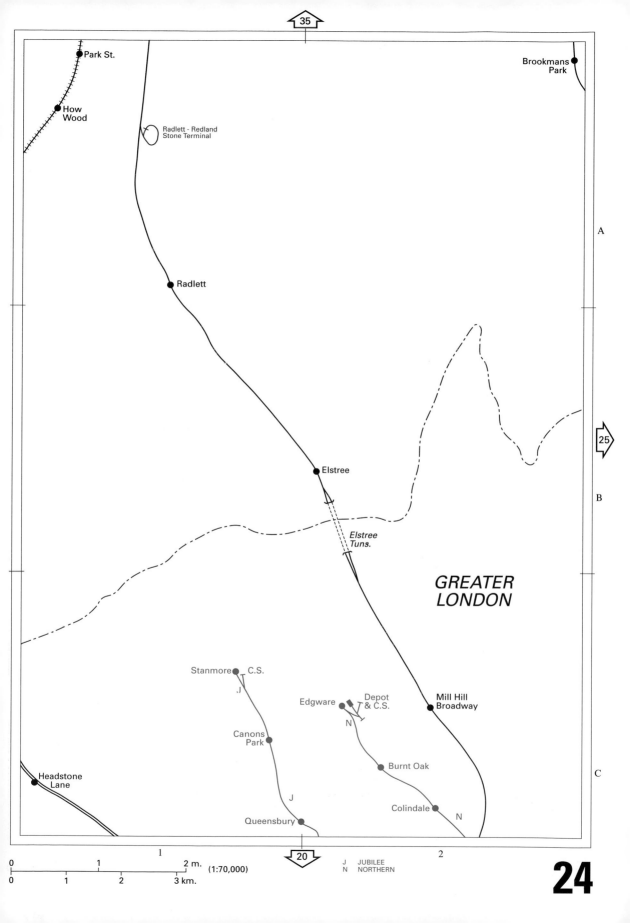

35

Park St.

Brookmans
Park

How
Wood

Radlett - Redland
Stone Terminal

A

Radlett

25

Elstree

B

Elstree
Tuns.

GREATER
LONDON

Stanmore ● C.S.
J

Depot
& C.S.
Edgware ●
N

Mill Hill
Broadway

Canons
Park ●

Burnt Oak ●

Headstone
Lane ●

C

J

Colindale ●   N

Queensbury ●

0   1   2 m.   (1:70,000)
0   1   2   3 km.

20

J   JUBILEE
N   NORTHERN

24

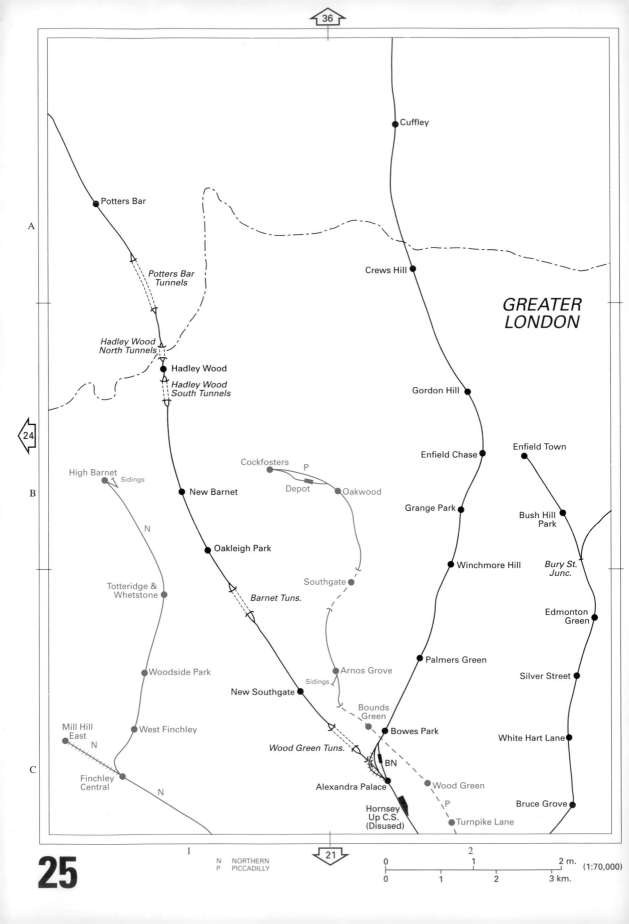

Cuffley

Potters Bar

A

Potters Bar
Tunnels

Crews Hill

*GREATER
LONDON*

Hadley Wood
North Tunnels

Hadley Wood

Hadley Wood
South Tunnels

Gordon Hill

24

Enfield Chase

Enfield Town

Cockfosters   P

High Barnet   Sidings

New Barnet

Depot   Oakwood

B

Grange Park

Bush Hill
Park

N

Winchmore Hill

Oakleigh Park

*Bury St.
Junc.*

Totteridge &
Whetstone

Barnet Tuns.

Southgate

Edmonton
Green

Woodside Park

Arnos Grove

Sidings

Palmers Green

Silver Street

New Southgate

Bounds
Green

Mill Hill
East

West Finchley

N

Bowes Park

White Hart Lane

Wood Green Tuns.

BN

Finchley
Central

N

C

Alexandra Palace

Wood Green

Bruce Grove

Hornsey
Up C.S.
(Disused)

P

Turnpike Lane

25

1

N   NORTHERN
P   PICCADILLY

2

0   1   2 m.

0   1   2   3 km.

(1:70,000)

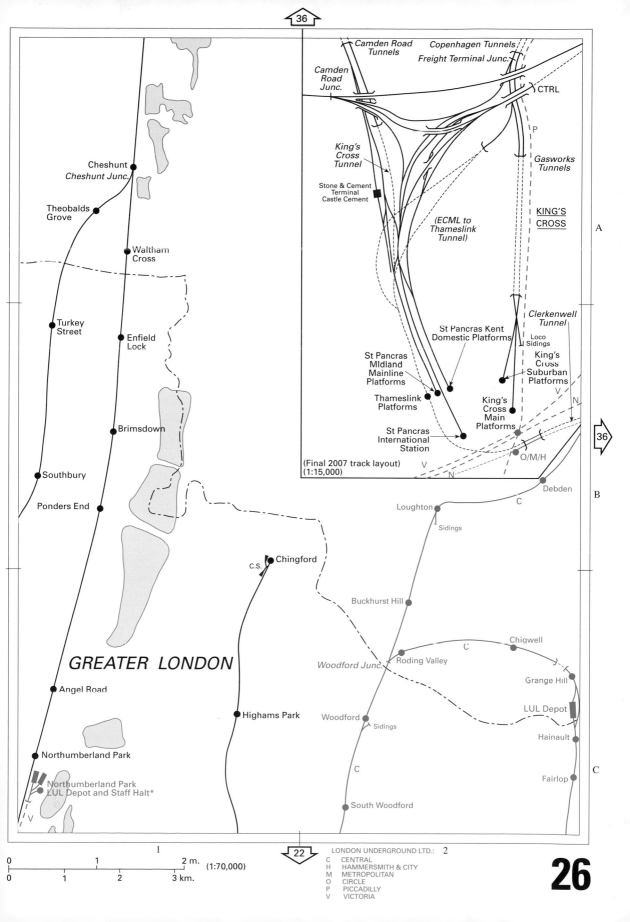

Camden Road
Tunnels

Copenhagen Tunnels

Freight Terminal Junc.

Camden
Road
Junc.

CTRL

P

King's
Cross
Tunnel

Gasworks
Tunnels

Stone & Cement
Terminal
Castle Cement

KING'S
CROSS

A

(ECML to
Thameslink
Tunnel)

Clerkenwell
Tunnel

Loco
Sidings

King's
Cross
Suburban
Platforms

St Pancras Kent
Domestic Platforms

St Pancras
Midland
Mainline
Platforms

King's
Cross
Main
Platforms

V

N

Thameslink
Platforms

St Pancras
International
Station

O/M/H

V

(Final 2007 track layout)
(1:15,000)

N

Cheshunt
Cheshunt Junc.

Theobalds
Grove

Waltham
Cross

Turkey
Street

Enfield
Lock

Brimsdown

Southbury

Ponders End

Chingford

C.S.

Debden

B

Loughton

Sidings

C

Buckhurst Hill

Chigwell

C

Roding Valley

Grange Hill

Woodford Junc.

LUL Depot

GREATER LONDON

Angel Road

Highams Park

Woodford

Sidings

Hainault

C

Northumberland Park

Fairlop

C

Northumberland Park
LUL Depot and Staff Halt*

V

South Woodford

0   1   2 m.   (1:70,000)

0   1   2   3 km.

LONDON UNDERGROUND LTD.: 2
C   CENTRAL
H   HAMMERSMITH & CITY
M   METROPOLITAN
O   CIRCLE
P   PICCADILLY
V   VICTORIA

26

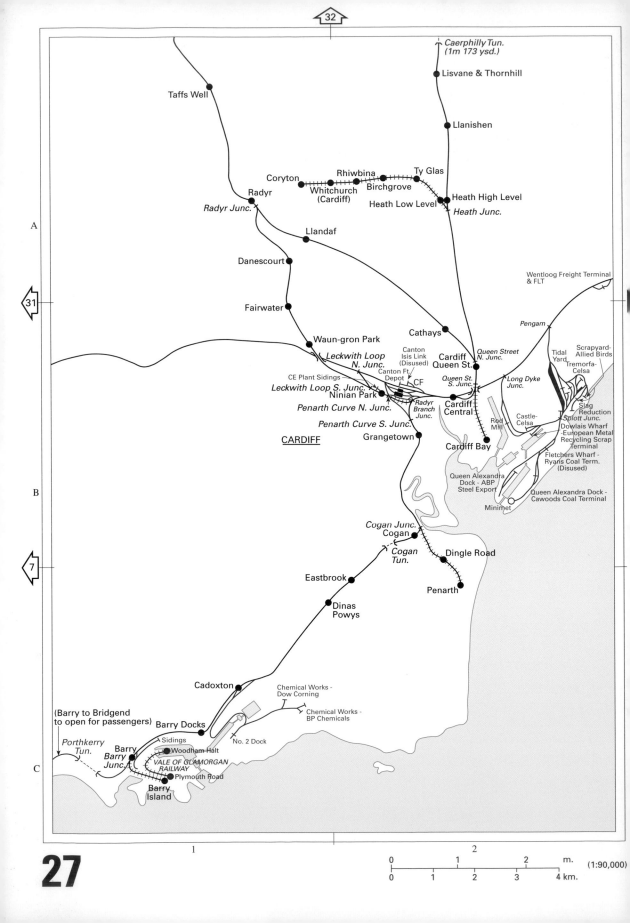

Caerphilly Tun.
(1m 173 ysd.)

Lisvane & Thornhill

Llanishen

Taffs Well

Coryton   Rhiwbina   Ty Glas
        Whitchurch   Birchgrove
Radyr   (Cardiff)
                Heath Low Level   Heath High Level
Radyr Junc.   Heath Junc.

A

Llandaf

Danescourt

Wentloog Freight Terminal
& FLT

31

Fairwater

Cathays   Pengam

                                    Queen Street
Waun-gron Park   Canton   N. Junc.   Tidal   Scrapyard-
        Leckwith Loop   Isis Link   Cardiff   Yard   Allied Birds
        N. Junc.   (Disused)   Queen St.   Tremorfa-
                         Canton Ft./   Celsa
CE Plant Sidings   Depot   CF
                                    Queen St.   Long Dyke
Leckwith Loop S. Junc.   S. Junc.   Junc.
        Ninian Park   Slag
Penarth Curve N. Junc.   Radyr   Cardiff   Red   Reduction
                         Branch   Central   Mill Castle-   Splott Junc.
        Penarth Curve S. Junc.   Junc.   Celsa
                                                            Dowlais Wharf
                                            Cardiff Bay   -European Metal
        Grangetown   Recycling Scrap
                                                            Terminal
CARDIFF   Fletchers Wharf -
                                            Queen Alexandra Ryans Coal Term.
                                            Dock - ABP   (Disused)
                                            Steel Export
B   Queen Alexandra Dock -
                                               Minimet   Cawoods Coal Terminal

                        Cogan Junc.
                        Cogan
                        Cogan
                        Tun.   Dingle Road

        Eastbrook
7   Penarth

        Dinas
        Powys

        Cadoxton

        Chemical Works -
        Dow Corning

                        Chemical Works -
                        BP Chemicals

(Barry to Bridgend
to open for passengers) Barry Docks
Porthkerry   Sidings   No. 2 Dock
Tun.   Barry   Woodham Halt
        Barry   VALE OF GLAMORGAN
        Junc.   RAILWAY
C   Plymouth Road
        Barry
        Island

27

1   2

0   1   2   m.
0   1   2   3   4 km.   (1:90,000)

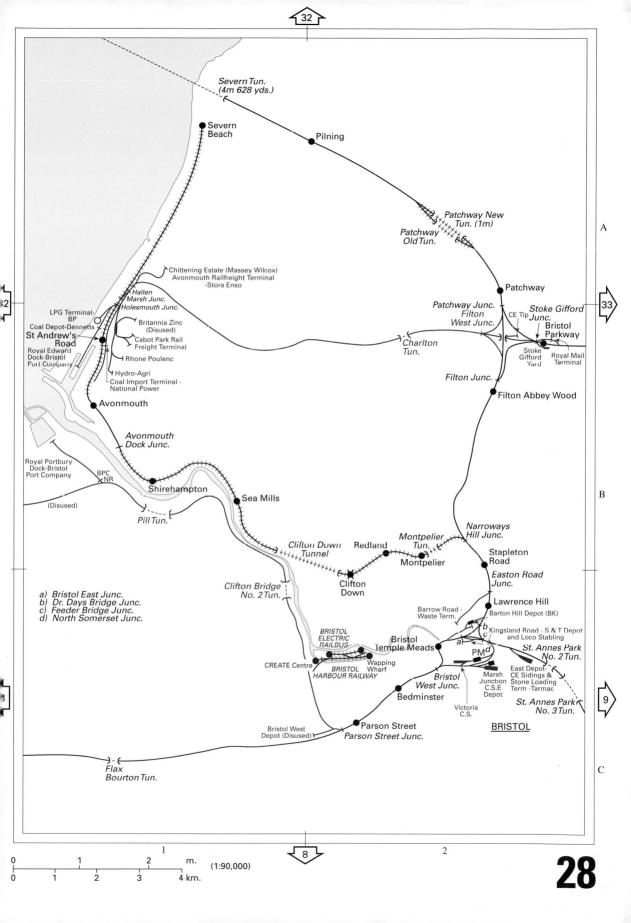

Severn Tun.
(4m 628 yds.)

Severn Beach

Pilning

Patchway New Tun. (1m)

Patchway Old Tun.

Patchway

Chittening Estate (Massey Wilcox)
Avonmouth Railfreight Terminal
-Stora Enso

Hallen Marsh Junc.
Holesmouth Junc.

Stoke Gifford Junc.

Patchway Junc.
Filton West Junc.

CE Tip

Bristol Parkway

LPG Terminal-BP
Coal Depot-Dennetts

Britannia Zinc (Disused)

St Andrew's Road

Cabot Park Rail Freight Terminal

Charlton Tun.

Stoke Gifford Yard

Royal Mail Terminal

Royal Edward Dock-Bristol Port Company

Rhone Poulenc

Filton Junc.

Hydro-Agri Coal Import Terminal - National Power

Filton Abbey Wood

Avonmouth

Avonmouth Dock Junc.

Royal Portbury Dock-Bristol Port Company

BPC NR

(Disused)

Shirehampton

Pill Tun.

Sea Mills

Narroways Hill Junc.

Clifton Down Tunnel

Redland

Montpelier Tun.

Stapleton Road

Montpelier

Easton Road Junc.

Clifton Bridge No. 2 Tun.

Clifton Down

Lawrence Hill

a) Bristol East Junc.
b) Dr. Days Bridge Junc.
c) Feeder Bridge Junc.
d) North Somerset Junc.

Barrow Road - Waste Term.

Barton Hill Depot (BK)

Kingsland Road - S & T Depot and Loco Stabling

b
c
a
d

St. Annes Park No. 2 Tun.

BRISTOL ELECTRIC RAILBUS

Bristol Temple Meads

PM

East Depot-CE Sidings & Stone Loading Term -Tarmac

CREATE Centre

BRISTOL HARBOUR RAILWAY

Wapping Wharf

Marsh Junction C.S.E Depot

St. Annes Park No. 3 Tun.

Bristol West Junc.

Bedminster

Victoria C.S.

BRISTOL

Bristol West Depot (Disused)

Parson Street
Parson Street Junc.

Flax Bourton Tun.

0   1   2   m.
0 1 2 3 4 km.

(1:90,000)

28

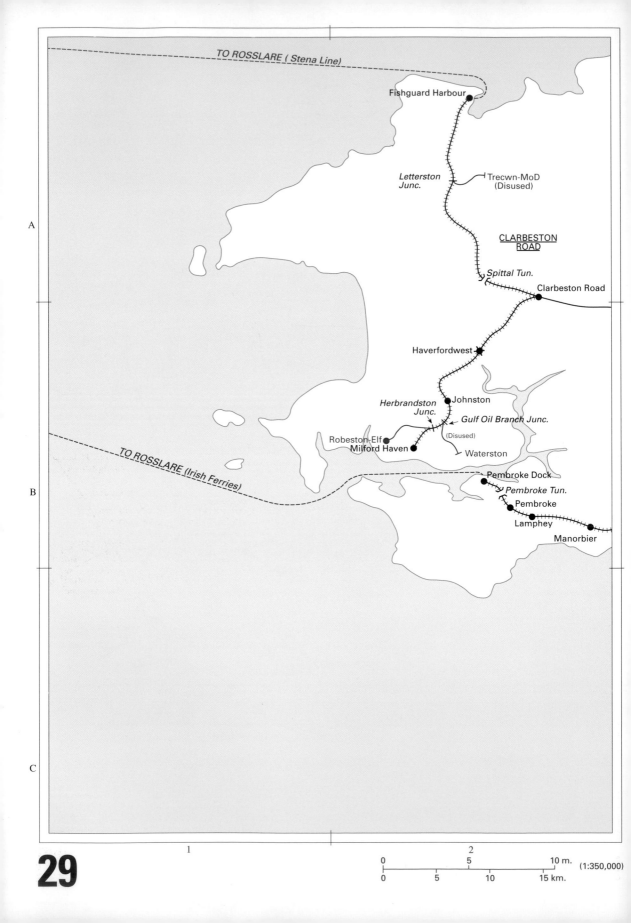

TO ROSSLARE (Stena Line)

Fishguard Harbour

Letterston Junc.

Trecwn-MoD
(Disused)

CLARBESTON
ROAD

Spittal Tun.

Clarbeston Road

Haverfordwest

Herbrandston Junc.

Johnston

Gulf Oil Branch Junc.

(Disused)

Robeston-Elf

Milford Haven

Waterston

Pembroke Dock

TO ROSSLARE (Irish Ferries)

Pembroke Tun.

Pembroke

Lamphey

Manorbier

A

B

C

1

2

0   5   10 m.

0   5   10   15 km.

(1:350,000)

29

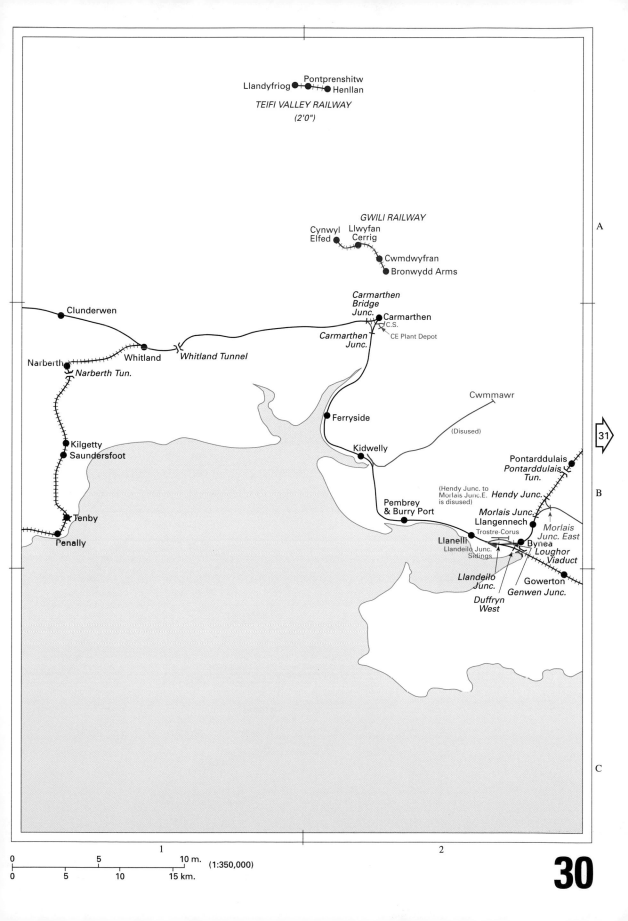

Llandyfriog ● ●Pontprenshitw
● Henllan

TEIFI VALLEY RAILWAY
(2'0")

GWILI RAILWAY

Cynwyl Llwyfan
Elfed Cerrig
● ●
●Cwmdwyfran
●Bronwydd Arms

A

Clunderwen ●

Carmarthen
Bridge
Junc.
●Carmarthen
C.S.
CE Plant Depot

Carmarthen
Junc.

Narberth ●
Whitland *Whitland Tunnel*
Narberth Tun.

●Ferryside

Cwmmawr

(Disused)

●Kilgetty
●Saundersfoot

●Kidwelly

Pontarddulais ●
Pontarddulais
Tun.

B

(Hendy Junc. to
Morlais Junc.E.
is disused) *Hendy Junc.*

●Tenby

Penally

Pembrey
& Burry Port ●

Morlais Junc.
Llangennech ●
Trostre-Corus *Morlais*
Junc. East

Llanelli ● ●Bynea
Llandeilo Junc. *Loughor*
Sidings *Viaduct*

Llandeilo
Junc. ●Gowerton
Genwen Junc.
Duffryn
West

31 ▷

C

0   5   10 m.
|———|———|———|———| (1:350,000)
0 5 10 15 km.

30

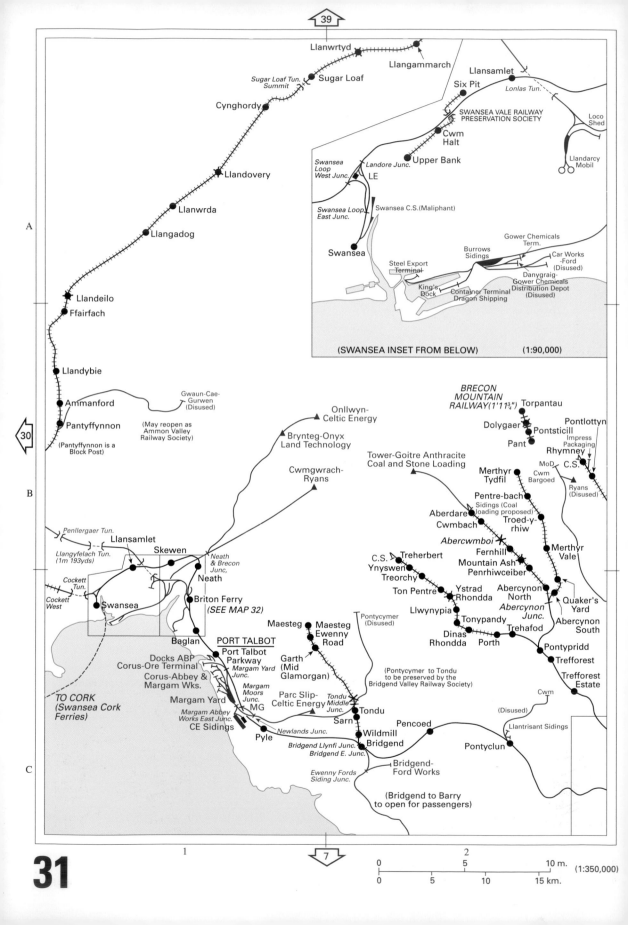

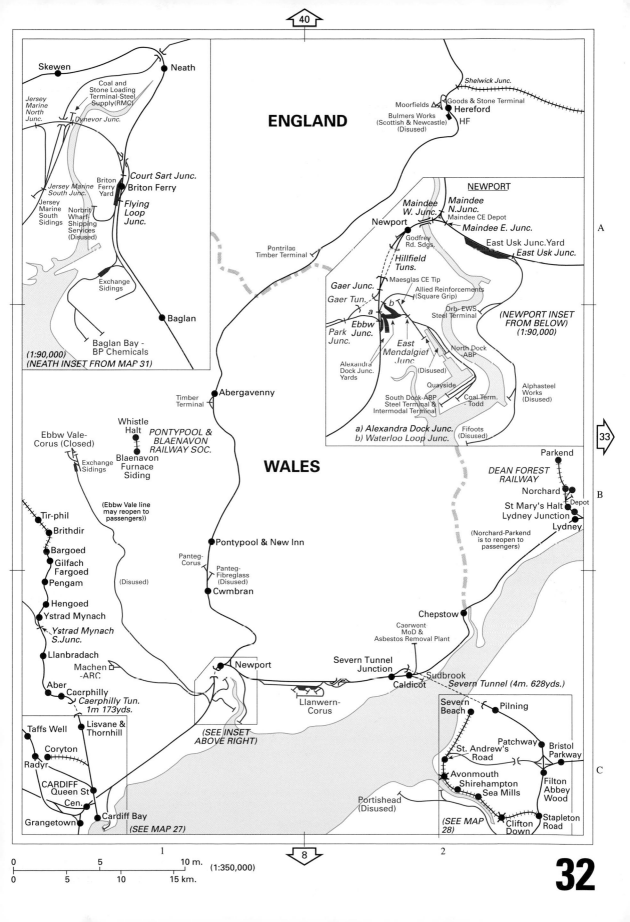

ENGLAND

WALES

NEWPORT

Skewen

Neath

Shelwick Junc.

Coal and Stone Loading Terminal-Steel Supply(RMC)

Moorfields △

Goods & Stone Terminal

Hereford

Jersey Marine North Junc.

Dynevor Junc.

Bulmers Works (Scottish & Newcastle) (Disused)

HF

Briton Ferry Yard

Court Sart Junc.

Jersey Marine South Junc.

Briton Ferry

Flying Loop Junc.

Maindee W. Junc.

Maindee N.Junc.

Maindee CE Depot

A

Jersey Marine South Sidings

Norbrit Wharf Shipping Services (Disused)

Newport

Godfrey Rd. Sdgs.

Maindee E. Junc.

East Usk Junc. Yard

East Usk Junc.

Hillfield Tuns.

Exchange Sidings

Pontrilas Timber Terminal

Maesglas CE Tip

Gaer Junc.

Allied Reinforcements (Square Grip)

Gaer Tun.

b

Orb- EWS Steel Terminal

(NEWPORT INSET FROM BELOW) (1:90,000)

Baglan

a

Ebbw Park Junc.

East Mendalgief Junc.

North Dock -ABP

Baglan Bay - BP Chemicals

Alexandra Dock Junc. Yards

(Disused)

Quayside

Alphasteel Works (Disused)

(1:90,000) (NEATH INSET FROM MAP 31)

South Dock-ABP Steel Terminal & Intermodal Terminal

Coal Term.- Todd

Abergavenny

Timber Terminal

a) Alexandra Dock Junc.
b) Waterloo Loop Junc.

Fifoots (Disused)

33

Whistle Halt

Parkend

Ebbw Vale- Corus (Closed)

PONTYPOOL & BLAENAVON RAILWAY SOC.

DEAN FOREST RAILWAY

Exchange Sidings

Norchard

B

Blaenavon Furnace Siding

St Mary's Halt

Depot

Tir-phil

(Ebbw Vale line may reopen to passengers))

Lydney Junction

Lydney

Brithdir

Bargoed

Pontypool & New Inn

(Norchard-Parkend is to reopen to passengers)

Gilfach Fargoed

Panteg- Corus

Pengam

Panteg- Fibreglass (Disused)

Hengoed

(Disused)

Cwmbran

Ystrad Mynach

Chepstow

Ystrad Mynach S.Junc.

Caerwent MoD & Asbestos Removal Plant

Llanbradach

Machen -ARC

Newport

Severn Tunnel Junction

Sudbrook

Aber

Caerphilly

Caerphilly Tun. 1m 173yds.

Caldicot

Severn Tunnel (4m. 628yds.)

Llanwern- Corus

Severn Beach

Pilning

Taffs Well

Lisvane & Thornhill

(SEE INSET ABOVE RIGHT)

Patchway

Coryton

St. Andrew's Road

Bristol Parkway

Radyr

C

CARDIFF Queen St Cen.

Avonmouth Shirehampton

Sea Mills

Filton Abbey Wood

Portishead (Disused)

Grangetown

Cardiff Bay

(SEE MAP 27)

(SEE MAP 28)

Clifton Down

Stapleton Road

0   1   10 m.

0   5   10   15 km.

(1:350,000)

32

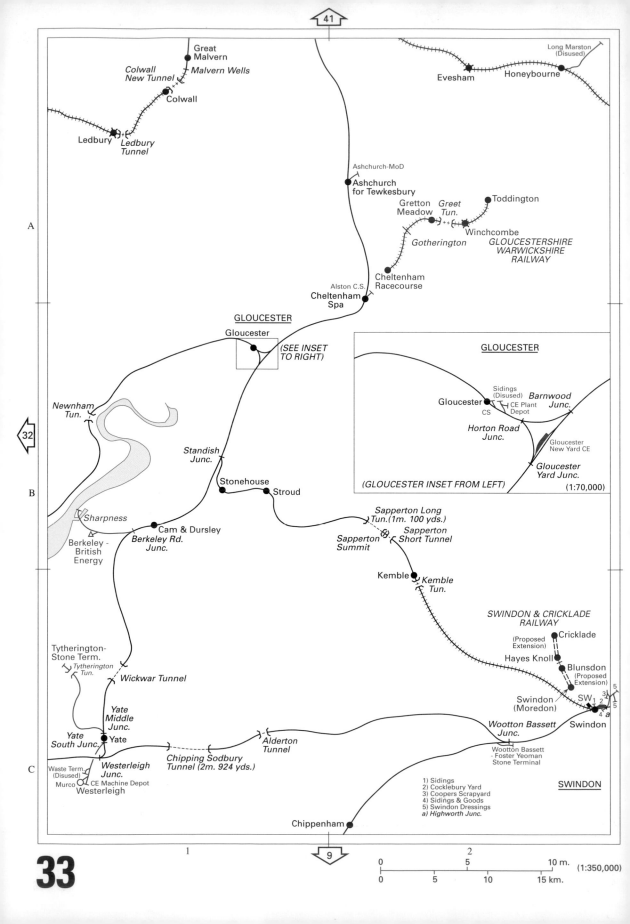

Great
Malvern

Malvern Wells

*Colwall
New Tunnel*

Colwall

Ledbury

*Ledbury
Tunnel*

Long Marston
(Disused)

Evesham

Honeybourne

Ashchurch-MoD

Ashchurch
for Tewkesbury

Gretton
Meadow

*Greet
Tun.*

Toddington

Winchcombe

Gotherington

**GLOUCESTERSHIRE
WARWICKSHIRE
RAILWAY**

Cheltenham
Racecourse

Alston C.S.

Cheltenham
Spa

A

GLOUCESTER

Gloucester

*(SEE INSET
TO RIGHT)*

*Newnham
Tun.*

32

GLOUCESTER

Gloucester

Sidings
(Disused)

*Barnwood
Junc.*

CS

CE Plant
Depot

*Horton Road
Junc.*

Gloucester
New Yard CE

*Gloucester
Yard Junc.*

(GLOUCESTER INSET FROM LEFT)

(1:70,000)

B

*Standish
Junc.*

Stonehouse

Stroud

*Sapperton Long
Tun.(1m. 100 yds.)*

*Sapperton
Short Tunnel*

*Sapperton
Summit*

Sharpness

*Berkeley -
British
Energy*

Cam & Dursley

*Berkeley Rd.
Junc.*

Kemble

*Kemble
Tun.*

**SWINDON & CRICKLADE
RAILWAY**

(Proposed
Extension)

Cricklade

Hayes Knoll

Blunsdon

(Proposed
Extension)

*Tytherington-
Stone Term.*

*Tytherington
Tun.*

Wickwar Tunnel

Swindon
(Moredon)

SW 1 2 3
4 5
a

Swindon

*Yate
Middle
Junc.*

*Yate
South Junc.*

Yate

*Alderton
Tunnel*

*Wootton Bassett
Junc.*

Wootton Bassett
- Foster Yeoman
Stone Terminal

C

Waste Term.
(Disused)

Murco

*Westerleigh
Junc.*

CE Machine Depot

Westerleigh

*Chipping Sodbury
Tunnel (2m. 924 yds.)*

1) Sidings
2) Cocklebury Yard
3) Coopers Scrapyard
4) Sidings & Goods
5) Swindon Dressings
a) Highworth Junc.

SWINDON

Chippenham

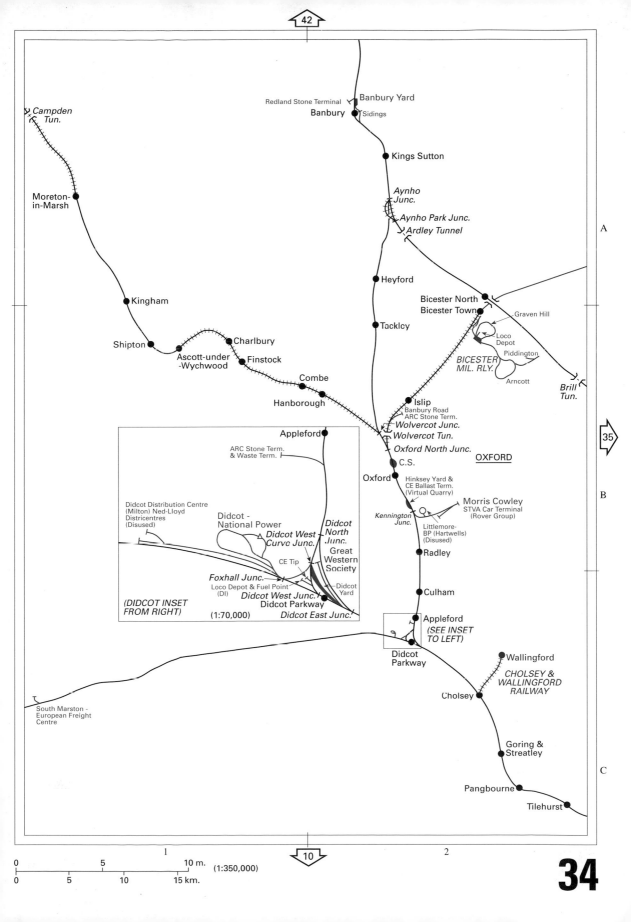

Campden Tun.

Moreton-in-Marsh

Kingham

Shipton

Ascott-under-Wychwood

Charlbury

Finstock

Combe

Hanborough

Appleford

Banbury Yard

Redland Stone Terminal

Banbury

Sidings

Kings Sutton

Aynho Junc.

Aynho Park Junc.

Ardley Tunnel

Heyford

Bicester North

Bicester Town

Graven Hill

Loco Depot

Piddington

BICESTER MIL. RLY.

Arncott

Brill Tun.

Tackley

Islip

Banbury Road ARC Stone Term.

Wolvercot Junc.

Wolvercot Tun.

Oxford North Junc.

OXFORD

C.S.

Oxford

Hinksey Yard & CE Ballast Term. (Virtual Quarry)

Morris Cowley

STVA Car Terminal (Rover Group)

Kennington Junc.

Littlemore-BP (Hartwells) (Disused)

Radley

Culham

Appleford

(SEE INSET TO LEFT)

Didcot Parkway

Wallingford

CHOLSEY & WALLINGFORD RAILWAY

Cholsey

Goring & Streatley

Pangbourne

Tilehurst

South Marston - European Freight Centre

Didcot Inset

ARC Stone Term. & Waste Term.

Didcot Distribution Centre (Milton) Ned-Lloyd Districentres (Disused)

Didcot - National Power

Didcot West Curve Junc.

Didcot North Junc.

Great Western Society

CE Tip

Foxhall Junc.

Loco Depot & Fuel Point (DI)

Didcot West Junc.

Didcot Parkway

Didcot Yard

Didcot East Junc.

(DIDCOT INSET FROM RIGHT)

(1:70,000)

0   5   10 m.

0   5   10   15 km.

(1:350,000)

BLETCHLEY inset:

Fenny Stratford
Flyover Junc.

Denbigh Hall
South Junc.

Alstom Works
(ZN)

Wolverton

CE & OLE
Depot
BY

ARC Stone
Terminal

C.S.

S & T
Sidings

Bletchley

Fenny
Stratford
Flyover Junc.

Bletchley
Junc.

RMC
Stone Term.

(1:90,000)
(BLETCHLEY INSET
FROM RIGHT)

BLETCHLEY

Milton
Keynes
Central

Woburn
Sands

Ridgmont

Marston Vale
(Ridgemont)

Aspley Guise

Bow Brickhill

Bletchley

Fenny Stratford

(SEE INSET TO LEFT)

(Used as a
train run-round)

(Disused)

Kempston
Hardwick

Forders Sidings
Shanks & McEwan Landfill

Elstow - Redland
Stone Terminal

Stewartby

Millbrook

Forders(Stewartby)
(Virtual Quarry)

Lidlington

Biggleswade

Plasmor
Brick
Terminal

Arlesey

Ampthill
Tuns.

Flitwick

Harlington

Cambridge Junc.
CE Plant Depot

Hitchin

Claydon L.N.E. Junc.

Calvert- Shanks &
McEwan Waste Terminal

Stonehenge
Works

LEIGHTON BUZZARD
RAILWAY (2' 0")

Linslade Tuns.

Leighton
Buzzard

Page's Park

Leagrave

Sidings

Limbury Rd.-
Tarmac Stone Term.

Luton

Luton Airport Parkway

Quainton Road*

Cheddington

GREAT WHIPSNADE RLY.
(2' 6")

Harpenden

Sidings

Aylesbury

Aylesbury Diesel Depot
(AL)

C.S.

Stoke
Mandeville

Tring
Summit

Tring

Haddenham &
Thame Parkway

Wendover

Northchurch
Tuns.

Berkhamsted

St. Albans
Abbey

St. Albans

Little
Kimble

Monks
Risborough

Hemel
Hempstead

Apsley

Park St.

(SEE MAP
24)

CHINNOR & PRINCES
RISBOROUGH RAILWAY
ASSOCIATION

Princes
Risborough

Dutchlands
Summit

Great
Missenden

Chesham

M

King's
Langley

Radlett

Chinnor

Wainhill

Saunderton
Summit

(Wainhill to Princes
Risborough to open 2006)

Saunderton

(MANTLES WOOD)

NR

LUL

Amersham

Chalfont
& Latimer

Chorleywood

Watford

Watford Junc.

(READING INSET FROM BELOW)

CE
Yard

Reading
Yard

CE
Sidings

Reading

Reading
New Junc.

Reading
West
Junc.

RG

C.S.

Westbury
Line Junc.

Reading
Spur Junc.

High Wycombe

Rickmansworth

Croxley
Green

M

Moor
Park

Edgware
Stanmore

J

N

Reading
West

Oxford Road Junc.

READING

Beaconsfield

Seer Green

Whitehouse
Tun.

Gerrards
Cross

Denham

(SEE MAP 23)

Harrow-on-
the- Hill

Rayners
Lane

M/P

Southcote
Junc.
(1:90,000)

Bourne End

Marlow

Cookham

Denham Golf
Club

West
Ruslip

C

Uxbridge

**GREATER
LONDON**

Henley-on-
Thames

Furze Platt

SLOUGH

Slough Estates-
Coal & Oil
Terminal

Redland
Stone Terminal

Shiplake

Maidenhead

Taplow

Slough

Langley

Iver

West
Drayton

Ealing
Bdy.

Wargrave

Burnham

Heathrow

(SEE MAP 20)

(SEE INSET
ABOVE)

Reading

Twyford

Windsor & Eton
Central

Windsor & Eton Riverside

Datchet

Sunnymeads

(SEE MAP 19)

P

Reading West

Wraysbury

Feltham

Richmond

LONDON UNDERGROUND LTD.: l

B	BAKERLOO	J	JUBILEE
C	CENTRAL	M	METROPOLITAN
O	CIRCLE	N	NORTHERN
D	DISTRICT	P	PICCADILLY
EL	EAST LONDON	V	VICTORIA
H	HAMMERSMITH & CITY	W	WATERLOO & CITY

OTHER SYSTEMS:
CT CROYDON TRAMLINK   DL DOCKLANDS

11

2

15

16

0   5   10 m.

0   5   10   15 km.

(1:350,000)

34

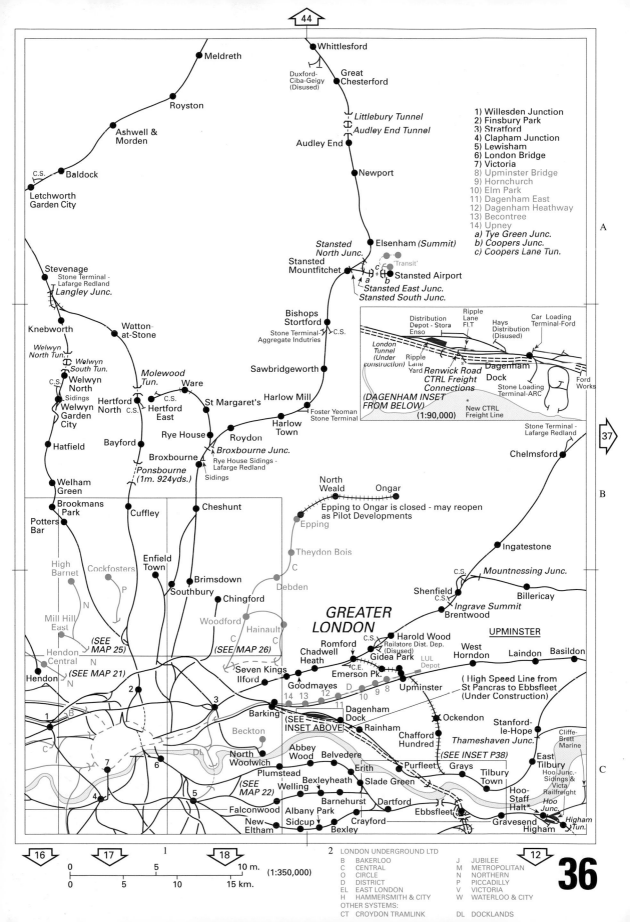

Meldreth

Whittlesford

Royston

Great Chesterford

Duxford-Ciba-Geigy (Disused)

Ashwell & Morden

Littlebury Tunnel
Audley End Tunnel

C.S.
Baldock

Audley End

Letchworth Garden City

Newport

1) Willesden Junction
2) Finsbury Park
3) Stratford
4) Clapham Junction
5) Lewisham
6) London Bridge
7) Victoria
8) Upminster Bridge
9) Hornchurch
10) Elm Park
11) Dagenham East
12) Dagenham Heathway
13) Becontree
14) Upney
a) Tye Green Junc.
b) Coopers Junc.
c) Coopers Lane Tun.

A

Elsenham (Summit)

Stevenage
Stone Terminal -
Lafarge Redland
Langley Junc.

Stansted North Junc.

Stansted Mountfitchet

c
d
'Transit'
a
b
Stansted Airport

Stansted East Junc.
Stansted South Junc.

Knebworth

Watton-at-Stone

Welwyn North Tun.

Bishops Stortford
Stone Terminal -
Aggregate Indutries
C.S.

Welwyn South Tun.

C.S.
Welwyn North

Molewood Tun.

Ware

Sawbridgeworth

Sidings
Welwyn Garden City

Hertford North
C.S.
Hertford East
C.S.

C.S.
St Margaret's

Harlow Mill

DAGENHAM INSET
(from below)

Distribution
Depot - Stora
Enso
Ripple
Lane
FLT
Hays
Distribution
(Disused)
Car Loading
Terminal-Ford

London Tunnel
(Under construction)
Ripple
Lane
Yard
Renwick Road
CTRL Freight
Connections
Dagenham
Dock

Ford
Works

Hatfield

Bayford

Rye House

Roydon

Harlow Town

Foster Yeoman
Stone Terminal

Stone Loading
Terminal-ARC
Stone Terminal -
Lafarge Redland

(DAGENHAM INSET
FROM BELOW)
(1:90,000)

* New CTRL
Freight Line

37

Welham Green

Broxbourne
Broxbourne Junc.
Ponsbourne
(1m. 924yds.)

Rye House Sidings -
Lafarge Redland
Sidings

Chelmsford

B

Brookmans Park

Cuffley

Cheshunt

North Weald

Ongar

Potters Bar

Epping

Epping to Ongar is closed - may reopen
as Pilot Developments

Ingatestone

High Barnet

Cockfosters
P

Enfield Town

Theydon Bois
C

Mountnessing Junc.

C.S.

Mill Hill East
N

Brimsdown
Southbury

Chingford

Debden

C

Woodford

Hainault
C   C

Shenfield
C.S.

Ingrave Summit
Billericay

Brentwood

Hendon Central
(SEE MAP 25)

N

(SEE MAP 26)

GREATER LONDON

UPMINSTER

Hendon

(SEE MAP 21)
N

Harold Wood
(Railtore Dist. Dep.
(Disused))

C.S.

Romford

Chadwell Heath

Gidea Park

West Horndon

Laindon

Basildon

2

3

Seven Kings
Ilford

Goodmayes

C.E.

Emerson Pk.

LUL
Depot

(High Speed Line from
St Pancras to Ebbsfleet
(Under Construction)

D

Upminster

14 13   12

10 9 8

1
B

Barking

11

Dagenham
Dock
(SEE
INSET ABOVE)

Ockendon

Stanford-le-Hope

Beckton

Rainham

Chafford
Hundred

Thameshaven Junc.

(SEE INSET P38)

Cliffe-
Brett
Marine

7

6

North Woolwich

Abbey Wood

Belvedere

Purfleet

Grays

Tilbury Town

East Tilbury

C

DL

Plumstead

Erith

Slade Green

Hoo Junc.-
Sidings &
Victa
Railfreight

4

5

(SEE MAP 22)

Bexleyheath

Welling

Barnehurst

Dartford

Ebbsfleet

Hoo-
Staff
Halt

*Hoo
Junc.*

Falconwood

Albany Park

Crayford

Gravesend

*Higham
Tun.*

New Eltham

Sidcup

Bexley

Crayford

Higham

B   BAKERLOO
C   CENTRAL
O   CIRCLE
D   DISTRICT
EL   EAST LONDON
H   HAMMERSMITH & CITY
OTHER SYSTEMS:
CT   CROYDON TRAMLINK

J   JUBILEE
M   METROPOLITAN
N   NORTHERN
P   PICCADILLY
V   VICTORIA
W   WATERLOO & CITY

DL   DOCKLANDS

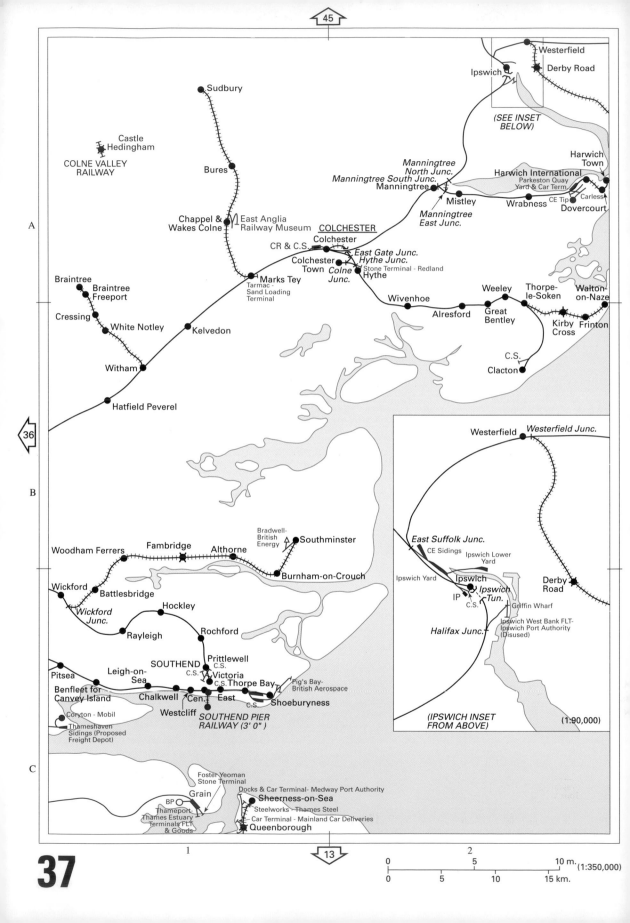

Sudbury

Castle Hedingham
COLNE VALLEY RAILWAY

Bures

Westerfield
Derby Road
Ipswich

(SEE INSET BELOW)

Harwich Town
Manningtree North Junc.
Manningtree South Junc.
Manningtree
Harwich International
Parkeston Quay Yard & Car Term.
CE Tip
Mistley
Wrabness
Carless
Dovercourt
Manningtree East Junc.

Chappel & Wakes Colne
East Anglia Railway Museum

COLCHESTER
Colchester
CR & C.S.
Colchester Town
East Gate Junc.
Hythe Junc.
Colne Junc.
Hythe
Stone Terminal - Redland

A

Marks Tey
Tarmac - Sand Loading Terminal

Braintree
Braintree Freeport
Cressing
White Notley
Kelvedon

Wivenhoe
Alresford
Great Bentley
Weeley
Thorpe-le-Soken
Walton-on-Naze
Kirby Cross
Frinton

Witham

C.S.
Clacton

Hatfield Peverel

36

B

Bradwell-British Energy
Southminster

Woodham Ferrers
Fambridge
Althorne
Burnham-on-Crouch

Wickford
Battlesbridge
Wickford Junc.

Hockley
Rochford

Rayleigh

Prittlewell
C.S.

Pitsea
Leigh-on-Sea
SOUTHEND
C.S.
Victoria
C.S. Thorpe Bay
Pig's Bay-British Aerospace

Benfleet for Canvey Island
Chalkwell
Cen.
East
Shoeburyness
C.S.
Westcliff
SOUTHEND PIER RAILWAY (3' 0")

Coryton - Mobil
Thameshaven Sidings (Proposed Freight Depot)

C

Foster Yeoman Stone Terminal
BP
Grain
Docks & Car Terminal- Medway Port Authority
Sheerness-on-Sea
Thameport-Thames Estuary Terminals FLT & Goods
Steelworks - Thames Steel
Car Terminal - Mainland Car Deliveries
C.S.
Queenborough

Ipswich Inset:

Westerfield
Westerfield Junc.

East Suffolk Junc.
CE Sidings
Ipswich Lower Yard

Ipswich Yard
Ipswich
Ipswich Tun.
IP
C.S.
Derby Road

Griffin Wharf

Halifax Junc.
Ipswich West Bank FLT-Ipswich Port Authority (Disused)

(IPSWICH INSET FROM ABOVE)
(1:90,000)

Talybont

Llanaber
(Block Post)

Barmouth

Barmouth Viaduct

Porth
Penrhyn — Morfa Mawddach

FAIRBOURNE
RAILWAY — *Gorsa* — Fairbourne
(1' 0¼") — Fairbourne

Llwyngwril

TALYLLYN RAILWAY (2' 3")
(Halts not shown)

CORRIS RAILWAY
(2' 3")

Maespoeth

Abergynolwyn — Nant
Quarry Siding — Gwernol
Dolgoch Falls

Tan-y-Coed
(Pantperthog)

(Proposed
Extension)

A

Tonfanau

Tywyn
Wharf — Brynglas

Rhydyronen
Tywyn Pendre

Machynlleth — Sidings
MN

Tywyn

Aberdovey Tuns.
No.3   No.2   No.1
No.4

Dovey Junction
(Block Post)

Aberdovey — Penhelig

**MACHYNLLETH RADIO
SIGNALLING CENTRE**

North
FLT

Trimley
Felixstowe

Felixstowe Beach Junc.

Docks-Felixstowe
Dock & Railway Co.

Felixstowe Docks
South
FLT

FELIXSTOWE - HARWICH
(Orwell & Harwich Nav. Co.)

HARWICH - HOEK VAN HOLLAND
INTERNATIONAL   (Stena Line)
PORT- ESBJERG (Scandinavian
Seaways)
- HAMBURG (Scandinavian
Seaways)

Borth (Block Post)

39

Cliff Lift
(4'10"gauge)

Shell
(Disused)

Aberystwyth

Glanrafon

Llanbadarn

Capel Bangor

Aberffrwd
Rheidol Falls
Rhiwfron

Nantyronen

Devil's
Bridge

VALE OF RHEIDOL RAILWAY (1' 11½")

B

(CTRL St Pancras to
Ebbsfleet under
construction - due
to open in 2007)

*West
Thurrock
Junc.*

Grays

Purfleet

Purfleet Thames Terminal
(Deep Water Wharf)

Foster Yeoman
Stone
Terminal

CE Ballast Term
(Virtual Quarry)

Tilbury FLT

Tilbury
Town

Slade
Green

Slade Green Junc.

C.S.

SG

Crayford Creek Junc.

(Thames Tun.
2.9km)

Tilbury Grain Terminal
Victa Railfreight &
Goods

*Tilbury
Railport
Junc.*

36

Perry Street
Fork Junc.

Crayford Spur
'A' Junc.

Tilbury
Northfleet
Hope FLT,
Docks and
Tilbury
Container
Services

Tilbury International
Railfreight Terminal
Victa Railfreight

Tilbury Riverside

36

Stone
Crossing

Proposed
Construction
Site/P.W. Depot

*Greenhithe
Tun.*

*Lower Thames & Medway
Boat Company*

C

Crayford
Spur 'B' — Dartford
Junc.

Dartford
C.S.

Greenhithe
for Bluewater

Swanscombe

Northfleet

Gravesend West St.

DARTFORD
(To close - control to
move to Ashford)

(INSET FROM MAP 36)
(1:90,000)

Ebbsfleet

Gravesend

Pepper Hill Tun.

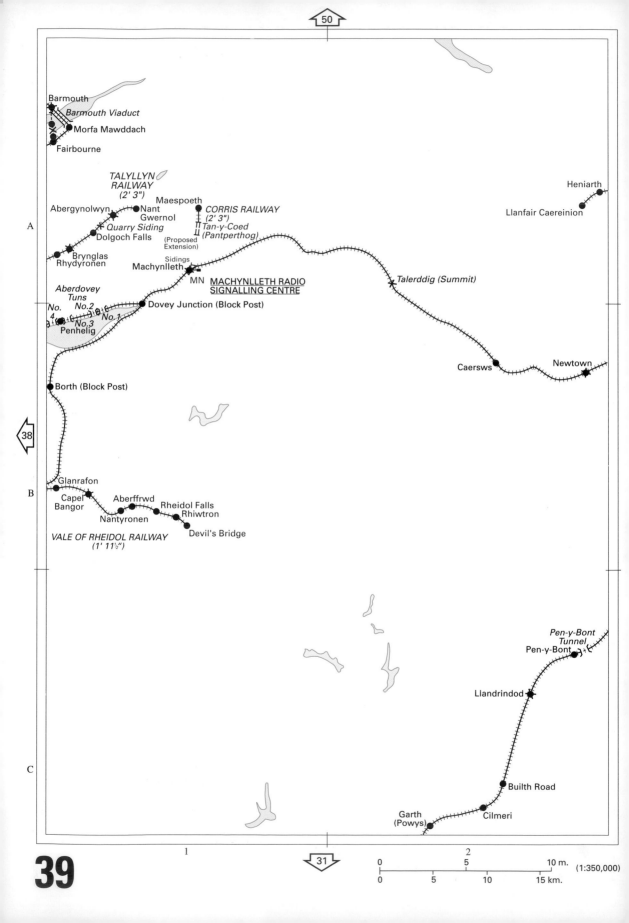

Barmouth

Barmouth Viaduct

Morfa Mawddach

Fairbourne

*TALYLLYN
RAILWAY
(2' 3")*

Maespoeth

Abergynolwyn — Nant
Gwernol

*CORRIS RAILWAY
(2' 3")*

Heniarth

Llanfair Caereinion

A

Quarry Siding

Tan-y-Coed
(Pantperthog)

Dolgoch Falls

(Proposed
Extension)

Brynglas
Rhydyronen

Sidings
Machynlleth

MN   **MACHYNLLETH RADIO
SIGNALLING CENTRE**

Talerddig (Summit)

*Aberdovey
Tuns*

No.   No.2
4   No.1

Dovey Junction (Block Post)

No.3
Penhelig

Caersws   Newtown

Borth (Block Post)

Glanrafon

B

Capel
Bangor

Aberffrwd

Rheidol Falls
Rhiwtron

Nantyronen

Devil's Bridge

*VALE OF RHEIDOL RAILWAY
(1' 11½")*

*Pen-y-Bont
Tunnel*
Pen-y-Bont

Llandrindod

C

Builth Road

Garth
(Powys)   Cilmeri

39

0   5   10 m.   (1:350,000)

0   5   10   15 km.

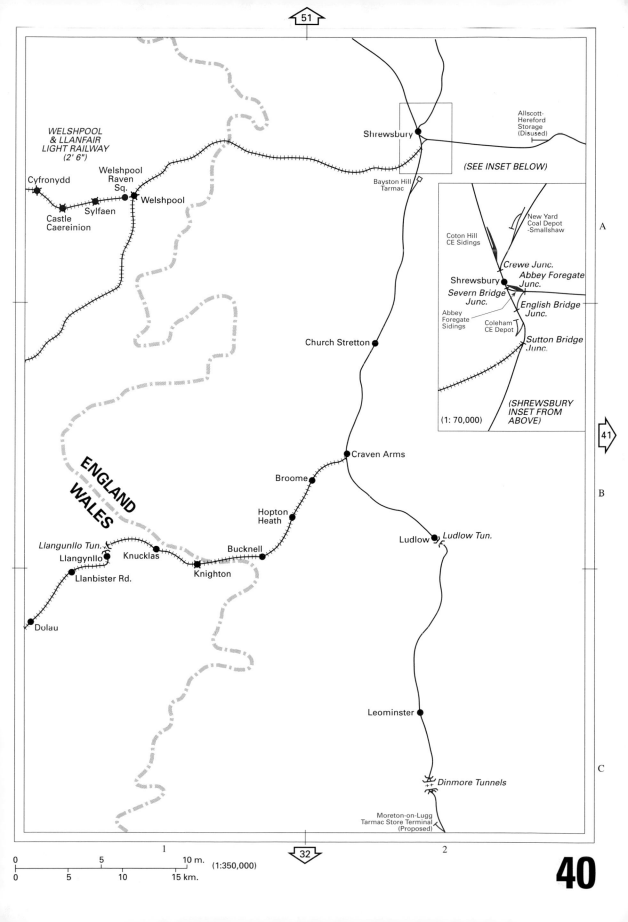

WELSHPOOL
& LLANFAIR
LIGHT RAILWAY
(2' 6")

Cyfronydd

Welshpool
Raven
Sq.

Welshpool

Castle
Caereinion

Sylfaen

Shrewsbury

Bayston Hill
Tarmac

Allscott-
Hereford
Storage
(Disused)

(SEE INSET BELOW)

New Yard
Coal Depot
-Smallshaw

Coton Hill
CE Sidings

Crewe Junc.

*Abbey Foregate
Junc.*

Shrewsbury

*Severn Bridge
Junc.*

*English Bridge
Junc.*

Abbey
Foregate
Sidings

Coleham
CE Depot

*Sutton Bridge
Junc.*

A

*(SHREWSBURY
INSET FROM
ABOVE)*

(1: 70,000)

Church Stretton

B

Craven Arms

Broome

Hopton
Heath

Ludlow   *Ludlow Tun.*

Llangunllo Tun.

Llangynllo

Knucklas

Bucknell

Llanbister Rd.

Knighton

ENGLAND

WALES

Dolau

Leominster

C

Dinmore Tunnels

Moreton-on-Lugg
Tarmac Store Terminal
(Proposed)

1   10 m.   (1:350,000)

0   5

0   5   10   15 km.

2

40

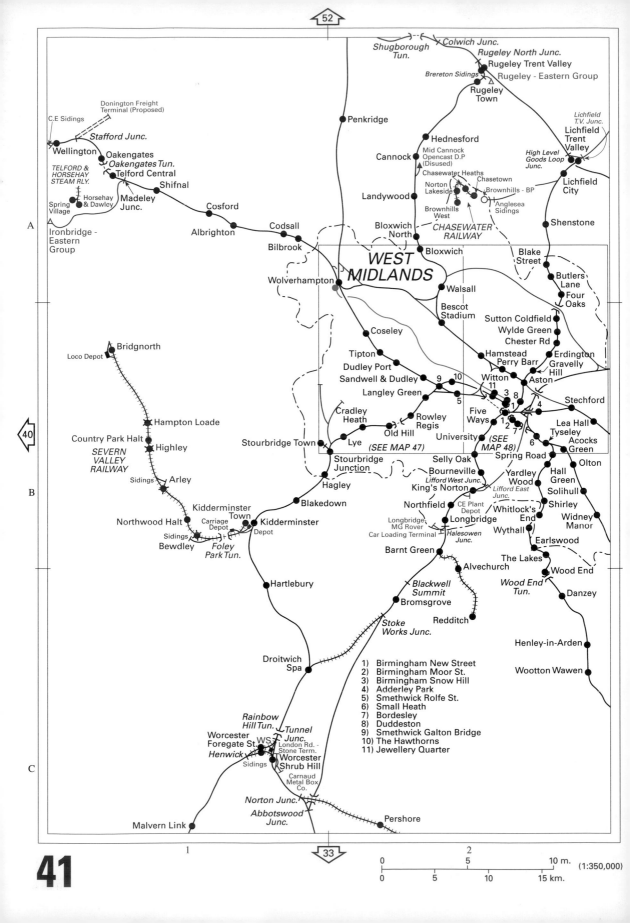

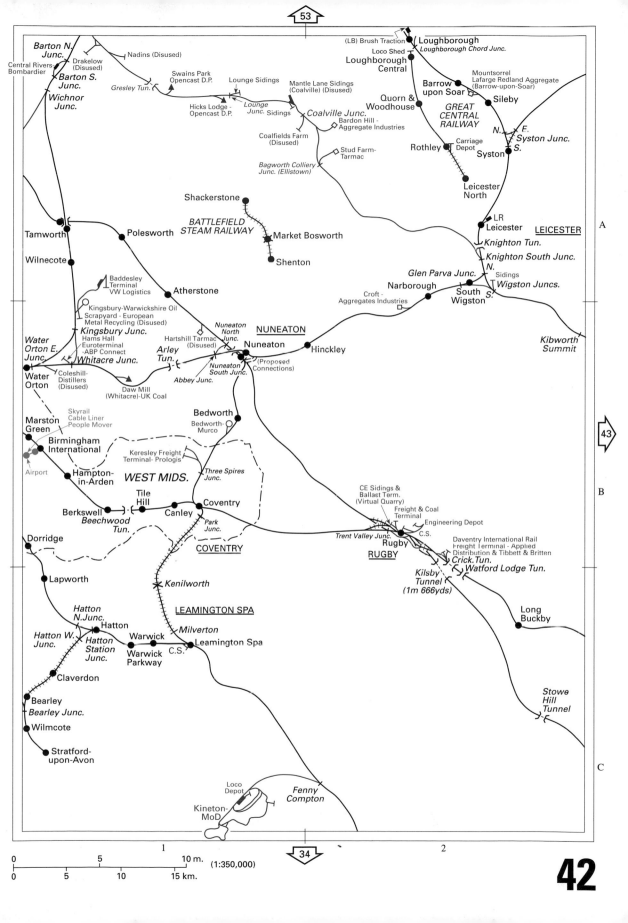

Barton N. Junc.
Central Rivers-Bombardier
Nadins (Disused)
Drakelow (Disused)
Barton S. Junc.
Wichnor Junc.
Gresley Tun.
Swains Park Opencast D.P.
Lounge Sidings
Mantle Lane Sidings (Coalville) (Disused)
Hicks Lodge - Opencast D.P.
Lounge Junc. Sidings
Coalville Junc.
Coalfields Farm (Disused)
Bardon Hill - Aggregate Industries
Stud Farm - Tarmac
Bagworth Colliery Junc. (Ellistown)

(LB) Brush Traction
Loughborough
Loco Shed
Loughborough Chord Junc.
Loughborough Central
Barrow upon Soar
Mountsorrel Lafarge Redland Aggregate (Barrow-upon-Soar)
Quorn & Woodhouse
Sileby
GREAT CENTRAL RAILWAY
N.
F.
Syston Junc.
Rothley
Carriage Depot
Syston
S.
Leicester North

Tamworth
Polesworth
Shackerstone
BATTLEFIELD STEAM RAILWAY
Market Bosworth
Shenton
Wilnecote

LR
Leicester
LEICESTER
A
Knighton Tun.
Knighton South Junc.
N.
Glen Parva Junc.
Sidings
Narborough
Wigston Juncs.
South Wigston
S.

Baddesley Terminal VW Logistics
Atherstone
Kingsbury-Warwickshire Oil
Scrapyard - European Metal Recycling (Disused)
Kingsbury Junc.
Hams Hall Euroterminal -ABP Connect
Hartshill Tarmac (Disused)
Nuneaton North Junc.
NUNEATON
Nuneaton
Hinckley
Croft - Aggregates Industries
Kibworth Summit

Water Orton E. Junc.
Whitacre Junc.
Arley Tun.
Nuneaton South Junc.
(Proposed Connections)
Water Orton
Coleshill-Distillers (Disused)
Daw Mill (Whitacre)-UK Coal
Abbey Junc.

Bedworth
Bedworth-Murco

Marston Green
Skyrail Cable Liner People Mover
Birmingham International
Keresley Freight Terminal- Prologis
Three Spires Junc.
Airport
Hampton-in-Arden
WEST MIDS.
43
B
CE Sidings & Ballast Term. (Virtual Quarry)
Freight & Coal Terminal
Engineering Depot

Dorridge
Berkswell
Tile Hill
Beechwood Tun.
Canley
Coventry
Park Junc.
COVENTRY
Trent Valley Junc.
Rugby
C.S.
RUGBY
Daventry International Rail Freight Terminal - Applied Distribution & Tibbett & Britten
Crick. Tun.
Watford Lodge Tun.
Kilsby Tunnel (1m 666yds)
Long Buckby

Lapworth
Kenilworth
LEAMINGTON SPA
Hatton N. Junc.
Hatton
Milverton
Hatton W. Junc.
Hatton Station Junc.
Warwick
Leamington Spa
Warwick Parkway
C.S.
Claverdon
Bearley
Bearley Junc.
Wilmcote
Stowe Hill Tunnel
C
Stratford-upon-Avon

Loco Depot
Fenny Compton
Kineton-MoD

0   5   10 m.
0   5   10   15 km.
(1:350,000)

1
2

42

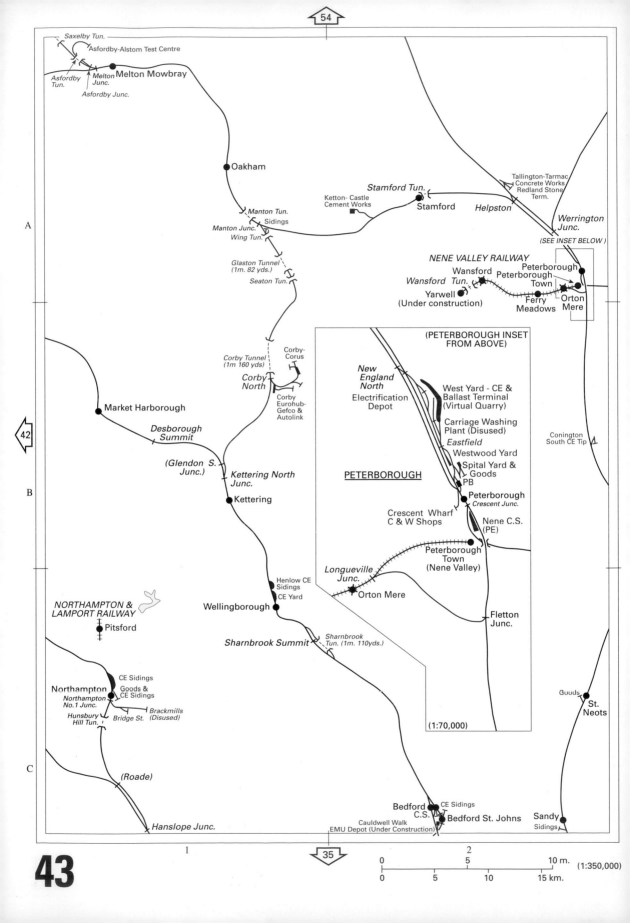

Saxelby Tun.

Asfordby-Alstom Test Centre

Asfordby Tun.

*Melton
Junc.* Melton Mowbray

Asfordby Junc.

Oakham

Stamford Tun.

Ketton- Castle
Cement Works

Stamford *Helpston*

Tallington-Tarmac
Concrete Works
Redland Stone
Term.

*Werrington
Junc.*

(SEE INSET BELOW)

Manton Tun.

Sidings

Manton Junc.

Wing Tun.

Glaston Tunnel
(1m. 82 yds.)

Seaton Tun.

NENE VALLEY RAILWAY

Wansford Tun.

Wansford

Yarwell
(Under construction)

Ferry
Meadows

Peterborough
Peterborough
Town

Orton
Mere

A

Corby-
Corus

*Corby Tunnel
(1m 160 yds.)*

*Corby
North*

Corby
Eurohub-
Gefco &
Autolink

(PETERBOROUGH INSET
FROM ABOVE)

*New
England
North*
Electrification
Depot

West Yard - CE &
Ballast Terminal
(Virtual Quarry)

Carriage Washing
Plant (Disused)

Eastfield

Westwood Yard

Spital Yard &
Goods

Conington
South CE Tip

Market Harborough

*Desborough
Summit*

PETERBOROUGH

PB

Peterborough
Crescent Junc.

42

*(Glendon S.
Junc.)*

*Kettering North
Junc.*

Kettering

Crescent Wharf
C & W Shops

Nene C.S.
(PE)

B

Henlow CE
Sidings

CE Yard

*Longueville
Junc.*

Peterborough
Town
(Nene Valley)

*NORTHAMPTON &
LAMPORT RAILWAY*

Pitsford

Wellingborough

Orton Mere

Fletton
Junc.

Sharnbrook Summit *Sharnbrook
Tun. (1m. 110yds.)*

Goods St.
Neots

CE Sidings

Northampton

Goods &
CE Sidings

*Northampton
No.1 Junc.*

Hunsbury
Hill Tun. Bridge St. Brackmills
(Disused)

(1:70,000)

C

(Roade)

Hanslope Junc.

Bedford
C.S.

CE Sidings

Bedford St. Johns

Sandy

Cauldwell Walk
EMU Depot (Under Construction)

Sidings

1 2

0 5 10 m.

0 5 10 15 km.

(1:350,000)

43

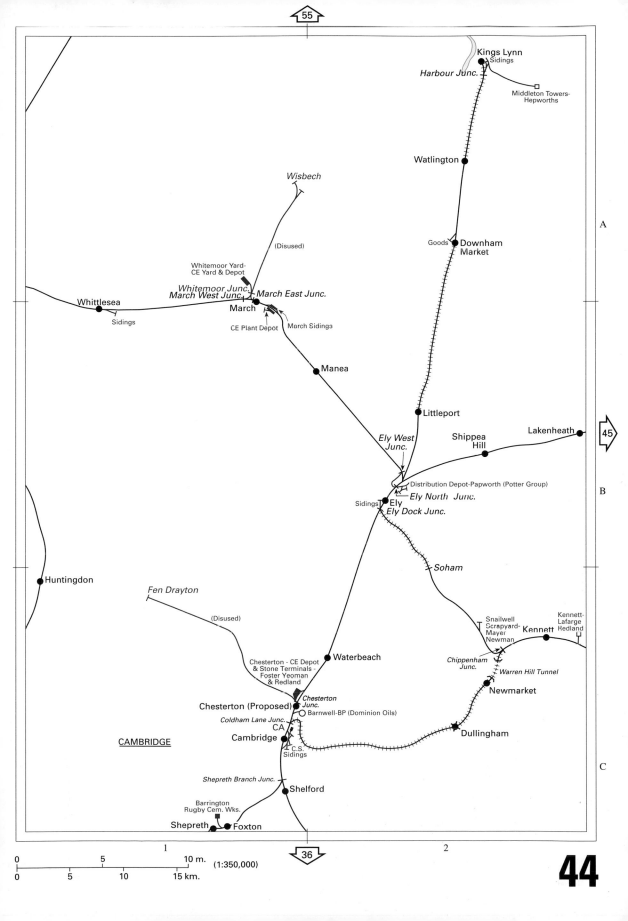

Kings Lynn
Sidings
Harbour Junc.
Middleton Towers-
Hepworths

Watlington

A

Goods Downham
Market

Wisbech

(Disused)

Whitemoor Yard-
CE Yard & Depot
Whitemoor Junc. March East Junc.
March West Junc.
Whittlesea March
Sidings CE Plant Depot March Sidings

Manea

Littleport

Lakenheath

*Ely West
Junc.*
Shippea
Hill

45

B

Distribution Depot-Papworth (Potter Group)
Ely North Junc.
Sidings Ely
Ely Dock Junc.

Soham

Kennett-
Lafarge
Redland
Snailwell
Scrapyard- Kennett
Mayer
Newman
*Chippenham
Junc.* *Warren Hill Tunnel*

Huntingdon

Fen Drayton

(Disused)

Waterbeach

Chesterton - CE Depot
& Stone Terminals -
Foster Yeoman
& Redland
*Chesterton
Junc.*
Chesterton (Proposed)
Barnwell-BP (Dominion Oils)
Coldham Lane Junc.
CA
CAMBRIDGE Cambridge
C.S.
Sidings

Newmarket

Dullingham

C

Shepreth Branch Junc.
Shelford

Barrington
Rugby Cem. Wks.
Shepreth Foxton

1

10 m.

(1:350,000)

0   5   10 m.
0   5   10   15 km.

36

2

44

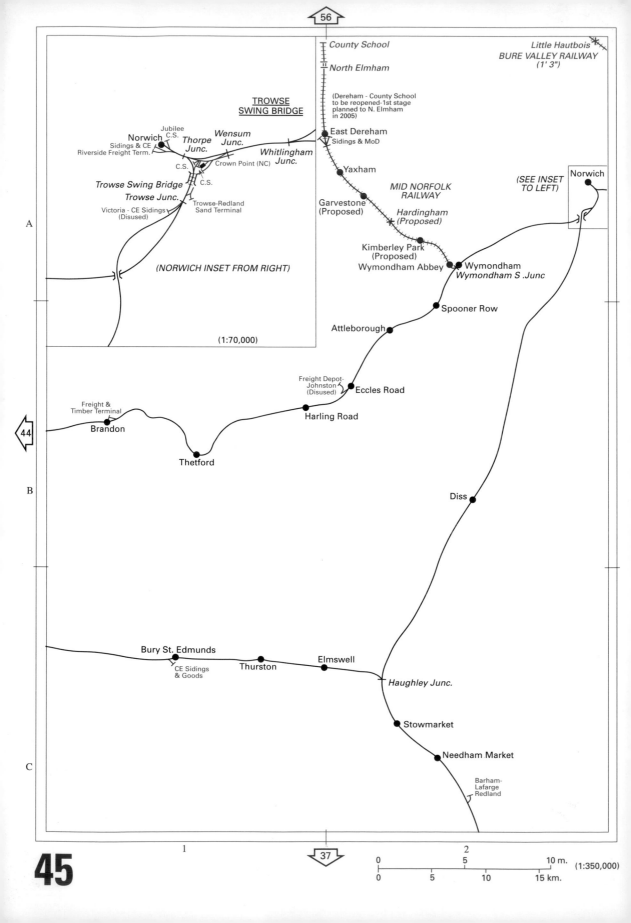

County School

North Elmham

Little Hautbois
BURE VALLEY RAILWAY
(1' 3")

**TROWSE
SWING BRIDGE**

(Dereham - County School
to be reopened-1st stage
planned to N. Elmham
in 2005)

Jubilee
C.S.

Norwich
Sidings & CE
Riverside Freight Term.

*Thorpe
Junc.*

*Wensum
Junc.*

East Dereham
Sidings & MoD

*Whitlingham
Junc.*

Crown Point (NC)

C.S.

Trowse Swing Bridge

C.S.

Trowse Junc.

Victoria - CE Sidings
(Disused)

Trowse-Redland
Sand Terminal

Yaxham

*MID NORFOLK
RAILWAY*

Garvestone
(Proposed)

*Hardingham
(Proposed)*

Kimberley Park
(Proposed)

*(SEE INSET
TO LEFT)*

Norwich

(NORWICH INSET FROM RIGHT)

Wymondham Abbey

Wymondham
Wymondham S .Junc

Spooner Row

Attleborough

(1:70,000)

A

Freight Depot-
Johnston
(Disused)

Eccles Road

Freight &
Timber Terminal

Brandon

Harling Road

Thetford

Diss

B

Bury St. Edmunds

CE Sidings
& Goods

Thurston

Elmswell

Haughley Junc.

Stowmarket

Needham Market

Barham-
Lafarge
Redland

C

2

0   5   10 m.
0   5   10   15 km.

(1:350,000)

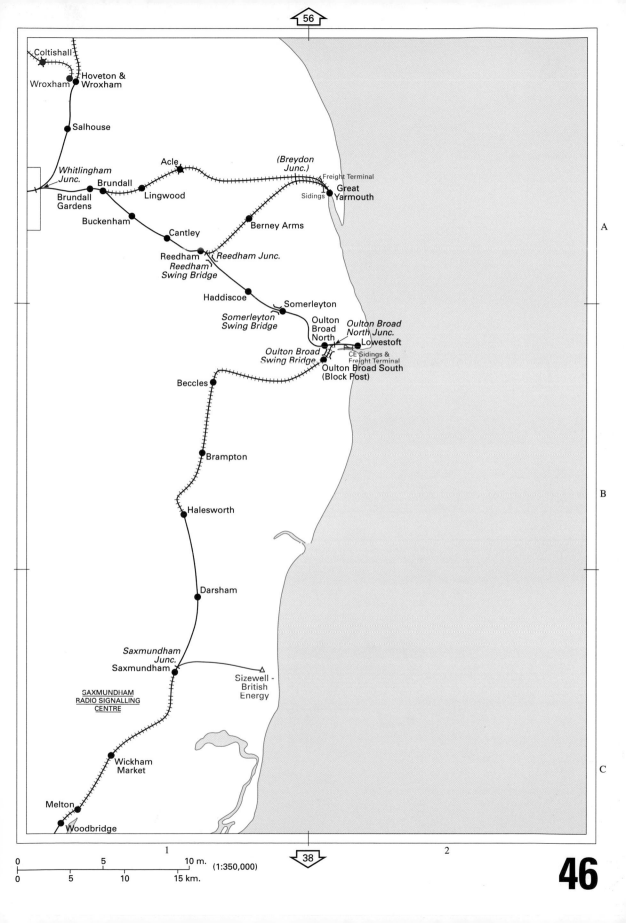

Coltishall

Hoveton &
Wroxham

Wroxham

Salhouse

*Whitlingham
Junc.*

Acle

*(Breydon
Junc.)*

Freight Terminal

Brundall

Lingwood

**Great
Yarmouth**

Sidings

Brundall
Gardens

Buckenham

Berney Arms

Cantley

A

Reedham

Reedham Junc.

*Reedham
Swing Bridge*

Haddiscoe

Somerleyton

*Somerleyton
Swing Bridge*

Oulton
Broad
North

*Oulton Broad
North Junc.*

Lowestoft

*Oulton Broad
Swing Bridge*

CE Sidings &
Freight Terminal

Oulton Broad South
(Block Post)

Beccles

Brampton

B

Halesworth

Darsham

*Saxmundham
Junc.*

Saxmundham

△ Sizewell -
British
Energy

SAXMUNDHAM
RADIO SIGNALLING
CENTRE

C

Wickham
Market

Melton

Woodbridge

1

10 m.

(1:350,000)

2

0   5   10 m.
0   5   10   15 km.

46

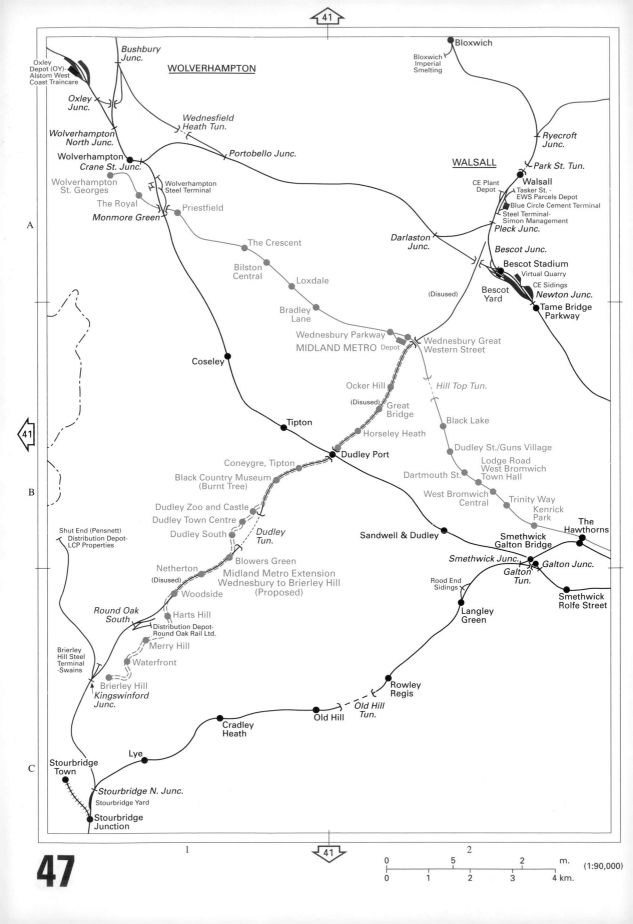

Bushbury Junc.

Oxley Depot (OY)-
Alstom West
Coast Traincare

Oxley Junc.

WOLVERHAMPTON

Bloxwich

Bloxwich
Imperial
Smelting

*Wednesfield
Heath Tun.*

*Wolverhampton
North Junc.*

Wolverhampton
Crane St. Junc.

Portobello Junc.

*Ryecroft
Junc.*

WALSALL

Park St. Tun.

Wolverhampton
St. Georges

Wolverhampton
Steel Terminal

The Royal

Monmore Green

Priestfield

Walsall

CE Plant
Depot

Tasker St. -
EWS Parcels Depot
Blue Circle Cement Terminal
Steel Terminal-
Simon Management

Pleck Junc.

A

The Crescent

*Darlaston
Junc.*

Bescot Junc.

Bilston
Central

Loxdale

Bescot Stadium
Virtual Quarry
CE Sidings

Bescot
Yard

Newton Junc.

Bradley
Lane

(Disused)

Tame Bridge
Parkway

Wednesbury Parkway
MIDLAND METRO Depot

Wednesbury Great
Western Street

Coseley

Ocker Hill

Hill Top Tun.

(Disused) Great
Bridge

Black Lake

Tipton

Horseley Heath

Dudley St./Guns Village

Dudley Port

Lodge Road
West Bromwich
Town Hall

Coneygre, Tipton

Dartmouth St.

Black Country Museum
(Burnt Tree)

West Bromwich
Central

Trinity Way
Kenrick
Park

B

Dudley Zoo and Castle
Dudley Town Centre

Sandwell & Dudley

The Hawthorns

Dudley South

*Dudley
Tun.*

Smethwick
Galton Bridge

Smethwick Junc.

Galton Junc.

Shut End (Pensnett)
Distribution Depot-
LCP Properties

Netherton

Blowers Green
Midland Metro Extension
Wednesbury to Brierley Hill
(Proposed)

*Galton
Tun.*

(Disused)

Woodside

Rood End
Sidings

Smethwick
Rolfe Street

*Round Oak
South*

Harts Hill

Distribution Depot-
Round Oak Rail Ltd.

Langley
Green

Brierley
Hill Steel
Terminal
-Swains

Merry Hill

Waterfront

Brierley Hill
*Kingswinford
Junc.*

Rowley
Regis

*Old Hill
Tun.*

Old Hill

Cradley
Heath

Lye

C

Stourbridge
Town

Stourbridge N. Junc.
Stourbridge Yard

Stourbridge
Junction

47

1

2

0   5   2   m.

0   1   2   3   4 km.

(1:90,000)

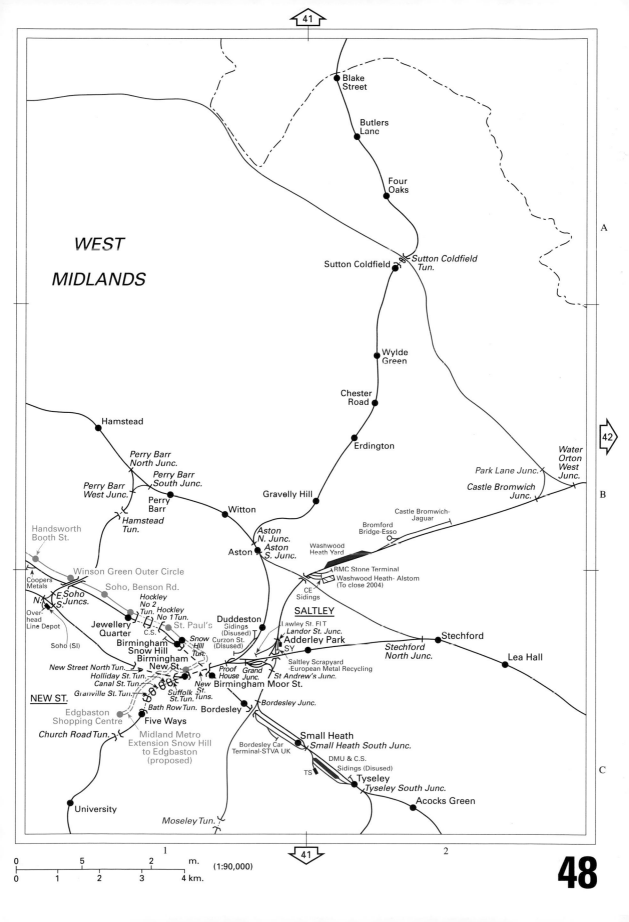

Blake
Street

Butlers
Lane

Four
Oaks

A

Sutton Coldfield
*Sutton Coldfield
Tun.*

WEST

MIDLANDS

Wylde
Green

Chester
Road

Hamstead

*Perry Barr
North Junc.*

*Perry Barr
South Junc.*

Erdington

42

*Water
Orton
West
Junc.*

*Perry Barr
West Junc.*

Park Lane Junc.

*Castle Bromwich
Junc.*

B

Perry
Barr

Witton

Gravelly Hill

*Hamstead
Tun.*

Handsworth
Booth St.

Winson Green Outer Circle

Coopers
Metals

Soho, Benson Rd.

N.( )
E.Soho
S.( ) Juncs.

Overhead
Line Depot

Soho (SI)

*Hockley
No 2
Tun.* *Hockley
No 1 Tun.*

Jewellery
Quarter

Birmingham
Snow Hill

*Snow
Hill
Tun.*

St. Paul's

C.S.

Birmingham
New St.

New Street North Tun.
Holliday St. Tun.
Canal St. Tun.

*Suffolk
St. Tun.*
Granville St. Tun.

Bath Row Tun.

NEW ST.

Edgbaston
Shopping Centre

Five Ways

Church Road Tun.

Midland Metro
Extension Snow Hill
to Edgbaston
(proposed)

University

Moseley Tun.

*Aston
N. Junc.*
*Aston
S. Junc.*

Aston

Duddeston
Sidings
(Disused)
Curzon St.
(Disused)

Lawley St. FLT
Landor St. Junc.

Adderley Park
SY

SALTLEY

Washwood
Heath Yard

CE
Sidings

RMC Stone Terminal
Washwood Heath- Alstom
(To close 2004)

Castle Bromwich-
Jaguar

Bromford
Bridge-Esso

Stechford

*Stechford
North Junc.*

Lea Hall

Saltley Scrapyard
-European Metal Recycling
St Andrew's Junc.

*Proof
House*
*Grand
Junc.*

New Birmingham Moor St.

Bordesley

Bordesley Junc.

Small Heath
Small Heath South Junc.

Bordesley Car
Terminal-STVA UK

DMU & C.S.
Sidings (Disused)

TS

Tyseley
Tyseley South Junc.

Acocks Green

C

0	5		

1 m.
(1:90,000)

| 0 | 1 | 2 | 3 | 4 km. |

2

48

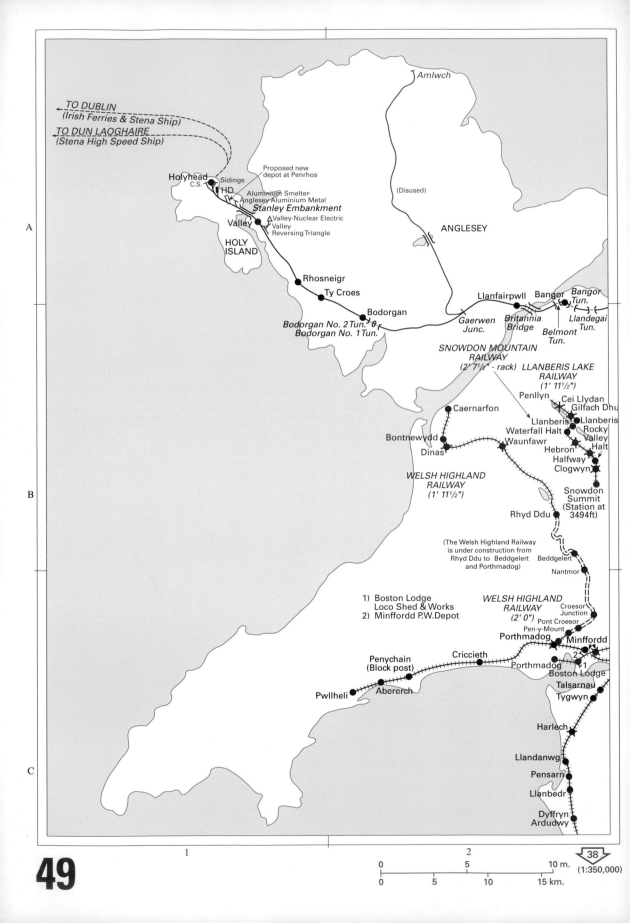

Amlwch

TO DUBLIN
(Irish Ferries & Stena Ship)

TO DUN LAOGHAIRE
(Stena High Speed Ship)

Proposed new
depot at Penrhos

Holyhead
C.S.   Sidings
HD
        Aluminium Smelter-
        Anglesey Aluminium Metal
        Stanley Embankment

(Disused)

ANGLESEY

Valley   Valley-Nuclear Electric
              Valley
HOLY   Reversing Triangle
ISLAND

Rhosneigr

Ty Croes

Bodorgan   Llanfairpwll   Bangor   *Bangor
                                              Tun.*
Bodorgan No. 2 Tun. &   Britannia   *Llandegai
Bodorgan No. 1 Tun.*   *Gaerwen   Bridge   Tun.*
                        Junc.*   *Belmont
                                  Tun.*

*SNOWDON MOUNTAIN
RAILWAY*
(2' 7½" - rack)   *LLANBERIS LAKE
                      RAILWAY*
                    (1' 11½")
                    Penllyn   Cei Llydan
                                 Gilfach Dhu
Caernarfon   Llanberis   Llanberis
                                 Rocky
Bontnewydd   Waterfall Halt   Valley Halt
                    Waunfawr
Dinas   Hebron
                    Halfway
                    Clogwyn
*WELSH HIGHLAND
RAILWAY*
(1' 11½")   Snowdon
                                 Summit
                    Rhyd Ddu   (Station at
                                 3494ft)

(The Welsh Highland Railway
is under construction from
Rhyd Ddu to Beddgelert   Beddgelert
and Porthmadog)
                             Nantmor

                             *WELSH HIGHLAND
                             RAILWAY*
1) Boston Lodge   *(2' 0")*
   Loco Shed & Works   Croesor
2) Minffordd P.W.Depot   Junction
                                    Pont Croesor
                                   Pen-y-Mount
                    Porthmadog   Minffordd
          Criccieth   2
Penychain   Porthmadog 1
(Block post)   Boston Lodge
                                          Talsarnau
Pwllheli   Abererch   Tygwyn

                                          Harlech

                                          Llandanwg
                                          Pensarn
                                          Llanbedr

                                          Dyffryn
                                          Ardudwy

A

B

C

1   2

38
(1:350,000)

0   5   10 m.

0   5   10   15 km.

49

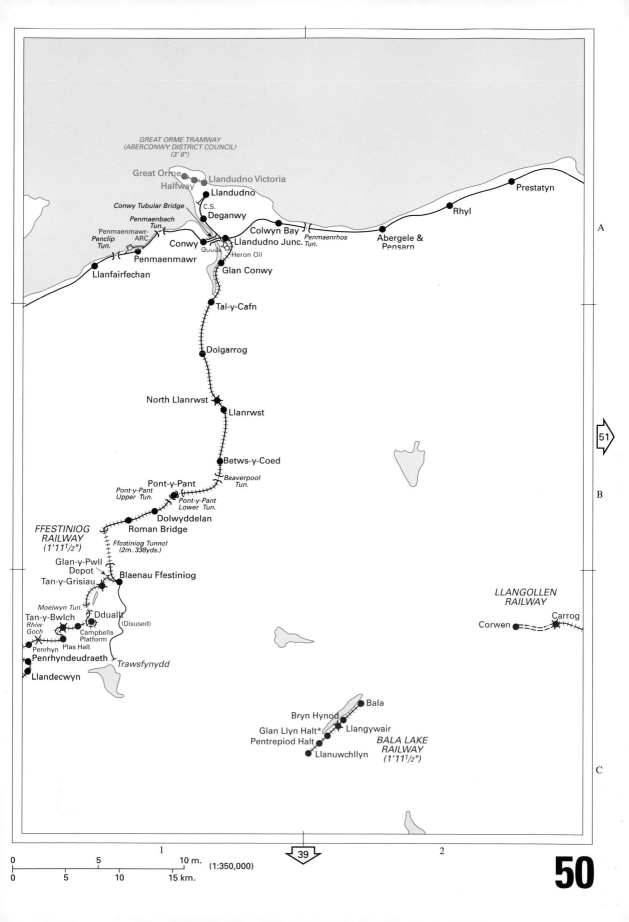

GREAT ORME TRAMWAY
(ABERCONWY DISTRICT COUNCIL)
(3' 6")

Great Orme
Halfway
Llandudno Victoria
Llandudno
C.S.
Conwy Tubular Bridge
Deganwy
Penmaenbach
Tun.
Penmaenmawr-
Penclip
Tun.
ARC
Colwyn Bay
Penmaenrhos
Tun.
Conwy
Quay
Llandudno Junc.
Heron Oil
Penmaenmawr
Glan Conwy
Llanfairfechan

Prestatyn
Rhyl
Abergele &
Pensarn

A

Tal-y-Cafn

Dolgarrog

North Llanrwst
Llanrwst

Betws-y-Coed

51

Pont-y-Pant
Beaverpool
Tun.

B

Pont-y-Pant
Upper Tun.
Pont-y-Pant
Lower Tun.
Dolwyddelan
Roman Bridge

FFESTINIOG
RAILWAY
(1'11¹/₂")
Ffestiniog Tunnel
(2m. 338yds.)

Glan-y-Pwll
Depot
Blaenau Ffestiniog
Tan-y-Grisiau

LLANGOLLEN
RAILWAY

Moelwyn Tun.
Tan-y-Bwlch
Dduallt
Carrog
Rhiw
Goch
(Disused)
Corwen
Campbells
Platform
Penrhyn
Plas Halt
Penrhyndeudraeth
Trawsfynydd

Llandecwyn

Bala
Bryn Hynod
Glan Llyn Halt*
Llangywair
Pentrepiod Halt
BALA LAKE
RAILWAY
(1'11¹/₂")
Llanuwchllyn

C

1
10 m.
39
2

0   5   10 m.   (1:350,000)
0   5   10   15 km.

50

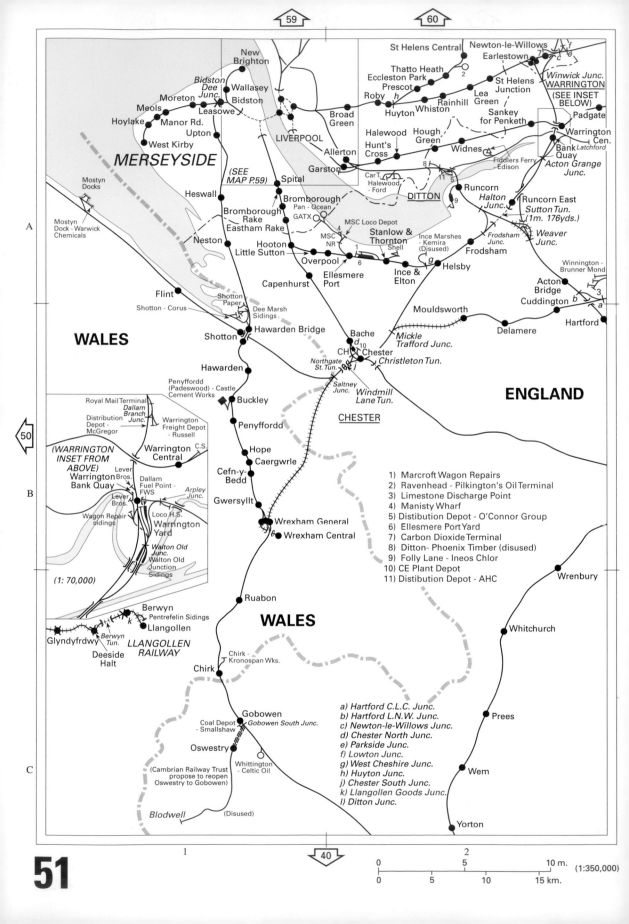

St Helens Central
Newton-le-Willows
Earlestown
Winwick Junc.
WARRINGTON
(SEE INSET BELOW)
Thatto Heath
Eccleston Park
Prescot
Roby
St Helens
Junction
Padgate
New
Brighton
Wallasey
Bidston
*Bidston
Dee Junc.*
Moreton
Leasowe
Meols
Bidston
Broad
Green
Huyton
Whiston
Rainhill
Lea Green
Sankey
for Penketh
Warrington
Cen.
Latchford
Hoylake
Manor Rd.
Upton
West Kirby
LIVERPOOL
Halewood
Hunt's
Cross
Hough
Green
Widnes
Bank
Quay
*Acton Grange
Junc.*
MERSEYSIDE
*(SEE
MAP P.59)*
Heswall
Spital
Garston
Allerton
Car T.
Halewood
- Ford
Fiddlers Ferry
- Edison
DITTON
Runcorn
Sutton Tun.
(1m. 176yds.)
Runcorn East
Mostyn
Docks
Bromborough
Pan - Ocean
GATX
MSC Loco Depot
*Halton
Junc.*
*Frodsham
Junc.*
*Weaver
Junc.*
Mostyn
Dock - Warwick
Chemicals
A
Bromborough
Rake
Eastham Rake
Neston
Stanlow &
Thornton
Shell
MSC
NR
Ince Marshes
- Kemira
(Disused)
Frodsham
*Winnington -
Brunner Mond*
Hooton
Little Sutton
Overpool
Ince &
Elton
Helsby
Acton
Bridge
Cuddington
Capenhurst
Ellesmere
Port
Mouldsworth
Delamere
Hartford
Flint
Shotton Paper
Shotton - Corus
Dee Marsh
Sidings
Shotton
Hawarden Bridge
Bache
*Mickle
Trafford Junc.*
Chester
CH
Christleton Tun.
WALES
Hawarden
*Northgate
St. Tun.*
*Saltney
Junc.*
*Windmill
Lane Tun.*
CHESTER
ENGLAND
Penyffordd
(Padeswood) - Castle
Cement Works
Buckley
Penyffordd
Royal Mail Terminal
*Dallam
Branch
Junc.*
Distribution
Depot -
McGregor
Warrington
Freight Depot
- Russell
Hope
Caergwrle
1) Marcroft Wagon Repairs
2) Ravenhead - Pilkington's Oil Terminal
3) Limestone Discharge Point
4) Manisty Wharf
5) Distibution Depot - O'Connor Group
6) Ellesmere Port Yard
7) Carbon Dioxide Terminal
8) Ditton- Phoenix Timber (disused)
9) Folly Lane - Ineos Chlor
10) CE Plant Depot
11) Distibution Depot - AHC
*(WARRINGTON
INSET FROM
ABOVE)*
Warrington
Bank Quay
Warrington
Central
C.S.
Lever
Bros.
Dallam
Fuel Point -
FWS
*Arpley
Junc.*
Cefn-y-
Bedd
Lever
Bros.
Wagon Repair
sidings
Warrington
Yard
Loco H.S.
*Walton Old
Junc.*
Walton Old
Junction
Sidings
Gwersyllt
Wrexham General
Wrexham Central
Wrenbury
(1: 70,000)
Berwyn
Pentrefelin Sidings
Llangollen
*Berwyn
Tun.*
Ruabon
WALES
Whitchurch
Glyndyfrdwy
Deeside
Halt
LLANGOLLEN
RAILWAY
Chirk
Chirk -
Kronospan Wks.
a) Hartford C.L.C. Junc.
b) Hartford L.N.W. Junc.
c) Newton-le-Willows Junc.
d) Chester North Junc.
e) Parkside Junc.
f) Lowton Junc.
g) West Cheshire Junc.
h) Huyton Junc.
j) Chester South Junc.
k) Llangollen Goods Junc.
l) Ditton Junc.
Prees
Gobowen
Gobowen South Junc.
Coal Depot
- Smallshaw
Oswestry
Whittington
- Celtic Oil
Wem
C
*(Cambrian Railway Trust
propose to reopen
Oswestry to Gobowen)*
Blodwell
(Disused)
Yorton

B

0   5   10 m.
0   5   10   15 km.
(1:350,000)

51

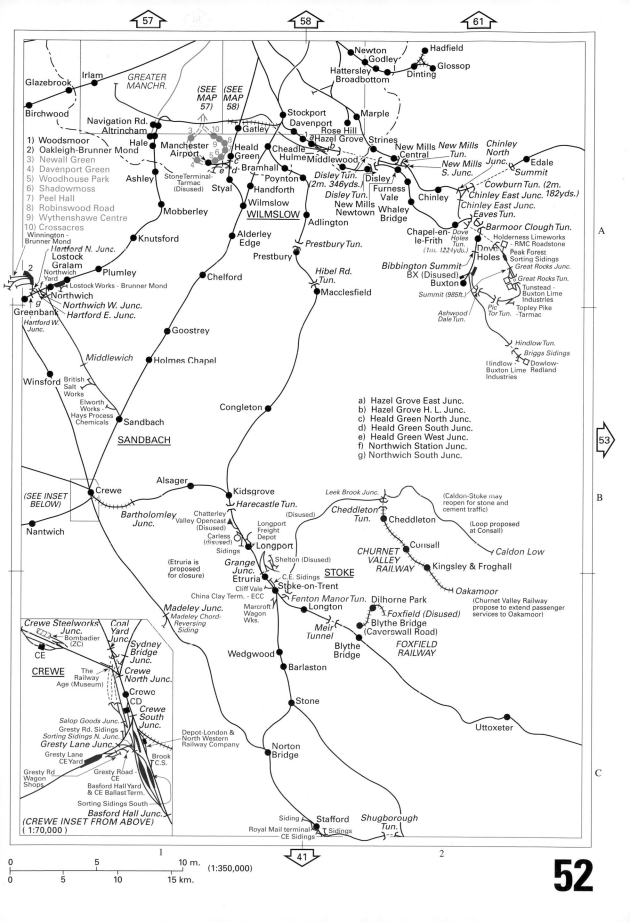

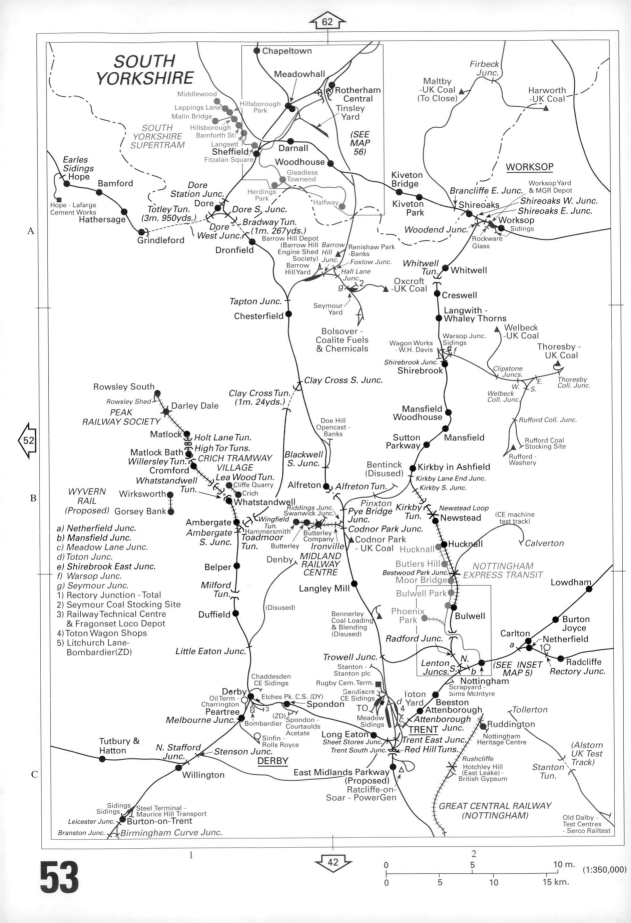

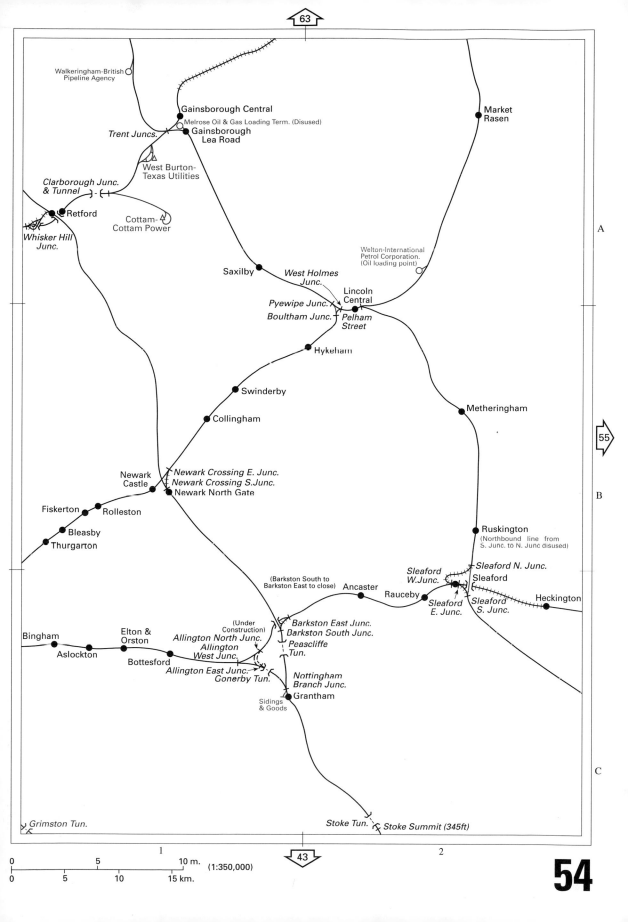

Walkeringham–British
Pipeline Agency

Gainsborough Central
Melrose Oil & Gas Loading Term. (Disused)
Trent Juncs. Gainsborough
Lea Road

West Burton–
Texas Utilities

*Clarborough Junc.
& Tunnel*

Retford

Cottam–
Cottam Power

*Whisker Hill
Junc.*

Market
Rasen

A

Welton–International
Petrol Corporation.
(Oil loading point)

Saxilby *West Holmes
Junc.*

Lincoln
Central
Pyewipe Junc.
Boultham Junc. Pelham
Street

Hykeham

Swinderby

Collingham

Metheringham

55

B

Newark
Castle

Newark Crossing E. Junc.
Newark Crossing S. Junc.
Newark North Gate

Fiskerton
Rolleston
Bleasby
Thurgarton

Ruskington
(Northbound line from
S. Junc. to N. Junc disused)

Sleaford N. Junc.
*Sleaford
W. Junc.* Sleaford

(Barkston South to
Barkston East to close) Ancaster
Rauceby *Sleaford
E. Junc.* *Sleaford
S. Junc.*
Heckington

(Under
Construction)
Barkston East Junc.
Barkston South Junc.
Allington North Junc.
*Allington
West Junc.* *Peascliffe
Tun.*

Bingham
Elton &
Orston
Aslockton
Bottesford
Allington East Junc.
Gonerby Tun. *Nottingham
Branch Junc.*
Sidings
& Goods Grantham

C

Grimston Tun.

Stoke Tun. *Stoke Summit (345ft)*

1
0   5   10 m.   (1:350,000)
0   5   10   15 km.

2

54

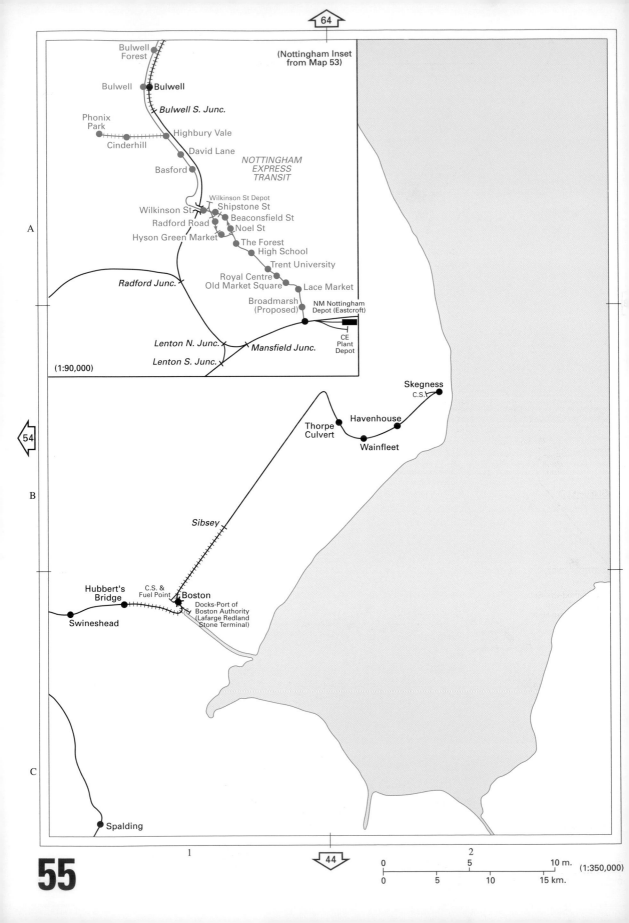

64

(Nottingham Inset
from Map 53)

Bulwell
Forest

Bulwell   **Bulwell**

Bulwell S. Junc.

Phonix
Park
                Highbury Vale
Cinderhill
                David Lane
Basford

*NOTTINGHAM
EXPRESS
TRANSIT*

Wilkinson St Depot
                Shipstone St
Wilkinson St   Beaconsfield St
Radford Road   Noel St
Hyson Green Market
                The Forest
                High School
                Trent University
Royal Centre
Old Market Square   Lace Market

Radford Junc. ✕

A

Broadmarsh
(Proposed)   NM Nottingham
                Depot (Eastcroft)

Lenton N. Junc. ✕   ✕ *Mansfield Junc.*

                CE
                Plant
                Depot

Lenton S. Junc. ✕

(1:90,000)

54

Skegness
C.S.

Havenhouse
Thorpe
Culvert
                Wainfleet

B

Sibsey ✕

Hubbert's   C.S. &
Bridge   Fuel Point   Boston
                              Docks-Port of
                              Boston Authority
                              (Lafarge Redland
Swineshead   Stone Terminal)

C

Spalding

55

1   44

0   2
0   5   10 m.
0   5   10   15 km.   (1:350,000)

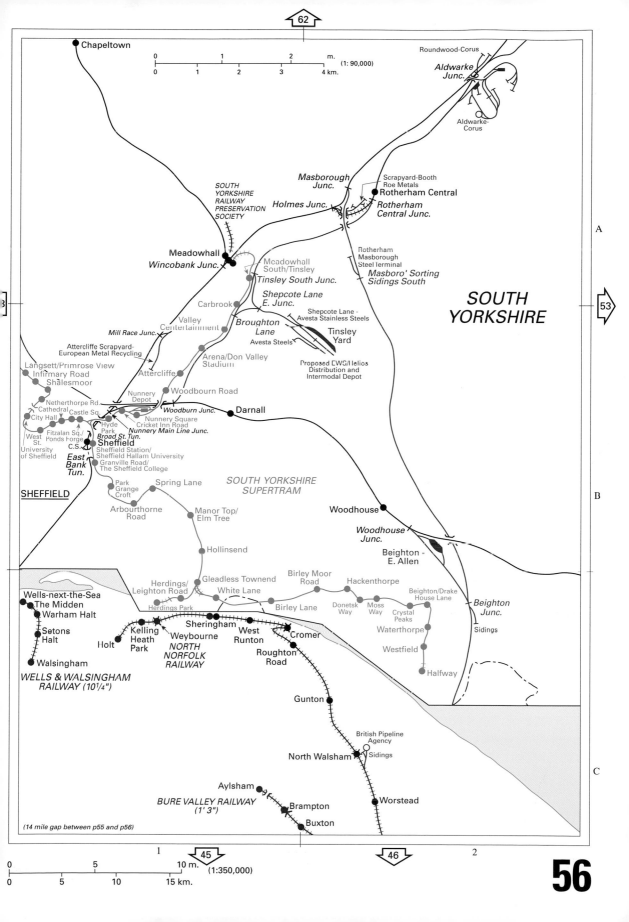

Chapeltown

0   1   2   m.
0   1   2   3   4 km.   (1: 90,000)

Roundwood-Corus

Aldwarke Junc.

Aldwarke-Corus

Masborough Junc.

Scrapyard-Booth
Roe Metals

Rotherham Central

Holmes Junc.

Rotherham
Central Junc.

SOUTH
YORKSHIRE
RAILWAY
PRESERVATION
SOCIETY

Meadowhall
Wincobank Junc.

Meadowhall
South/Tinsley

Tinsley South Junc.

Rotherham
Masborough
Steel Terminal

Masboro' Sorting
Sidings South

A

Shepcote Lane
E. Junc.

Carbrook

Valley
Centertainment

Broughton
Lane

Shepcote Lane -
Avesta Stainless Steels

Tinsley
Yard

Mill Race Junc.

Attercliffe Scrapyard-
European Metal Recycling

Arena/Don Valley
Stadium

Avesta Steels

Proposed CWS/Helios
Distribution and
Intermodal Depot

Attercliffe

Langsett/Primrose View
Infirmary Road
Shalesmoor

Woodbourn Road

Nunnery
Depot

Netherthorpe Rd
Cathedral Castle Sq.
City Hall

Hyde
Park

Woodburn Junc.

Darnall

Nunnery Square
Cricket Inn Road

West
St.
University
of Sheffield

Fitzalan Sq./
Ponds Forge

Nunnery Main Line Junc.

Broad St. Tun.

C.S.

Sheffield

Sheffield Station/
Sheffield Hallam University
Granville Road/
The Sheffield College

East
Bank
Tun.

Park
Grange
Croft

Spring Lane

SOUTH YORKSHIRE
SUPERTRAM

SHEFFIELD

Arbourthorne
Road

Manor Top/
Elm Tree

Woodhouse

B

Hollinsend

Woodhouse
Junc.

Beighton -
E. Allen

Herdings/
Leighton Road

Gleadless Townend

White Lane

Birley Moor
Road

Hackenthorpe

Beighton/Drake
House Lane

Beighton
Junc.

Herdings Park

Birley Lane

Donetsk
Way

Moss
Way

Crystal
Peaks

Waterthorpe

Sidings

Wells-next-the-Sea
The Midden
Warham Halt

Setons
Halt

Walsingham

Holt

Kelling
Heath
Park

Weybourne

NORTH
NORFOLK
RAILWAY

Sheringham

West
Runton

Cromer

Roughton
Road

Westfield

Halfway

WELLS & WALSINGHAM
RAILWAY (10¼")

Gunton

British Pipeline
Agency

North Walsham

Sidings

C

Aylsham

BURE VALLEY RAILWAY
(1' 3")

Brampton

Buxton

Worstead

(14 mile gap between p55 and p56)

0   5   10 m.
0   5   10   15 km.   (1:350,000)

1   2

56

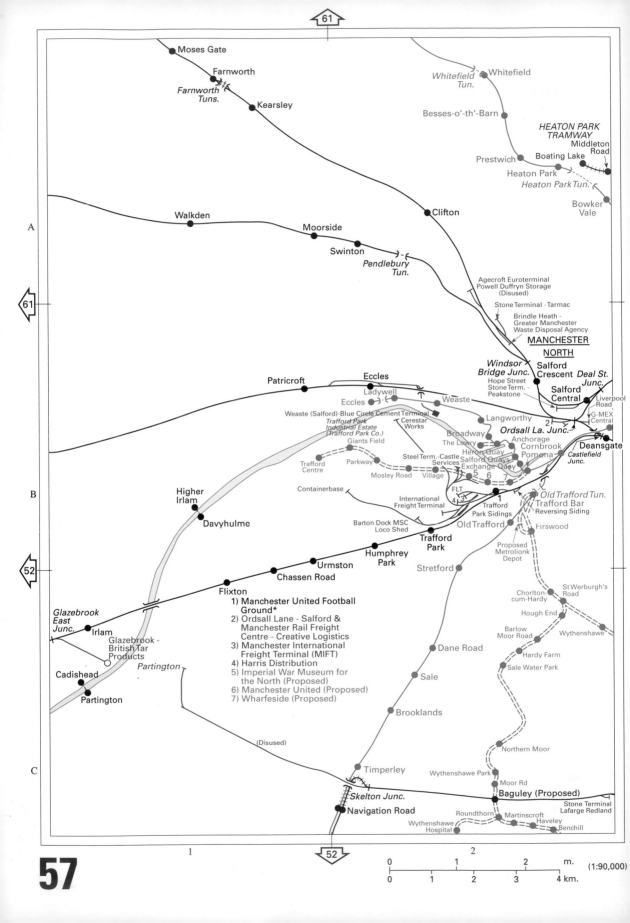

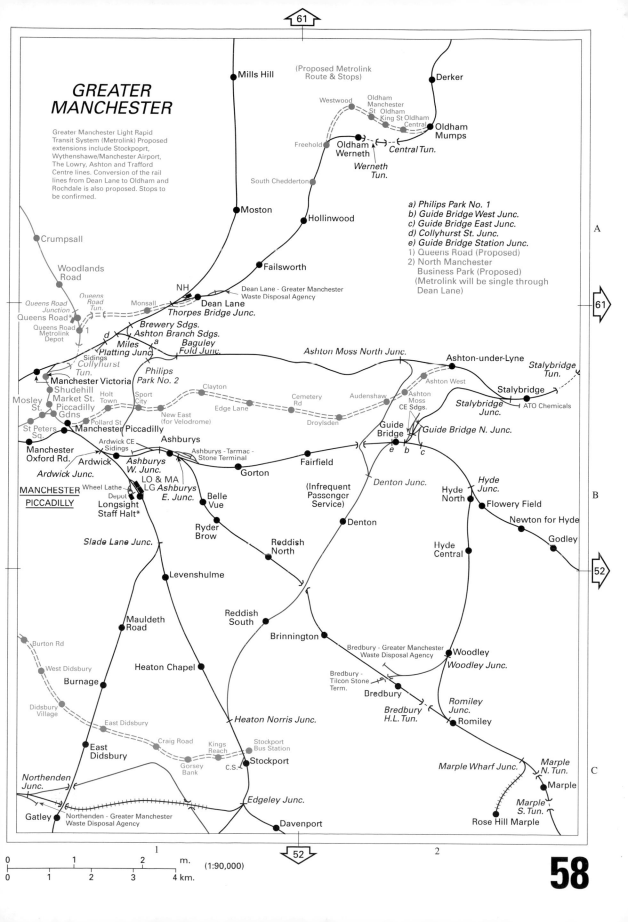

GREATER MANCHESTER

Greater Manchester Light Rapid
Transit System (Metrolink) Proposed
extensions include Stockpoprt,
Wythenshawe/Manchester Airport,
The Lowry, Ashton and Trafford
Centre lines. Conversion of the rail
lines from Dean Lane to Oldham and
Rochdale is also proposed. Stops to
be confirmed.

(Proposed Metrolink
Route & Stops)

Mills Hill

Derker

Westwood

Oldham
Manchester
St Oldham
King St Oldham
Central

Oldham
Mumps

Freehold

Oldham
Werneth

Central Tun.

*Werneth
Tun.*

South Chedderton

Moston

Hollinwood

a) Philips Park No. 1
b) Guide Bridge West Junc.
c) Guide Bridge East Junc.
d) Collyhurst St. Junc.
e) Guide Bridge Station Junc.
1) Queens Road (Proposed)
2) North Manchester
   Business Park (Proposed)
(Metrolink will be single through
Dean Lane)

Failsworth

Crumpsall

Woodlands
Road

NH

Dean Lane - Greater Manchester
Waste Disposal Agency

*Queens Road
Junction*

*Queens
Road
Tun.*

Monsall

Dean Lane

Queens Road

Queens Road
Metrolink
Depot

1

d

Thorpes Bridge Junc.

Brewery Sdgs.

Ashton Branch Sdgs.

a

Baguley
Fold Junc.

*Miles
Platting Junc.*

Ashton Moss North Junc.

Ashton-under-Lyne

*Stalybridge
Tun.*

Sidings

*Collyhurst
Tun.*

Manchester Victoria

Shudehill

Market St.

Mosley
St.

Piccadilly
Gdns

Philips
Park No. 2

Holt
Town

Sport
City

Clayton

Edge Lane

Cemetery
Rd

Ashton West

Audenshaw

Ashton
Moss
CE Sdgs.

Stalybridge

*Stalybridge
Junc.*

ATO Chemicals

New East
(for Velodrome)

Droylsden

Pollard St

St Peters
Sq.

Manchester Piccadilly

Ashburys

Guide
Bridge

Guide Bridge N. Junc.

Manchester
Oxford Rd.

Ardwick

Ardwick Junc.

Ardwick CE
Sidings

*Ashburys
W. Junc.*

Ashburys - Tarmac -
Stone Terminal

Fairfield

e   b   c

Gorton

**MANCHESTER
PICCADILLY**

Wheel Lathe

LO & MA
LG *Ashburys
E. Junc.*

Depot

Belle
Vue

(Infrequent
Passenger
Service)

Denton Junc.

Hyde
North

*Hyde
Junc.*

Longsight
Staff Halt*

Ryder
Brow

Denton

Flowery Field

Newton for Hyde

Hyde
Central

Slade Lane Junc.

Reddish
North

Godley

Levenshulme

Mauldeth
Road

Reddish
South

Brinnington

Bredbury - Greater Manchester
Waste Disposal Agency

Woodley

Woodley Junc.

Burton Rd

West Didsbury

Heaton Chapel

Bredbury -
Tilcon Stone
Term.

Bredbury

*Romiley
Junc.*

Burnage

Didsbury
Village

*Bredbury
H.L. Tun.*

Romiley

East Didsbury

Craig Road

Kings
Reach

Stockport
Bus Station

Heaton Norris Junc.

Marple Wharf Junc.

*Marple
N. Tun.*

Marple

East
Didsbury

Gorsey
Bank

C.S.

Stockport

*Marple
S. Tun.*

*Northenden
Junc.*

Gatley

Northenden - Greater Manchester
Waste Disposal Agency

Edgeley Junc.

Davenport

Rose Hill Marple

A

61

B

52

C

0   1   2   m.
0   1   2   3   4 km.
(1:90,000)

1   2

52

58

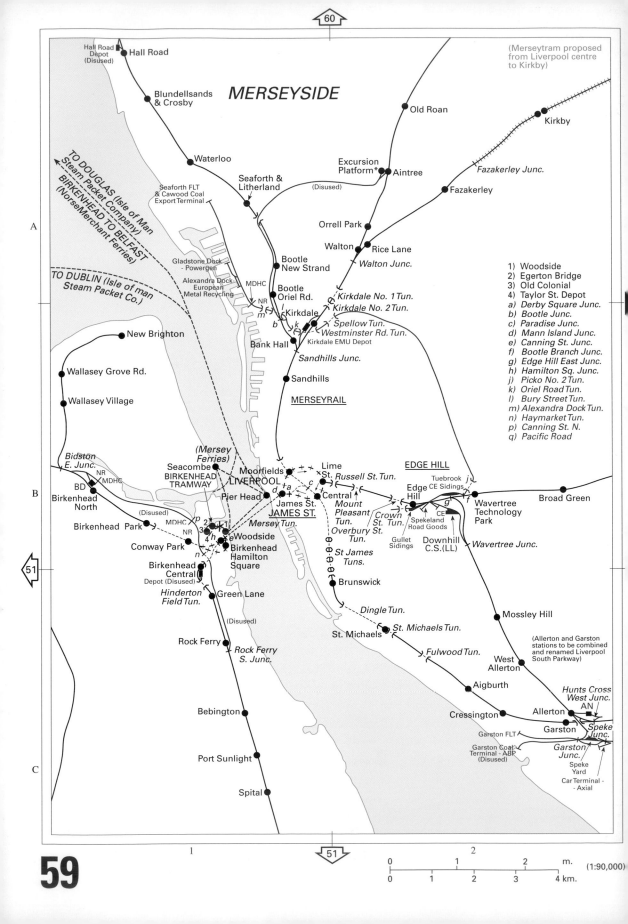

(Merseytram proposed
from Liverpool centre
to Kirkby)

Hall Road
Depot
(Disused)   Hall Road

MERSEYSIDE

Blundellsands
& Crosby

Old Roan

Kirkby

Waterloo

Excursion
Platform*   Aintree

Fazakerley Junc.

Seaforth &
Litherland

Seaforth FLT
& Cawood Coal
Export Terminal

(Disused)

Fazakerley

A

TO DOUGLAS (Isle of Man
Steam Packet Company)
BIRKENHEAD TO BELFAST
(Norse Merchant Ferries)

Orrell Park

Walton   Rice Lane

Walton Junc.

Gladstone Dock
- Powergen

Alexandra Dock -
European
Metal Recycling

MDHC

NR

Bootle
New Strand

Bootle
Oriel Rd.

Kirkdale No. 1 Tun.

Kirkdale No. 2 Tun.

Spellow Tun.

TO DUBLIN (Isle of man
Steam Packet Co.)

New Brighton

Wallasey Grove Rd.

Wallasey Village

l   Kirkdale

m   b   k

Bank Hall

Westminster Rd. Tun.

Kirkdale EMU Depot

Sandhills Junc.

Sandhills

MERSEYRAIL

1) Woodside
2) Egerton Bridge
3) Old Colonial
4) Taylor St. Depot
a) Derby Square Junc.
b) Bootle Junc.
c) Paradise Junc.
d) Mann Island Junc.
e) Canning St. Junc.
f) Bootle Branch Junc.
g) Edge Hill East Junc.
h) Hamilton Sq. Junc.
j) Picko No. 2 Tun.
k) Oriel Road Tun.
l) Bury Street Tun.
m) Alexandra Dock Tun.
n) Haymarket Tun.
p) Canning St. N.
q) Pacific Road

B

*Bidston
E. Junc.*

NR

MDHC

BD

Birkenhead
North

(Disused)

Birkenhead Park

Conway Park

MDHC

NR

*(Mersey
Ferries)*

Seacombe
BIRKENHEAD
TRAMWAY

LIVERPOOL

Pier Head

Moorfields

Lime
St.

Russell St. Tun.

EDGE HILL

Tuebrook
CE Sidings

j

Edge
Hill

g

f

Broad Green

Wavertree
Technology
Park

p   2
3   4 h

1

James St.

JAMES ST.

Mersey Tun.

Woodside

Birkenhead
Hamilton
Square

d   a

Central

c

*Mount
Pleasant
Tun.*

*Crown
St. Tun.*

*Overbury St.
Tun.*

Spekeland
Road Goods

CE

Gullet
Sidings

Downhill
C.S. (LL)

Wavertree Junc.

n

Birkenhead
Central
Depot (Disused)

*Hinderton
Field Tun.*

Green Lane

(Disused)

Rock Ferry

*Rock Ferry
S. Junc.*

*St James
Tuns.*

Brunswick

Dingle Tun.

St. Michaels

St. Michaels Tun.

Fulwood Tun.

Mossley Hill

(Allerton and Garston
stations to be combined
and renamed Liverpool
South Parkway)

West
Allerton

Bebington

Aigburth

*Hunts Cross
West Junc.*

AN

Port Sunlight

Cressington

Allerton

Garston

*Speke
Junc.*

C

Spital

Garston FLT

Garston Coal
Terminal - ABP
(Disused)

*Garston
Junc.*

Speke
Yard

Car Terminal -
- Axial

51

1

2

51

0   1   2   m.

0   1   2   3   4 km.

(1:90,000)

59

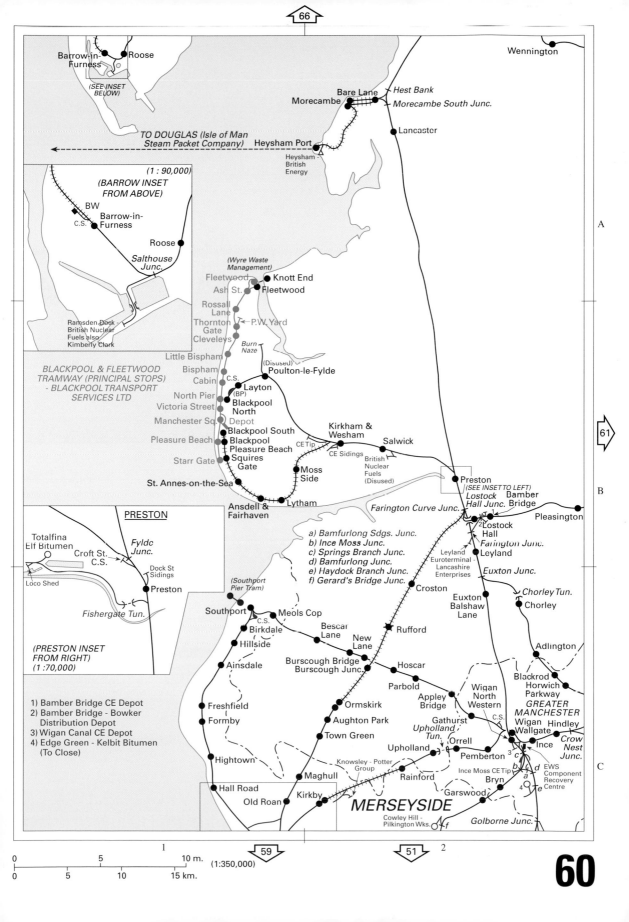

Wennington

Barrow-in-Furness   Roose

(SEE INSET BELOW)

Bare Lane   Hest Bank

Morecambe   Morecambe South Junc.

TO DOUGLAS (Isle of Man
Steam Packet Company)   Heysham Port   Lancaster

Heysham –
British
Energy

(1 : 90,000)

(BARROW INSET
FROM ABOVE)

BW
C.S.   Barrow-in-
Furness

Roose

Salthouse
Junc.

Ramsden Dock –
British Nuclear
Fuels also
Kimberly Clark

A

(Wyre Waste
Management)

Fleetwood   Knott End
Ash St.   Fleetwood
Rossall
Lane
Thornton   ← P.W. Yard
Gate
Cleveleys
Burn
Little Bispham   *Naze*

BLACKPOOL & FLEETWOOD   Bispham   (Disused)
TRAMWAY (PRINCIPAL STOPS)   Cabin   Poulton-le-Fylde
- BLACKPOOL TRANSPORT   C.S.
SERVICES LTD   Layton
North Pier   (BP)
Victoria Street   Blackpool
Manchester Sq.   North
Depot   Kirkham &
Blackpool South   Wesham
Pleasure Beach   Blackpool
Pleasure Beach   Salwick
Starr Gate   Squires   CE Tip
Gate   CE Sidings   British
Moss   Nuclear
St. Annes-on-the-Sea   Side   Fuels
(Disused)   Preston   61

Ansdell &   *(SEE INSET TO LEFT)*
Fairhaven   Lytham   Lostock   Bamber
Faringate Curve Junc.   Hall Junc.   Bridge
B

PRESTON   Pleasington

Totalfina   *Fylde*   1
Elf Bitumen   *Junc.*   2   Lostock
Croft St.   Hall
C.S.   *Faringate Junc.*
Dock St   Leyland
Loco Shed   Sidings   a) Bamfurlong Sdgs. Junc.   *Euxton Junc.*
Preston   b) Ince Moss Junc.   Leyland
Fishergate Tun.   c) Springs Branch Junc.   Euroterminal -
d) Bamfurlong Junc.   Lancashire   *Chorley Tun.*
e) Haydock Branch Junc.   Enterprises   Chorley
(PRESTON INSET   f) Gerard's Bridge Junc.   Croston   Euxton
FROM RIGHT)   Balshaw
(1 :70,000)   *(Southport*   Lane   Adlington
Pier Tram)
Southport   Meols Cop
1) Bamber Bridge CE Depot   Birkdale   Bescar   Blackrod
2) Bamber Bridge - Bowker   C.S.   Lane   Rufford   Horwich
Distribution Depot   Hillside   New   Parkway
3) Wigan Canal CE Depot   Lane
4) Edge Green - Kelbit Bitumen   Ainsdale   Burscough Bridge   Hoscar   Wigan
(To Close)   Burscough Junc.   North   **GREATER**
Parbold   Western   Gathurst   **MANCHESTER**
Freshfield   Appley   C.S.
Ormskirk   Bridge   Wigan   Hindley
Formby   Aughton Park   *Upholland*   Wallgate
Town Green   *Tun.*   Orrell   Ince   *Crow*
Upholland   Pemberton   3   *Nest*
Hightown   Knowsley - Potter   Ince Moss CE Tip   c   *Junc.*
Group   Rainford   b   d   EWS
Maghull   Garswood   a   Component
Hall Road   4   e   Recovery
Old Roan   Kirkby   **MERSEYSIDE**   Bryn   Centre   C

Cowley Hill -   Golborne Junc.
Pilkington Wks.   f

1   2

0   5   10 m.
(1:350,000)
0   5   10   15 km.   **60**

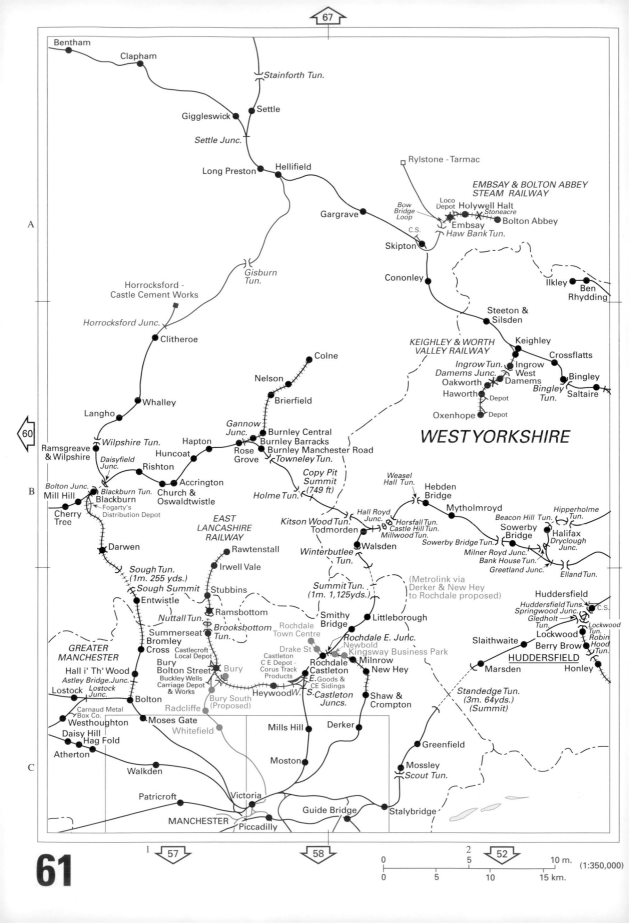

Bentham

Clapham

Stainforth Tun.

Settle

Giggleswick

Settle Junc.

Long Preston   Hellifield

Rylstone - Tarmac

EMBSAY & BOLTON ABBEY
STEAM RAILWAY

Bow
Bridge
Loop   Loco
Depot   Holywell Halt
Stoneacre
Embsay   Bolton Abbey
C.S.   *Haw Bank Tun.*

Gargrave

Skipton

Cononley

Ilkley   Ben
Rhydding

A

Horrocksford -
Castle Cement Works

Gisburn
Tun.

Horrocksford Junc.

Clitheroe

Steeton &
Silsden

Keighley   Crossflatts

KEIGHLEY & WORTH
VALLEY RAILWAY

Ingrow Tun.   Ingrow
West
Damems Junc.   Damems
Oakworth
Haworth   *Bingley*
Tun.   Saltaire
Bingley
Depot
Oxenhope   Depot

WEST YORKSHIRE

Whalley

Langho

Colne

Nelson

Brierfield

60

Ramsgreave
& Wilpshire   *Wilpshire Tun.*

Hapton   *Gannow*
Junc.   Burnley Central
Burnley Barracks
Burnley Manchester Road
Towneley Tun.
Rose
Grove

Daisyfield
Junc.   Huncoat
Rishton

Copy Pit
Summit
(749 ft)

Weasel
Hall Tun.   Hebden
Bridge   Mytholmroyd
Hipperholme
Tun.
Beacon Hill Tun.

Bolton Junc.   *Blackburn Tun.*
Mill Hill   Blackburn
Fogarty's
Distribution Depot   Church &
Oswaldtwistle
Accrington   *Holme Tun.*   *Hall Royd*
Junc.   *Horsfall Tun.*
Castle Hill Tun.
Millwood Tun.   Sowerby
Bridge   Halifax
Dryclough
Junc.

B

Cherry
Tree   *EAST*
LANCASHIRE
RAILWAY   *Kitson Wood Tun.*
Todmorden   *Sowerby Bridge Tun.*   *Milner Royd Junc.*
Bank House Tun.
Greetland Junc.   *Elland Tun.*

Darwen   Rawtenstall   *Winterbutlee*
Tun.   Walsden

Sough Tun.
(1m. 255 yds.)   Irwell Vale   Huddersfield
Sough Summit   Stubbins   *Summit Tun.*
(1m. 1,125yds.)   (Metrolink via
Derker & New Hey
to Rochdale proposed)   *Huddersfield Tuns.*
Springwood Junc.
Gledholt
Tun.   C.S.
Lockwood
Entwistle   Ramsbottom   Smithy
Bridge   Littleborough   Slaithwaite   Lockwood   *Tun.*
Robin
Berry Brow   *Hood Tun.*
Nuttall Tun.   Rochdale
Town Centre   *Rochdale E. Junc.*
Newbold
Kingsway Business Park
Drake St   **HUDDERSFIELD**
Brooksbottom
Tun.   Milnrow   Marsden   Honley
Summerseat
Bromley
Cross   Castlecroft
Local Depot   Rochdale
Castleton   New Hey
Bury
Bolton Street   Castleton
C E Depot -
Corus Track
Products   E.Goods &
CE Sidings
Shaw &
Crompton
GREATER
MANCHESTER   Bury
Buckley Wells
Carriage Depot
& Works   HeywoodW.   *S.Castleton*
Juncs.

Hall i' Th' Wood
Astley Bridge.Junc.
Lostock   *Lostock*
Junc.   Bury South
(Proposed)   *Standedge Tun.*
(3m. 64yds.)
(Summit)
Bolton
Radcliffe
Carnaud Metal
Box Co.   Greenfield
Westhoughton   Moses Gate
Daisy Hill   Whitefield   Mills Hill   Derker
Hag Fold   Moston   Mossley
Atherton   *Scout Tun.*

C

Walkden

Patricroft   Victoria   Guide Bridge   Stalybridge

MANCHESTER   Piccadilly

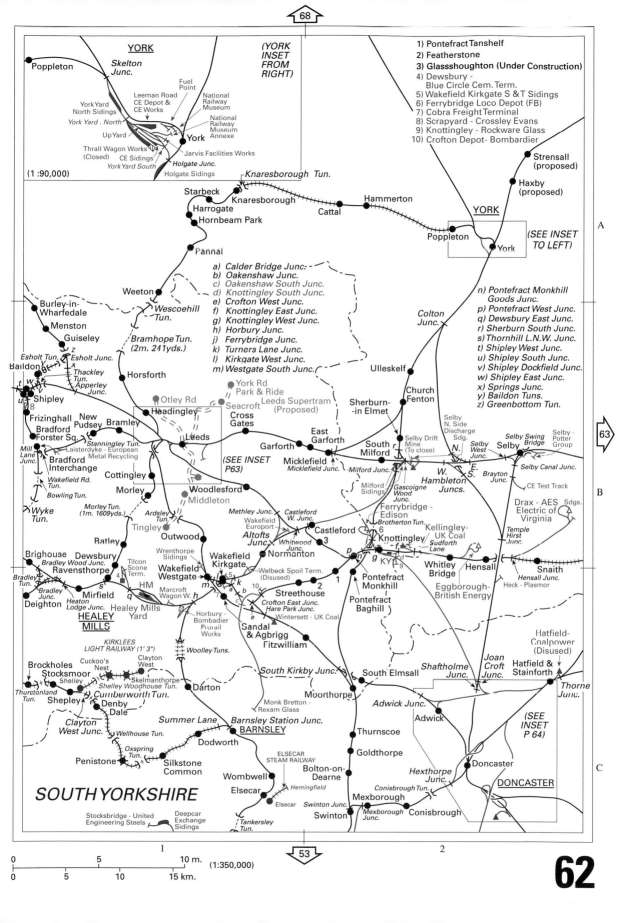

Bridlington Quay
Bridlington

Headingley

(LEEDS INSET FROM MAP 62)

Leeds Supertram
(Proposed)

Fforde
Green

**WEST
YORKS.**

Headingley
Centre

Burley Park

St. James'
Hosp.

University

Nafferton

Driffield

Headrow
Bus
Sta.

Marsh Lane-
Tilcon Stone
Terminal

*Richmond
Hill Tun.*

A

1) Leeds (Whitehall)
Temporary Station

Armley Junc.

City
Sq.

*Neville
Hill
West
Junc.*

Neville
Hill
(NL)

Hutton
Cranswick

*Whitehall
Junc.*

Leeds

1

Leeds W. Junc.

Armouries
Mus.

Neville
Hill Up
Sidings

1) Dawes Coak Ovens
2) Santon-Foreign Ore Term.
3) Scunthorpe Trent Yard
4) Loco Shed-Corus
5) Sinter Plant
a) Walton St. Junc.
b) West Parade N. Junc.
c) Hessle Road Junc.
d) Anlaby Road Junc.
e) Trent Junc.
f) Hessle East Junc.
g) North Lincoln Junc.

*Copley Hill
E. Junc.
Holbeck
Junc.*

*Engine
Shed
Junc.*

Shell

*Copley Hill
W. Junc.*

*Whitehall
Road S & T
Sidings*

Moor Row
(Hunslet)

Hunslet East

Cross Green-
Tarmac Stone Terminal

Arram

*Holbeck-CE
Plant Depot*

Shed

Hunslet
Centre

Cottingley

Scrapyard (Disused)
Parkside Junc.
Hunslet
Sidings
(Disused)

Midland Road Loco Depot- London
and North Western Railway Co. (LD)

Stone Term.-RMC

Stourton FLT

Beverley

**MIDDLETON
RAILWAY**

Belle
Isle

Stourton
Park &
Ride

D & F
Steels

Steel Terminal
-Corus

(1:90,000)

Park Halt

Cottingham

62

Wressle

Howden

Eastrington

Gilberdyke

Broomfleet

Springbank
North Junc.

a b
c
d

BG
Hull

Hedon
Road
Sidings

Kingston
Coal Term.

B

Goole-Guardian
Glass

Saltmarshe

Brough

Sidings

Sidings

Hull King
George Dock
-ABP

Saltend -
BP Chems.

Melton- Omya
Croxton & Garry

Ferriby

Hessle

Dairycoates-Tarmac
Stone Term.

*Potters
Grange Junc.*

Goole

*Goole
Swing Bridge*

Freight
Terminal
(Disused)

New Holland

Rawcliffe

Docks- Goole Railfreight
Goole Yard

Barton-on-Humber

Barrow
Haven

Oxmarsh Crossing

Goxhill

*Engine
Shed
Junc.*

Killingholme

(SEE INSET P 64)

Thornton
Abbey

Roxby Landfill Site -
Waste Management

Immingham

Thorne
North

*Dragonby
Sidings*

Plant Depot-
Grant Rail

Scunthorpe Coal Term.-Corus
Anchor Yard

Ulceby

Habrough

Thorne
South

Flixborough Wharf-
Faber Prest Ports

*Normanby
Park*

3 g

Brocklesby Junc.

Foreign Ore Branch Junc.

Crowle

Althorpe

Scunthorpe

Sidings

e

1

Scunthorpe
(Anchor Works)
-Corus

Barnetby

Sidings

CE
Sidings

Entrance A

4

2

Appleby-Frodingham RPS Excursion Platform
Heavy Section Mill-Corus

5

**SOUTH
YORKS.**

Allied Steel
& Wire

Blast
Furnaces

Basic
Oxygen
Steel Plant

Brigg

Wrawby Junc.

**Corus Steelworks
Scunthorpe Complex**

SCUNTHORPE
(Barnetby-Gainsborough
passenger service
operates Sats. only)

C

*Kirton
Lime
Sidings*

Kirton Tun.

Northorpe

Kirton
Lindsey

1

0   2
5   10 m.   (1:350,000)
0   5   10   15 km.

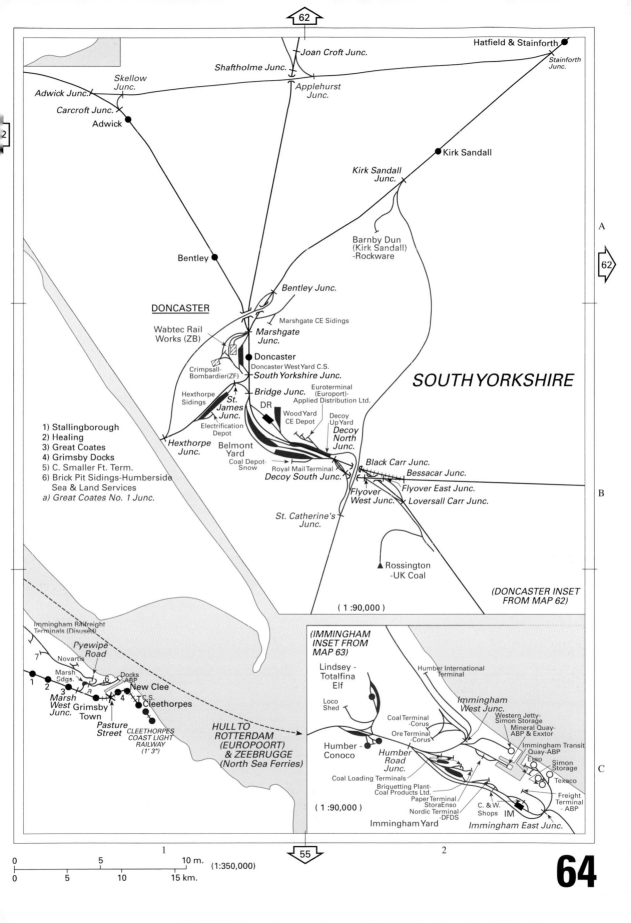

Hatfield & Stainforth

Stainforth Junc.

Joan Croft Junc.

Shaftholme Junc.

Applehurst Junc.

Skellow Junc.

Adwick Junc.

Carcroft Junc.

Adwick

Kirk Sandall

Kirk Sandall Junc.

62

A

Barnby Dun
(Kirk Sandall)
-Rockware

Bentley

Bentley Junc.

DONCASTER

Marshgate CE Sidings

Wabtec Rail
Works (ZB)

Marshgate Junc.

Doncaster

Doncaster West Yard C.S.

Crimpsall-
Bombardier (ZF)

South Yorkshire Junc.

Hexthorpe Sidings

Bridge Junc.

Euroterminal
(Europort)-
Applied Distribution Ltd.

SOUTH YORKSHIRE

St. James Junc.

Electrification Depot

DR

Wood Yard
CE Depot

Decoy
Up Yard

Decoy North Junc.

Hexthorpe Junc.

Belmont Yard

Coal Depot-
Snow

Royal Mail Terminal

Decoy South Junc.

Black Carr Junc.

Bessacar Junc.

Flyover East Junc.

Flyover West Junc.

Loversall Carr Junc.

B

1) Stallingborough
2) Healing
3) Great Coates
4) Grimsby Docks
5) C. Smaller Ft. Term.
6) Brick Pit Sidings-Humberside
   Sea & Land Services
a) Great Coates No. 1 Junc.

St. Catherine's Junc.

Rossington
-UK Coal

*(DONCASTER INSET
FROM MAP 62)*

(1 :90,000)

Immingham Railfreight
Terminals (Disused)

Pyewipe Road

7

Novartis

Marsh
Sdgs.

1

2

3

a

6

Docks
ABP

New Clee

*Marsh
West
Junc.*

4

Grimsby Town

T.C.S.

Cleethorpes

Pasture Street

CLEETHORPES
COAST LIGHT
RAILWAY
(1' 3")

HULL TO
ROTTERDAM
(EUROPOORT)
& ZEEBRUGGE
(North Sea Ferries)

*(IMMINGHAM
INSET FROM
MAP 63)*

Lindsey -
Totalfina
Elf

Humber International
Terminal

Loco
Shed

Coal Terminal
-Corus

*Immingham
West Junc.*

Western Jetty-
Simon Storage

Mineral Quay-
ABP & Exxtor

Ore Terminal
-Corus

Humber -
Conoco

*Humber
Road
Junc.*

Immingham Transit
Quay-ABP

Esso

Simon
Storage

Coal Loading Terminals

Texaco

Briquetting Plant-
Coal Products Ltd.

Paper Terminal
StoraEnso

Nordic Terminal
-DFDS

C. & W.
Shops

IM

Freight
Terminal - ABP

C

(1 :90,000)

Immingham Yard

Immingham East Junc.

0   5   10 m.   (1:350,000)

0   5   10   15 km.

1

2

2

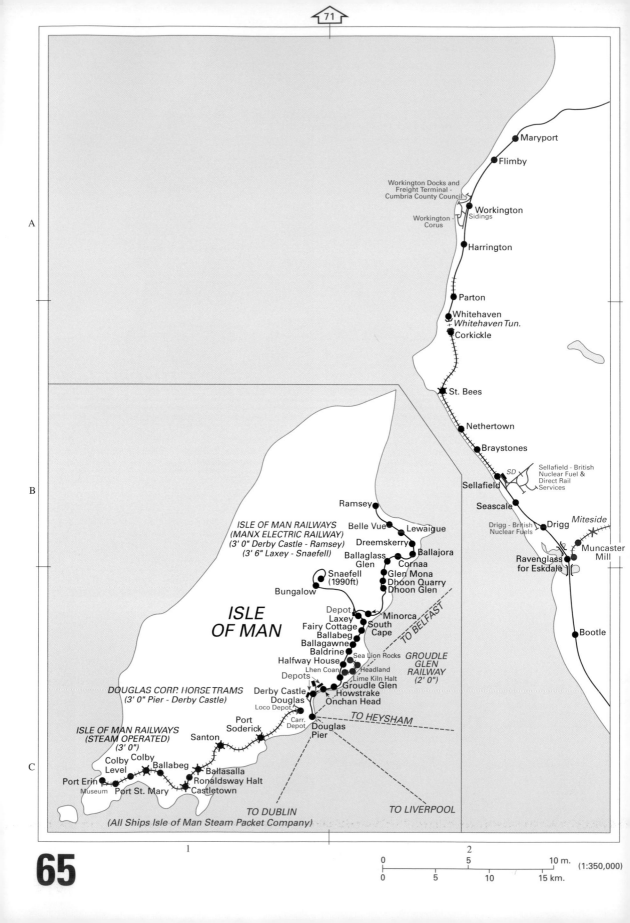

Maryport

Flimby

Workington Docks and
Freight Terminal -
Cumbria County Council

Workington
Corus

Sidings

Workington

A

Harrington

Parton

Whitehaven
Whitehaven Tun.
Corkickle

St. Bees

Nethertown

Braystones

Sellafield - British
Nuclear Fuel &
Direct Rail
Services

SD

Sellafield

B

Seascale

Drigg *Miteside*

Drigg - British
Nuclear Fuels

Ramsey

Muncaster
Mill

Belle Vue   Lewaigue

Ravenglass
for Eskdale

ISLE OF MAN RAILWAYS
(MANX ELECTRIC RAILWAY)
(3' 0" Derby Castle - Ramsey)
(3' 6" Laxey - Snaefell)

Dreemskerry

Ballaglass
Glen

Ballajora

Cornaa

Glen Mona

Dhoon Quarry

Dhoon Glen

Snaefell
(1990ft)

Bungalow

*ISLE
OF MAN*

Depot

Minorca

TO BELFAST

Laxey

Fairy Cottage   South
Cape

Ballabeg

Ballagawne

Bootle

Baldrine

Sea Lion Rocks

*GROUDLE
GLEN
RAILWAY
(2' 0")*

Halfway House

Lhen Coan   Headland

Depots

Lime Kiln Halt

DOUGLAS CORP. HORSE TRAMS
(3' 0" Pier - Derby Castle)

Derby Castle
Douglas

Groudle Glen

Howstrake

Onchan Head

Loco Depot

Port
Soderick

Carr.
Depot

Douglas
Pier

TO HEYSHAM

ISLE OF MAN RAILWAYS
(STEAM OPERATED)
(3' 0")

Santon

Colby   Colby
Level   Ballabeg

Port Erin

Ballasalla

Museum   Port St. Mary

Ronaldsway Halt
Castletown

C

TO DUBLIN

TO LIVERPOOL

(All Ships Isle of Man Steam Packet Company)

65

1   2

0   5   10 m.

0   5   10   15 km.

(1:350,000)

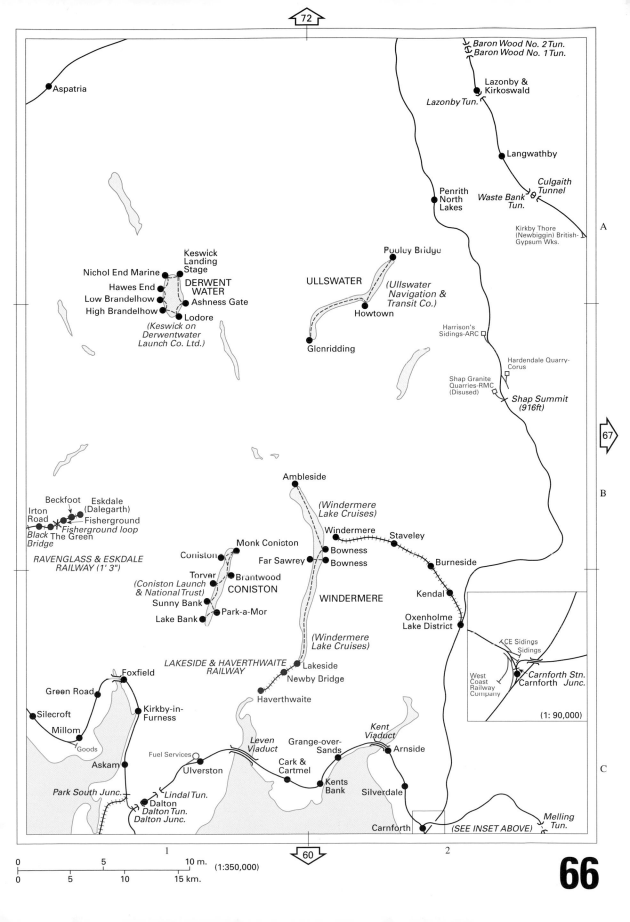

Baron Wood No. 2 Tun.
Baron Wood No. 1 Tun.

Lazonby &
Kirkoswald

Lazonby Tun.

Langwathby

Culgaith Tunnel

Penrith
North
Lakes

Waste Bank Tun.

Kirkby Thore
(Newbiggin) British-
Gypsum Wks.

A

Aspatria

Keswick
Landing
Stage

Nichol End Marine

Hawes End

Low Brandelhow

High Brandelhow

DERWENT
WATER

Ashness Gate

Lodore

*(Keswick on
Derwentwater
Launch Co. Ltd.)*

ULLSWATER

Pooley Bridge

*(Ullswater
Navigation &
Transit Co.)*

Howtown

Glenridding

Harrison's
Sidings-ARC

Hardendale Quarry-
Corus

Shap Granite
Quarries-RMC
(Disused)

*Shap Summit
(916ft)*

67

B

Ambleside

*(Windermere
Lake Cruises)*

Beckfoot

Eskdale
(Dalegarth)

Irton
Road

Fisherground

Fisherground loop

Black The Green
Bridge

*RAVENGLASS & ESKDALE
RAILWAY (1' 3")*

Monk Coniston

Coniston

Windermere

Staveley

Bowness

Far Sawrey

Bowness

Burnside

Torver

Brantwood

CONISTON

Kendal

*(Coniston Launch
& National Trust)*

Sunny Bank

WINDERMERE

Oxenholme
Lake District

Lake Bank

Park-a-Mor

*(Windermere
Lake Cruises)*

CE Sidings
Sidings

*LAKESIDE & HAVERTHWAITE
RAILWAY*

Lakeside

Newby Bridge

West
Coast
Railway
Company

*Carnforth Stn.
Carnforth Junc.*

Foxfield

Haverthwaite

(1: 90,000)

Green Road

Kirkby-in-
Furness

Silecroft

Leven
Viaduct

Grange-over-
Sands

Kent
Viaduct

Millom

Goods

Fuel Services

Arnside

Askam

Ulverston

Cark &
Cartmel

C

Park South Junc.

Lindal Tun.

Dalton

*Dalton Tun.
Dalton Junc.*

Kents
Bank

Silverdale

Carnforth

(SEE INSET ABOVE)

*Melling
Tun.*

0   1   10 m.   (1:350,000)

0   5   10   15 km.

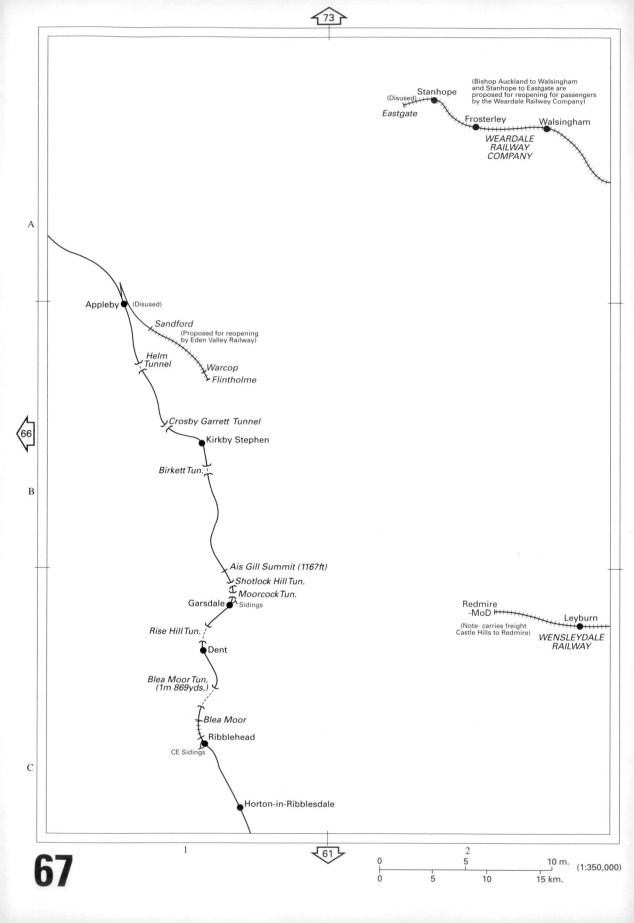

(Bishop Auckland to Walsingham
and Stanhope to Eastgate are
proposed for reopening for passengers
by the Weardale Railway Company)

Eastgate (Disused) Stanhope

Frosterley Walsingham

*WEARDALE
RAILWAY
COMPANY*

A

Appleby (Disused)

Sandford

(Proposed for reopening
by Eden Valley Railway)

*Helm
Tunnel*

Warcop

Flintholme

Crosby Garrett Tunnel

Kirkby Stephen

Birkett Tun.

B

Ais Gill Summit (1167ft)

Shotlock Hill Tun.

Moorcock Tun.

Garsdale Sidings

Redmire
-MoD Leyburn

(Note- carries freight
Castle Hills to Redmire)

*WENSLEYDALE
RAILWAY*

Rise Hill Tun.

Dent

*Blea Moor Tun.
(1m 869yds.)*

Blea Moor

Ribblehead

CE Sidings

C

Horton-in-Ribblesdale

67

0   2
5   10 m.
0   5   10   15 km.   (1:350,000)

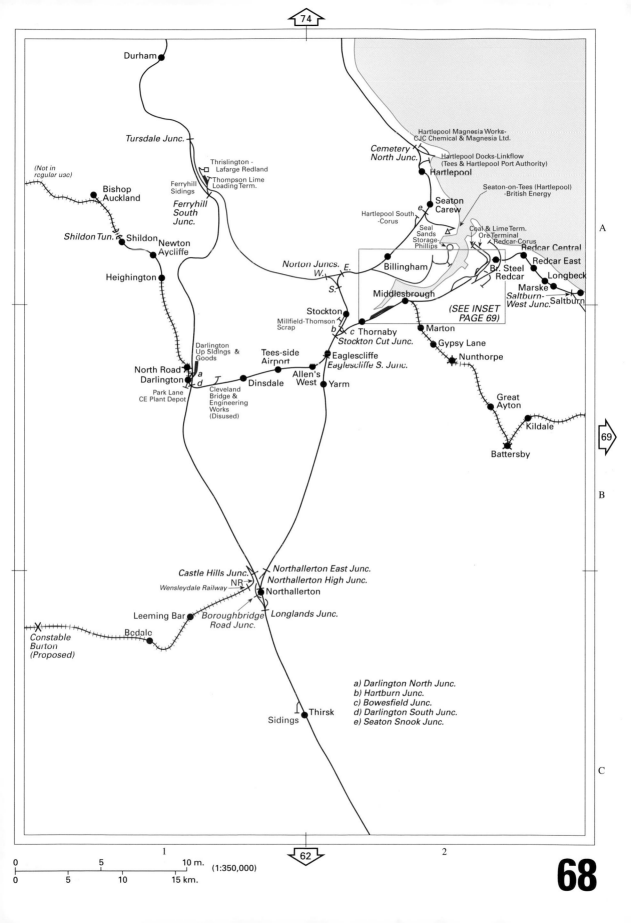

Durham

Tursdale Junc.

(Not in regular use)

Bishop Auckland

Thrislington - Lafarge Redland
Thompson Lime Loading Term.

Ferryhill Sidings

Ferryhill South Junc.

Shildon Tun. — Shildon
Newton Aycliffe

Heighington

Hartlepool Magnesia Works-
CJC Chemical & Magnesia Ltd.

Cemetery North Junc.

Hartlepool Docks-Linkflow
(Tees & Hartlepool Port Authority)

Hartlepool

Seaton Carew

Seaton-on-Tees (Hartlepool)
-British Energy

Hartlepool South
-Corus

e

Seal Sands
Storage-
Phillips

Coal & Lime Term.
Ore Terminal
Redcar-Corus

Br. Steel
Redcar

Redcar Central

Redcar East

Longbeck

Marske

Saltburn-
West Junc.

Saltburn

Norton Juncs.
W.   E.
S.

Billingham

Middlesbrough

(SEE INSET PAGE 69)

Marton

Gypsy Lane

Nunthorpe

Stockton

Millfield-Thomson
Scrap

b
c Thornaby
Stockton Cut Junc.

Great Ayton

Kildale

Battersby

Darlington Up Sidings & Goods

North Road
Darlington

a

d

Park Lane
CE Plant Depot

Cleveland Bridge &
Engineering Works
(Disused)

Dinsdale

Tees-side Airport

Allen's West

Eaglescliffe
Eaglescliffe S. Junc.

Yarm

Castle Hills Junc.
Wensleydale Railway
NR

Northallerton East Junc.
Northallerton High Junc.
Northallerton

Leeming Bar

Boroughbridge
Road Junc.

Longlands Junc.

Bedale

Constable Burton
(Proposed)

Sidings   Thirsk

a) Darlington North Junc.
b) Hartburn Junc.
c) Bowesfield Junc.
d) Darlington South Junc.
e) Seaton Snook Junc.

0   5   10 m.
0   5   10   15 km.   (1:350,000)

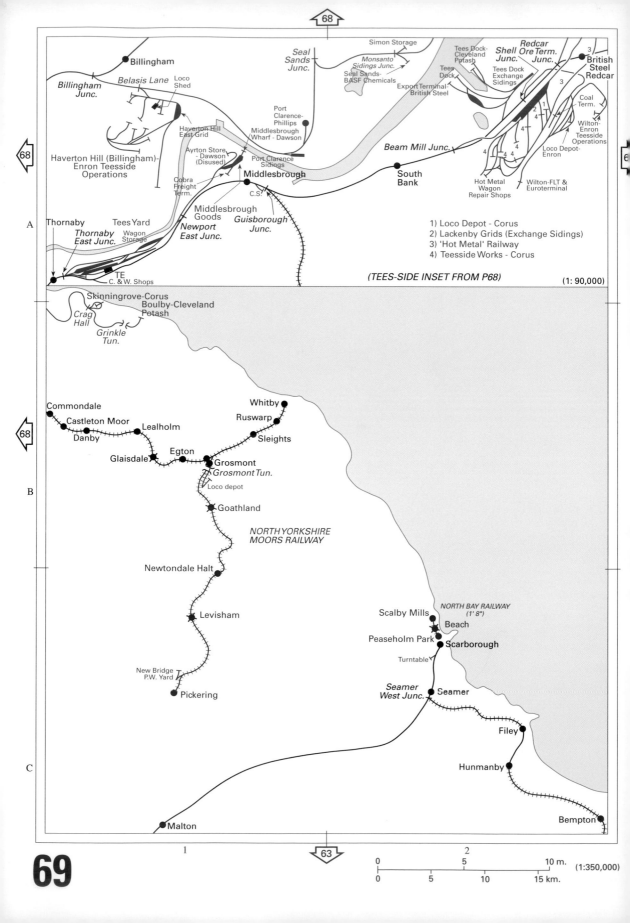

68

68

68

Billingham

Billingham Junc.

Belasis Lane

Loco Shed

Haverton Hill East Grid

Haverton Hill (Billingham)-Enron Teesside Operations

Ayrton Store - Dawson (Disused)

Cobra Freight Term.

Port Clarence Sidings

Port Clarence-Phillips

Middlesbrough Wharf - Dawson

Middlesbrough

C.S.

Seal Sands Junc.

Simon Storage

Monsanto Sidings Junc.

Seal Sands-BASF Chemicals

Tees Dock-Cleveland Potash

Tees Dock Exchange Sidings

Export Terminal-British Steel

Tees Dock

Redcar Ore Term.

Shell Ore Term.

Redcar Shell Ore Term. Junc.

3

British Steel Redcar

Coal Term.

3

1

2

4

4

4

Wilton-Enron Teesside Operations

Loco Depot-Enron

4

4

4

Hot Metal Wagon Repair Shops

Wilton-FLT & Euroterminal

Beam Mill Junc.

South Bank

A

Thornaby

Tees Yard

Thornaby East Junc.

Wagon Storage

Middlesbrough Goods

Newport East Junc.

Guisborough Junc.

TE
C. & W. Shops

1) Loco Depot - Corus
2) Lackenby Grids (Exchange Sidings)
3) 'Hot Metal' Railway
4) Teesside Works - Corus

(TEES-SIDE INSET FROM P68)

(1: 90,000)

Skinningrove-Corus

Boulby-Cleveland Potash

Crag Hall

Grinkle Tun.

68

Commondale

Castleton Moor

Danby

Lealholm

Glaisdale

Egton

Whitby

Ruswarp

Sleights

Grosmont

Grosmont Tun.

Loco depot

B

Goathland

NORTH YORKSHIRE MOORS RAILWAY

Newtondale Halt

Levisham

New Bridge P.W. Yard

Pickering

Scalby Mills

NORTH BAY RAILWAY (1' 8")

Beach

Peaseholm Park

Scarborough

Turntable

Seamer West Junc.

Seamer

Filey

C

Hunmanby

Malton

Bempton

69

1

63

2

0   5   10 m.

0   5   10   15 km.

(1:350,000)

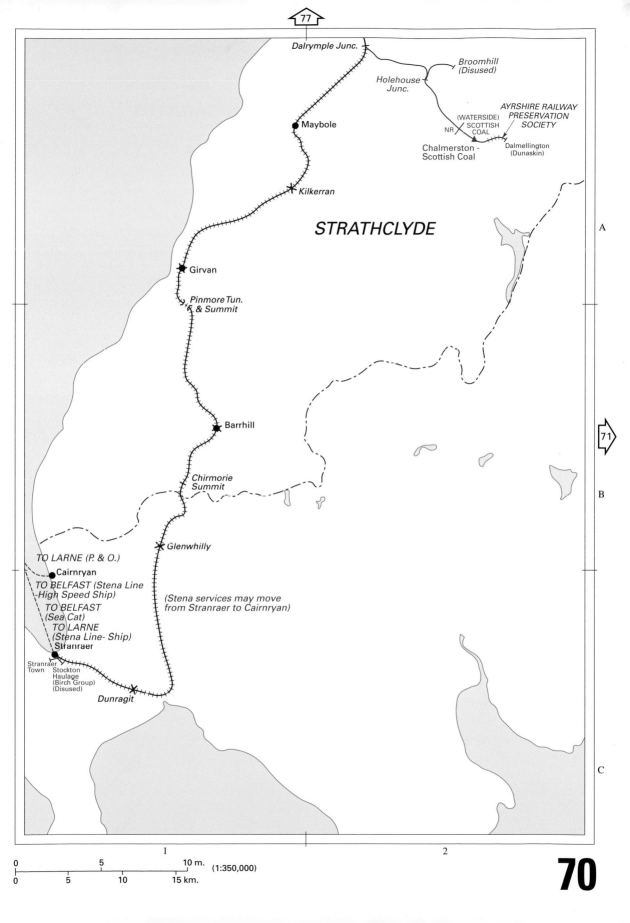

Dalrymple Junc.

Broomhill (Disused)

Holehouse Junc.

●Maybole

(WATERSIDE) SCOTTISH COAL

AYRSHIRE RAILWAY PRESERVATION SOCIETY

NR

Chalmerston - Scottish Coal

Dalmellington (Dunaskin)

✖ Kilkerran

STRATHCLYDE

A

★ Girvan

Pinmore Tun. & Summit

★ Barrhill

B

Chirmorie Summit

71

✖ Glenwhilly

TO LARNE (P. & O.)

●Cairnryan

TO BELFAST (Stena Line -High Speed Ship)

(Stena services may move from Stranraer to Cairnryan)

TO BELFAST (Sea Cat)

TO LARNE (Stena Line- Ship)

●Stranraer

Stranraer Town

Stockton Haulage (Birch Group) (Disused)

✖

Dunragit

C

1

2

0   5   10 m.   (1:350,000)

0   5   10   15 km.

70

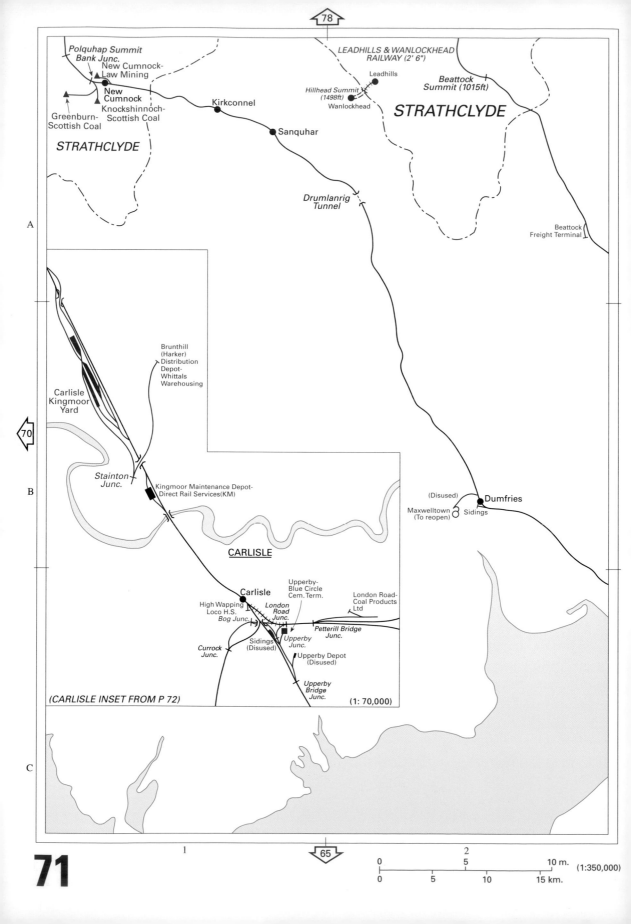

Polquhap Summit
Bank Junc.
New Cumnock-
Law Mining
New
Cumnock
Greenburn-
Scottish Coal
Knockshinnoch-
Scottish Coal

STRATHCLYDE

Kirkconnel

Sanquhar

*Drumlanrig
Tunnel*

LEADHILLS & WANLOCKHEAD
RAILWAY (2' 6")

Leadhills

*Hillhead Summit
(1498ft)*
Wanlockhead

*Beattock
Summit (1015ft)*

STRATHCLYDE

Beattock
Freight Terminal

A

Brunthill
(Harker)
Distribution
Depot-
Whittals
Warehousing

Carlisle
Kingmoor
Yard

70

*Stainton
Junc.*

Kingmoor Maintenance Depot-
Direct Rail Services(KM)

B

(Disused)
Maxwelltown
(To reopen)

Sidings

Dumfries

CARLISLE

Carlisle

High Wapping
Loco H.S.
Bog Junc.

*London
Road
Junc.*

Upperby-
Blue Circle
Cem. Term.

London Road-
Coal Products
Ltd

*Petterill Bridge
Junc.*

*Currock
Junc.*

Sidings
(Disused)

*Upperby
Junc.*

Upperby Depot
(Disused)

*Upperby
Bridge
Junc.*

(CARLISLE INSET FROM P 72)

(1: 70,000)

C

71

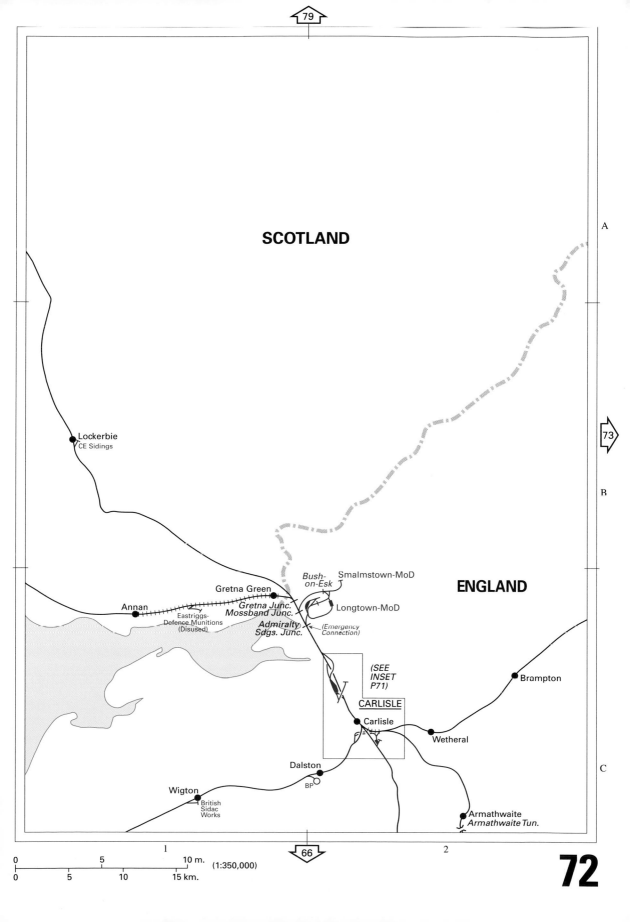

SCOTLAND

ENGLAND

Lockerbie
CE Sidings

A

B

Bush-
on-Esk   Smalmstown-MoD

Gretna Green

Annan   *Gretna Junc.*   Longtown-MoD
                 Mossband Junc.
        Eastriggs-
        Defence Munitions   *Admiralty*   (Emergency
        (Disused)   *Sdgs. Junc.*   Connection)

*(SEE
INSET
P71)*   Brampton

CARLISLE

Carlisle

Wetheral

C

Dalston

BP

Wigton

British
Sidac
Works

Armathwaite
Armathwaite Tun.

1   2

0   5   10 m.   (1:350,000)
0   5   10   15 km.

SCOTLAND

ENGLAND

A

72

B

Haltwhistle   Bardon Mill

Whitchester
Tun.   Plenmellor D.P.-RJB
                (Melkridge) (Disused)   Haydon
                                               Bridge

Hexham   Corbridge   Prudhoe   Wylam
          Goods &
          Timber
          Terminal

                Riding
                Mill   Stocksfield

                                        TYNE
                                        & WEAR

SOUTH TYNEDALE
RAILWAY
(2' 0")

Slaggyford
(Proposed Extension)

Kirkhaugh   Gilderdale (Temporarily closed)

          Alston

C

80

67

1

2

0   5   10 m.

0   5   10   15 km.   (1:350,000)

73

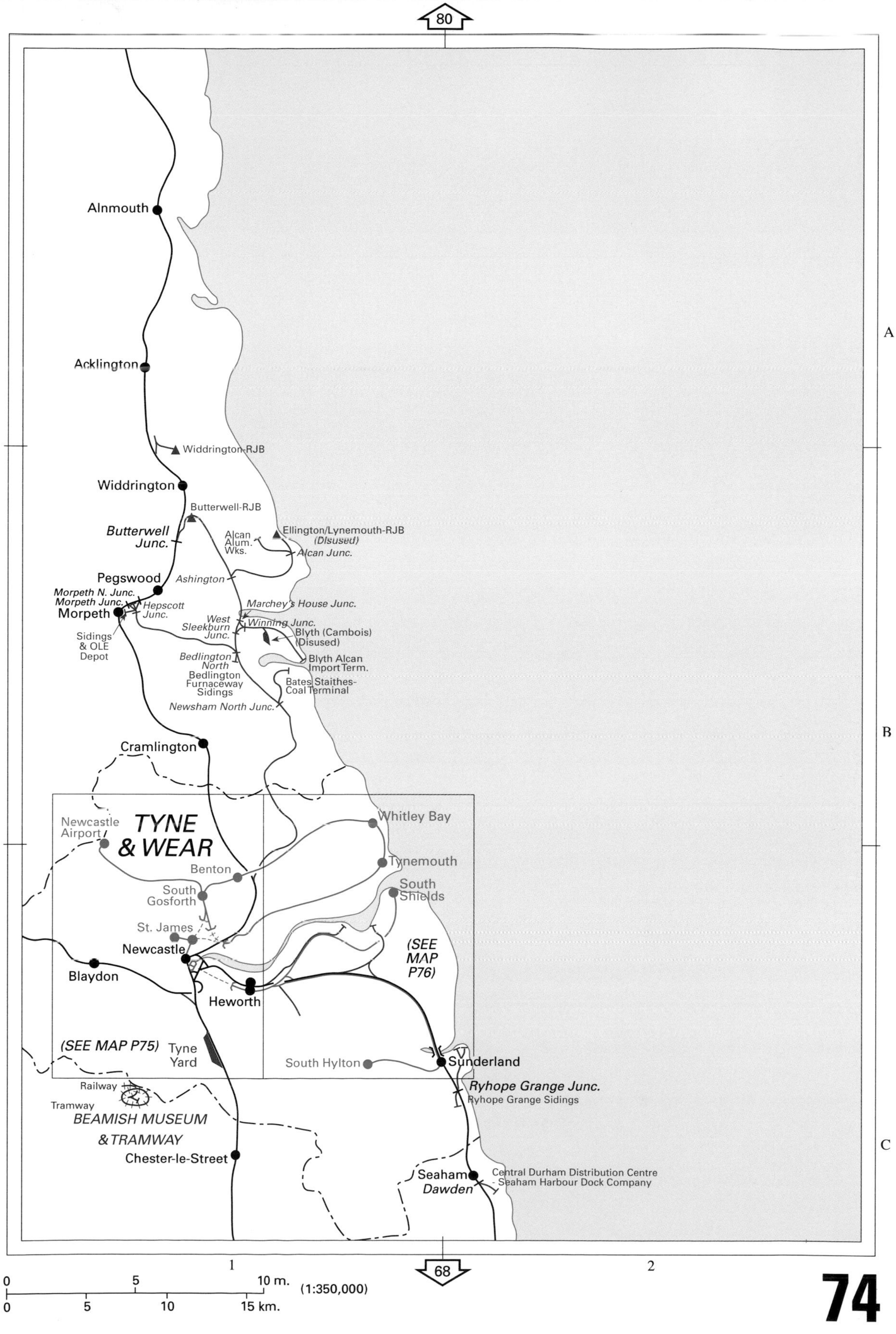

Alnmouth

Acklington

▲ Widdrington-RJB

Widdrington

Butterwell-RJB ▲

Butterwell
Junc.

Alcan
Alum.
Wks. ▲ Ellington/Lynemouth-RJB
(Disused)
Alcan Junc.

Pegswood   *Ashington*

Morpeth N. Junc.
Morpeth Junc.   Hepscott   *Marchey's House Junc.*
Morpeth   Junc.   *West*   *Winning Junc.*
Sleekburn   Blyth (Cambois)
Sidings   *Junc.*   *(Disused)*
& OLE   Blyth Alcan
Depot   Import Term.
Bedlington   Bates Staithes-
North   Coal Terminal
Bedlington
Furnaceway
Sidings
Newsham North Junc.

Cramlington

B

Newcastle
Airport   **TYNE**   Whitley Bay
& WEAR
Benton   Tynemouth
South   South
Gosforth   Shields
St. James
(SEE
Newcastle   *MAP*
P76)
Blaydon
Heworth

(SEE MAP P75)   Tyne   South Hylton   Sunderland
Yard
Railway   *Ryhope Grange Junc.*
Tramway   Ryhope Grange Sidings
BEAMISH MUSEUM
& TRAMWAY
Chester-le-Street   Seaham   Central Durham Distribution Centre
Dawden   Seaham Harbour Dock Company

C

0   5   10 m.   (1:350,000)
0   5   10   15 km.

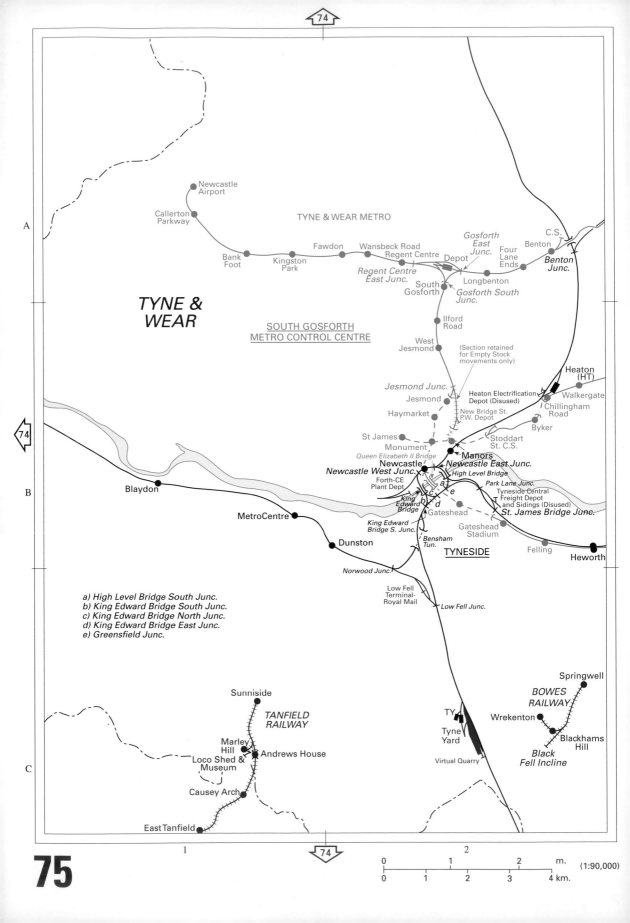

TYNE & WEAR METRO

C.S.

Newcastle
Airport

Callerton
Parkway

A

*Gosforth
East
Junc.*

Benton

Four
Lane
Ends

*Benton
Junc.*

Fawdon
Wansbeck Road
Regent Centre

Depot

Bank
Foot

Kingston
Park

*Regent Centre
East Junc.*

South
Gosforth

Longbenton

*Gosforth South
Junc.*

TYNE &
WEAR

SOUTH GOSFORTH
METRO CONTROL CENTRE

Ilford
Road

West
Jesmond

(Section retained
for Empty Stock
movements only)

Heaton
(HT)

Jesmond Junc.

Jesmond

Heaton Electrification
Depot (Disused)

Walkergate

Chillingham
Road

Haymarket

New Bridge St.
P.W. Depot

Byker

St James

Stoddart
St. C.S.

Monument

Manors

Queen Elizabeth II Bridge

Newcastle

Newcastle East Junc.

Newcastle West Junc.

High Level Bridge

Forth-CE
Plant Dept

Park Lane Junc.

a

c   e

Blaydon

*King
Edward
Bridge*

b   d

Gateshead

Tyneside Central
Freight Depot
and Sidings (Disused)

St. James Bridge Junc.

B

MetroCentre

*King Edward
Bridge S. Junc.*

Gateshead
Stadium

Dunston

*Bensham
Tun.*

TYNESIDE

Felling

Heworth

Norwood Junc.

Low Fell
Terminal-
Royal Mail

Low Fell Junc.

a) High Level Bridge South Junc.
b) King Edward Bridge South Junc.
c) King Edward Bridge North Junc.
d) King Edward Bridge East Junc.
e) Greensfield Junc.

Springwell

Sunniside

*BOWES
RAILWAY*

*TANFIELD
RAILWAY*

TY

Wrekenton

Marley
Hill

Andrews House

Tyne
Yard

Blackhams
Hill

Loco Shed &
Museum

*Black
Fell Incline*

C

Causey Arch

Virtual Quarry

East Tanfield

1

2

0   1   2   m.

(1:90,000)

0   1   2   3   4 km.

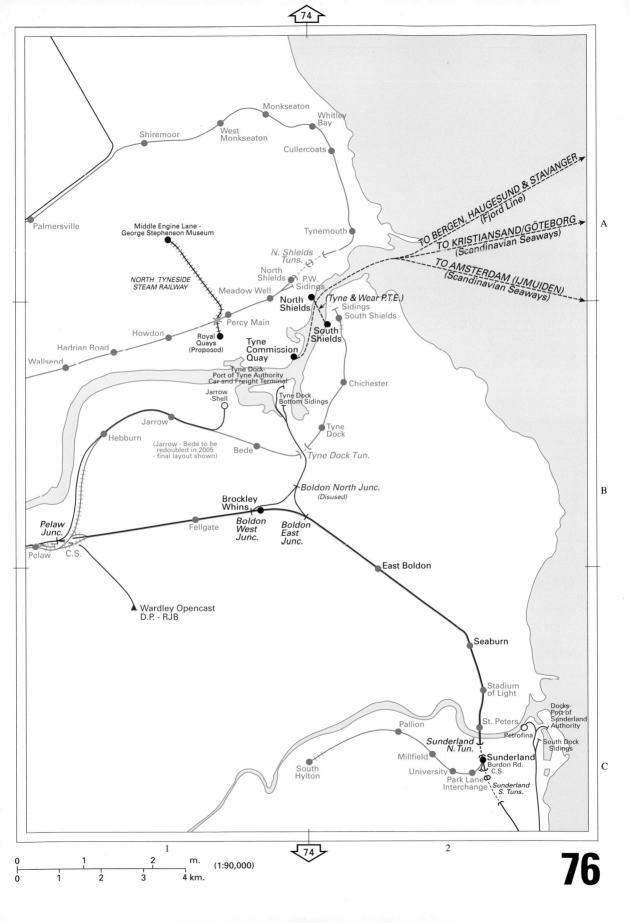

Monkseaton

Whitley
Bay

West
Monkseaton

Shiremoor

Cullercoats

Palmersville

TO BERGEN, HAUGESUND & STAVANGER
(Fiord Line)

TO KRISTIANSAND/GÖTEBORG
(Scandinavian Seaways)

A

Tynemouth

TO AMSTERDAM (IJMUIDEN)
(Scandinavian Seaways)

Middle Engine Lane -
George Stephenson Museum

N. Shields
Tuns.

NORTH TYNESIDE
STEAM RAILWAY

North
Shields

P.W.
Sidings

Meadow Well

North
Shields

Tyne & Wear P.T.E.

Sidings
South Shields

Percy Main

South
Shields

Howdon

Royal
Quays
(Proposed)

Tyne
Commission
Quay

Hadrian Road

Wallsend

Tyne Dock -
Port of Tyne Authority
Car and Freight Terminal

Chichester

Jarrow
-Shell

Tyne Dock
Bottom Sidings

Jarrow

Tyne Dock

Hebburn

(Jarrow - Bede to be
redoubled in 2005
- final layout shown)

Bede

Tyne Dock Tun.

Boldon North Junc.
(Disused)

Brockley
Whins

B

Pelaw
Junc.

Fellgate

Boldon
West
Junc.

Boldon
East
Junc.

Pelaw

C.S.

East Boldon

Wardley Opencast
D.P. - RJB

Seaburn

Stadium
of Light

Docks-
Port of
Sunderland
Authority

Pallion

St. Peters

Petrofina

South Dock
Sidings

Sunderland
N. Tun.

Millfield

Sunderland
Burdon Rd.
C.S.

C

University

South
Hylton

Park Lane
Interchange

Sunderland
S. Tuns.

0   1   2   m.   (1:90,000)

0   1   2   3   4 km.

1

2

76

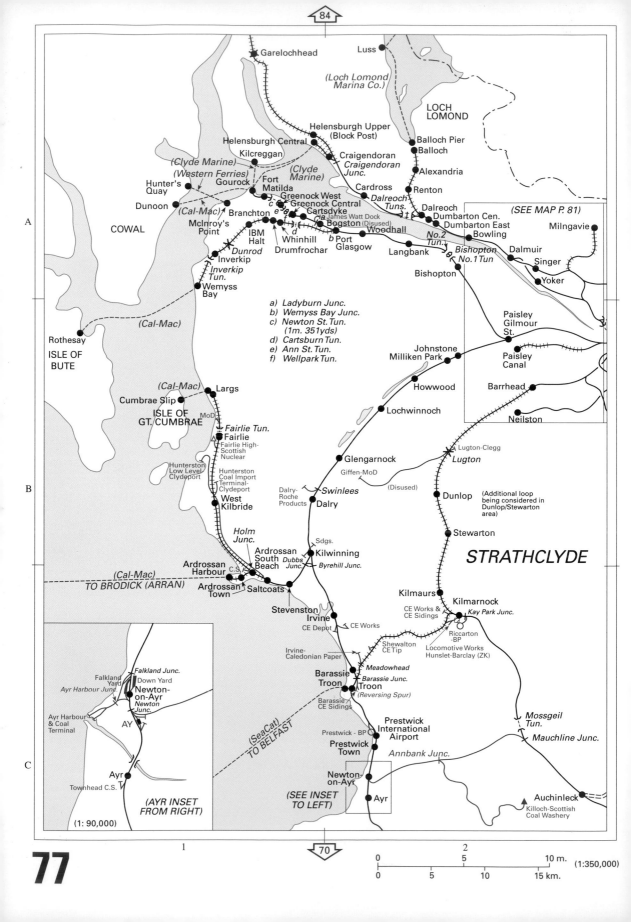

Garelochhead

Luss

(Loch Lomond
Marina Co.)

LOCH
LOMOND

Helensburgh Upper
(Block Post)

Balloch Pier
Balloch

Helensburgh Central

Kilcreggan

Craigendoran
*Craigendoran
Junc.*

Alexandria

(Clyde Marine)
(Western Ferries)

Cardross

Renton

Hunter's
Quay

Fort
Matilda

Gourock

(Clyde
Marine)

*Dalreoch
Tuns.*

Dalreoch

Dunoon

Greenock West
Greenock Central

(Cal-Mac)

Cartsdyke

c

Dumbarton Cen.
Dumbarton East

(SEE MAP P. 81)

Milngavie

Branchton

e

James Watt Dock

Bowling

McInroy's
Point

g

Bogston (Disused)

b

Woodhall

*No.2
Tun.*

Dalmuir

Singer

COWAL

IBM
Halt

Whinhill

Drumfrochar

Port
Glasgow

Langbank

*Bishopton
No.1 Tun*

Yoker

Dunrod

Inverkip

d

Bishopton

*Inverkip
Tun.*

Wemyss
Bay

Paisley
Gilmour
St.

a) Ladyburn Junc.
b) Wemyss Bay Junc.
c) Newton St. Tun.
   (1m. 351yds)
d) Cartsburn Tun.
e) Ann St. Tun.
f) Wellpark Tun.

Johnstone
Milliken Park

Paisley
Canal

Rothesay

ISLE OF
BUTE

(Cal-Mac)

Howwood

Barrhead

Lochwinnoch

Neilston

(Cal-Mac)

Largs

Cumbrae Slip

ISLE OF
GT. CUMBRAE

MoD

Glengarnock

Lugton-Clegg

Lugton

Fairlie Tun.
Fairlie

Fairlie High-
Scottish
Nuclear

Giffen-MoD

(Disused)

Dunlop

(Additional loop
being considered in
Dunlop/Stewarton
area)

Hunterston
Low Level
Clydeport

Hunterston
Coal Import
Terminal-
Clydeport

Dalry-
Roche
Products

Swinlees

Dalry

Stewarton

West
Kilbride

*Holm
Junc.*

Sdgs.

STRATHCLYDE

Ardrossan
South
Beach

*Dubbs
Junc.*

Kilwinning

Byrehill Junc.

Kilmaurs

CE Works &
CE Sidings

Ardrossan
Harbour

C.S.

Kilmarnock

Kay Park Junc.

(Cal-Mac)
TO BRODICK (ARRAN)

Ardrossan
Town

Saltcoats

Riccarton
-BP

Stevenston

Irvine

CE Depot

CE Works

Locomotive Works
Hunslet-Barclay (ZK)

Irvine-
Caledonian Paper

Shewalton
CE Tip

*Mossgeil
Tun.*

Falkland
Yard

Falkland Junc.

Down Yard

Newton-
on-Ayr

Ayr Harbour Junc.

*Newton
Junc.*

AY

Barassie
Troon

Meadowhead

Barassie Junc.

Troon

(Reversing Spur)

Mauchline Junc.

Barassie
CE Sidings

Prestwick
International
Airport

(SeaCat)
TO BELFAST

Prestwick - BP

Annbank Junc.

Ayr Harbour
& Coal
Terminal

Prestwick
Town

Ayr

Townhead C.S.

Newton-
on-Ayr

(SEE INSET
TO LEFT)

Auchinleck

(AYR INSET
FROM RIGHT)

Ayr

Killoch-Scottish
Coal Washery

(1: 90,000)

1

0   5   10 m.   (1:350,000)

0   5   10   15 km.

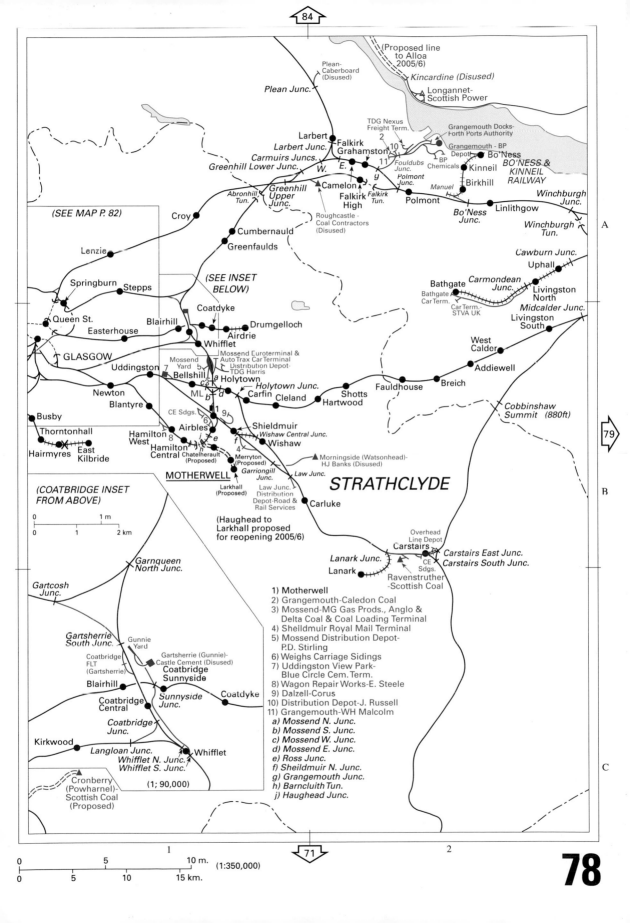

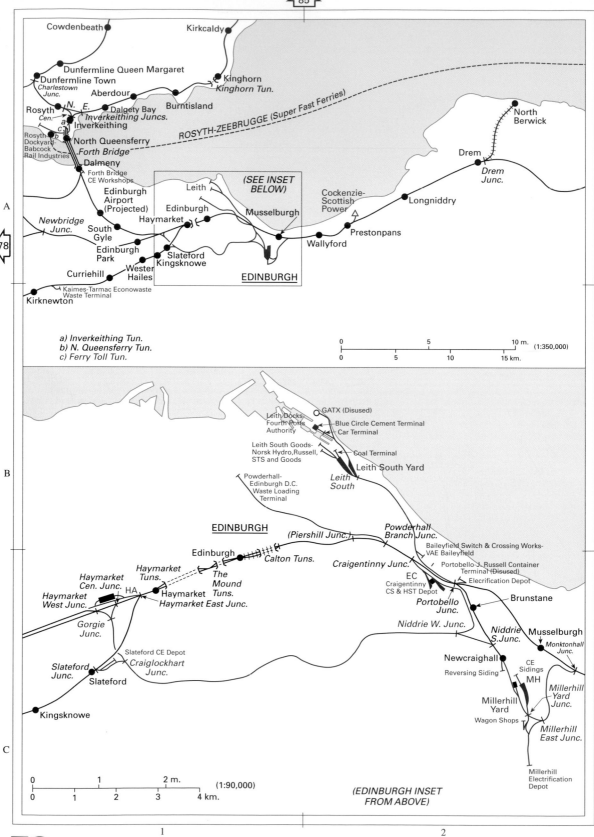

Cowdenbeath

Kirkcaldy

Dunfermline Queen Margaret

Dunfermline Town
Charlestown Junc.
Rosyth
Cen.
N. E.
Aberdour
Kinghorn
Kinghorn Tun.
Burntisland

Dalgety Bay
Inverkeithing Juncs.
Inverkeithing
a)
b)
c)
Rosyth
Dockyard-
Babcock
Rail Industries
North Queensferry
Forth Bridge
Dalmeny
*Forth Bridge
CE Workshops*

ROSYTH-ZEEBRUGGE (Super Fast Ferries)

North
Berwick

Drem
*Drem
Junc.*

A

*Newbridge
Junc.*
Edinburgh
Airport
(Projected)
South
Gyle
Edinburgh
Park
Wester
Hailes
Edinburgh
Haymarket
Slateford
Kingsknowe
Leith
Edinburgh
Musselburgh
(SEE INSET
BELOW)

Cockenzie-
Scottish
Power
Longniddry

Prestonpans
Wallyford

EDINBURGH

78

Curriehill
Kaimes-Tarmac Econowaste
Waste Terminal
Kirknewton

a) *Inverkeithing Tun.*
b) *N. Queensferry Tun.*
c) *Ferry Toll Tun.*

0   5   10 m.
0   5   10   15 km.   (1:350,000)

B

Leith Docks-
Fourth Ports
Authority
GATX (Disused)
Blue Circle Cement Terminal
Car Terminal

Leith South Goods-
Norsk Hydro, Russell,
STS and Goods
Coal Terminal

Powderhall-
Edinburgh D.C.
Waste Loading
Terminal
Leith
South
Leith South Yard

EDINBURGH

Edinburgh
Calton Tuns.
Piershill Junc.
Powderhall
Branch Junc.
Baileyfield Switch & Crossing Works-
VAE Baileyfield
Portobello J. Russell Container
Terminal (Disused)
Elecrification Depot

Haymarket
Cen. Junc.
*Haymarket
Tuns.*
HA
Haymarket
West Junc.
*Gorgie
Junc.*
Haymarket
*The
Mound
Tuns.*
Haymarket East Junc.
Craigentinny Junc.
EC
*Craigentinny
CS & HST Depot*
*Portobello
Junc.*
Brunstane

Niddrie W. Junc.
Niddrie
S.Junc.
Musselburgh
*Monktonhall
Junc.*

Slateford CE Depot
*Craiglockhart
Junc.*
*Slateford
Junc.*
Slateford
Newcraighall
Reversing Siding
CE
Sidings
MH
*Millerhill
Yard
Junc.*

Kingsknowe
Millerhill
Yard
Wagon Shops
*Millerhill
East Junc.*

C

Millerhill
Electrification
Depot

0   1   2 m.
0   1   2   3   4 km.   (1:90,000)

(EDINBURGH INSET
FROM ABOVE)

1   2

79

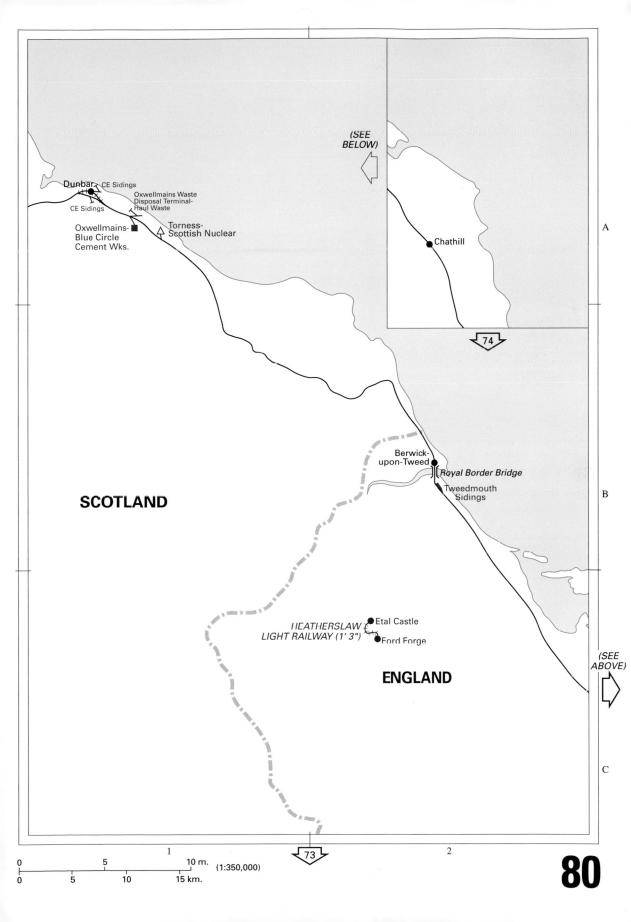

CE Sidings

Dunbar

CE Sidings

Oxwellmains Waste
Disposal Terminal-
Haul Waste

Oxwellmains-
Blue Circle
Cement Wks.

Torness-
Scottish Nuclear

(SEE
BELOW)

Chathill

A

74

SCOTLAND

Berwick-
upon-Tweed

Royal Border Bridge

Tweedmouth
Sidings

B

HEATHERSLAW
LIGHT RAILWAY (1' 3")

Etal Castle

Ford Forge

ENGLAND

(SEE
ABOVE)

C

1

2

73

0   5   10 m.

0   5   10   15 km.

(1:350,000)

80

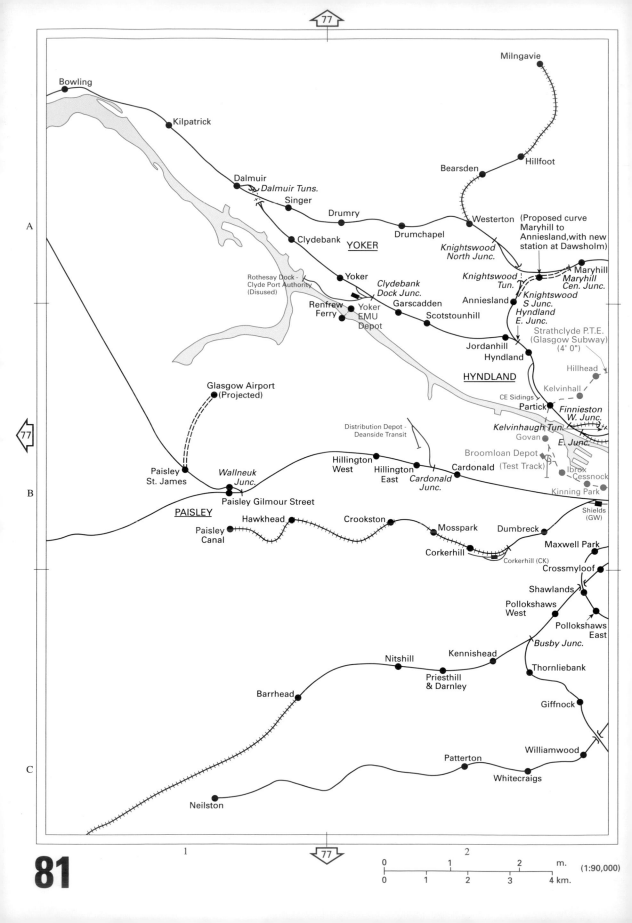

Milngavie

Bowling

Kilpatrick

Hillfoot

Dalmuir
Dalmuir Tuns.
Singer
Drumry
Drumchapel
Bearsden
Westerton

A

Clydebank
YOKER
(Proposed curve
Maryhill to
Anniesland, with new
station at Dawsholm)

*Knightswood
North Junc.*

Yoker
*Clydebank
Dock Junc.*
*Knightswood
Tun.*
Maryhill
*Maryhill
Cen. Junc.*

Rothesay Dock -
Clyde Port Authority
(Disused)

Renfrew
Ferry
Yoker
EMU
Depot
Garscadden
Scotstounhill
Anniesland
*Knightswood
S Junc.*
*Hyndland
E. Junc.*

Jordanhill
Hyndland

HYNDLAND

Strathclyde P.T.E.
(Glasgow Subway)
(4' 0")

Hillhead
Kelvinhall

CE Sidings
Partick
*Finnieston
W. Junc.*

Glasgow Airport
(Projected)

Distribution Depot -
Deanside Transit

Kelvinhaugh Tun.
Govan
E. Junc.

Broomloan Depot
(Test Track)
Ibrox
Cessnock

Paisley
St. James
*Wallneuk
Junc.*
Hillington
West
Hillington
East
Cardonald
*Cardonald
Junc.*

Kinning Park

B

Paisley Gilmour Street
PAISLEY
Shields
(GW)

Hawkhead
Crookston
Mosspark
Dumbreck
Maxwell Park

Paisley
Canal
Corkerhill
Corkerhill (CK)
Crossmyloof

Shawlands
Pollokshaws
West
Pollokshaws
East

Nitshill
Kennishead
Busby Junc.
Thornliebank

Priesthill
& Darnley

Barrhead
Giffnock

Williamwood

Patterton
C
Whitecraigs

Neilston

81

1

2

| 0 | | 1 | | 2 | m. |
| 0 | 1 | 2 | 3 | 4 | km. |

(1:90,000)

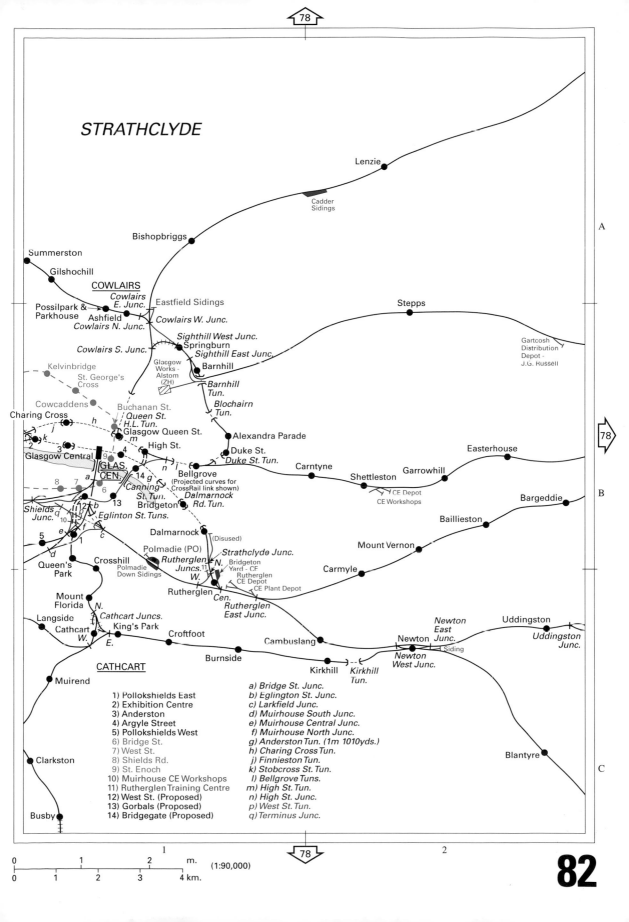

ISLE OF SKYE

Kylerhea • • Glenelg

CANNA •

RUM

Armadale •

• Inverie

(Bruce Watt Cruises)

Mallaig

LOCH NEVIS

(Cal-Mac)

Morar •

(Cal-Mac)

• Tarbet

EIGG

Arisaig

Beasdale
Beasdale Tuns.

A

Borrodale Tun.
Lochailort Tun.

Glenfinnan

Locheilside

(M. Grant)

Lochailort

Glenfinnan

MUCK

(Cal-Mac)

(Loch Shiel Cruises)

TO LOCHBOISDALE (SOUTH UIST)

LOCH SHIEL

ARDNAMURCHAN

Acharacle

TO CASTLEBAY (BARRA)

Kilchoan

Ardgour •

(Cal-Mac)

(Cal-Mac)

COLL

Tobermory

MORVERN

Lismore

Port
Appin

TIREE •

ISLAND
OF
MULL

(Cal-Mac)

Lochaline

(Cal-Mac)

Lismore

B

ULVA

Fishnish

Shell
(Disused)

STAFFA

STRATHCLYDE

Craignure
Tarmstedt

(Cal-Mac)

Connel Ferry
(Block Post)

Taynuilt
Pier

IONA

Torosay
Castle

Oban

Taynuilt

(Cal-Mac)

Fionnphort

MULL & WEST HIGHLAND
RAILWAY (10 ¼")

Goods &
Timber
Loading
Term.

Timber
Loading
Term.

Isle
of Seil

Isle
of Luing

(Cal-Mac)

C

COLONSAY •

JURA

TO PORT ASKAIG
(ISLAY)

1

2

0   10   20 m.

0   10   20   30 km.

(1:700,000)

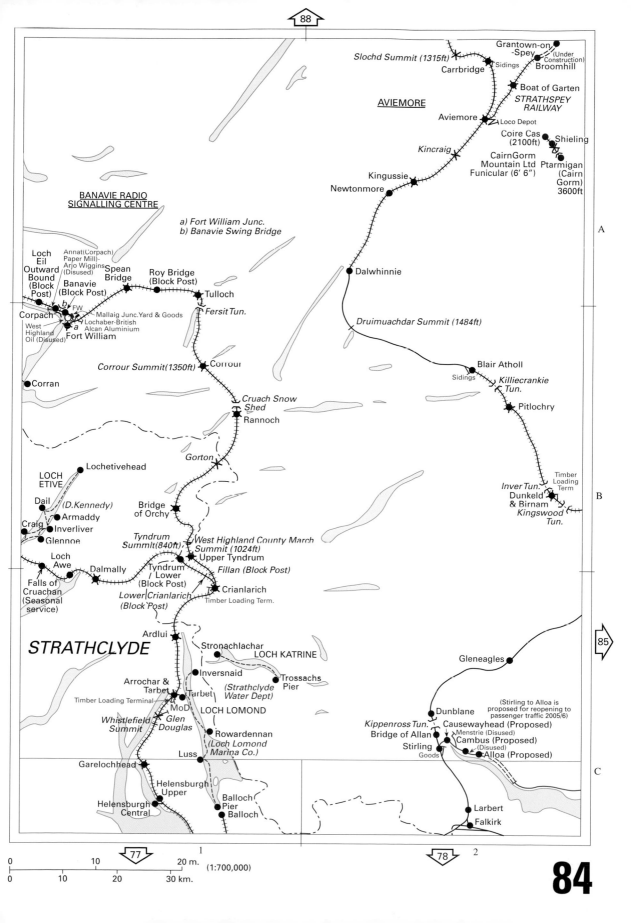

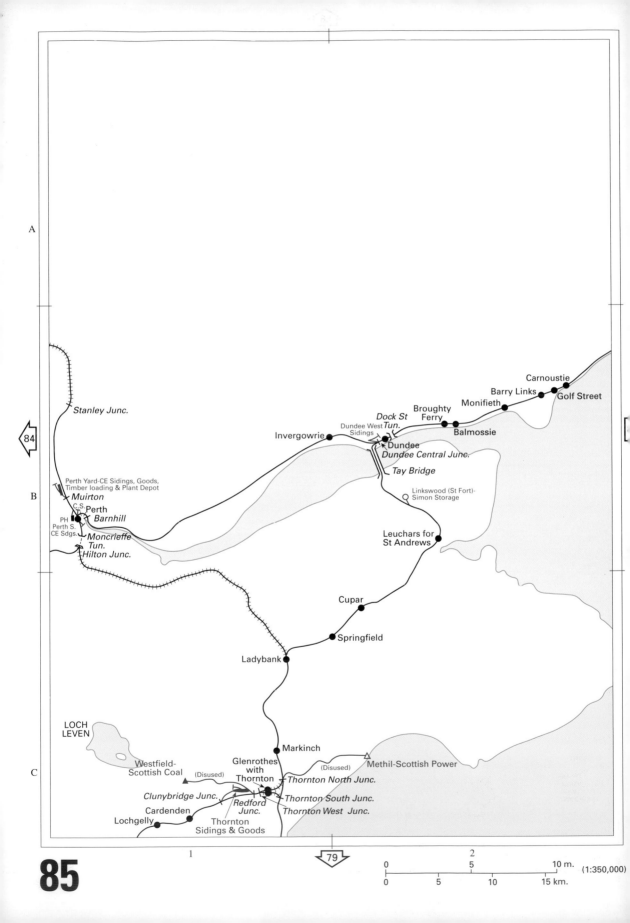

Stanley Junc.

Carnoustie
Barry Links
Golf Street
Monifieth
Broughty Ferry
Balmossie

Dock St Tun.
Dundee West Sidings
Dundee
Dundee Central Junc.
Tay Bridge

Invergowrie

Linkswood (St Fort)-
Simon Storage

Perth Yard-CE Sidings, Goods,
Timber loading & Plant Depot
Muirton
C.S.
Perth
Barnhill
PH
Perth S.
CE Sdgs.
*Moncrieffe
Tun.*
Hilton Junc.

Leuchars for
St Andrews

Cupar

Springfield

Ladybank

LOCH
LEVEN

Markinch

Methil-Scottish Power

Westfield-
Scottish Coal
(Disused)

Glenrothes
with
Thornton
Thornton North Junc.
(Disused)

Clunybridge Junc.
*Redford
Junc.*
Thornton South Junc.
Thornton West Junc.

Cardenden
Lochgelly
Thornton
Sidings & Goods

84

79

85

0   5   10 m.
0   5   10   15 km.
(1:350,000)

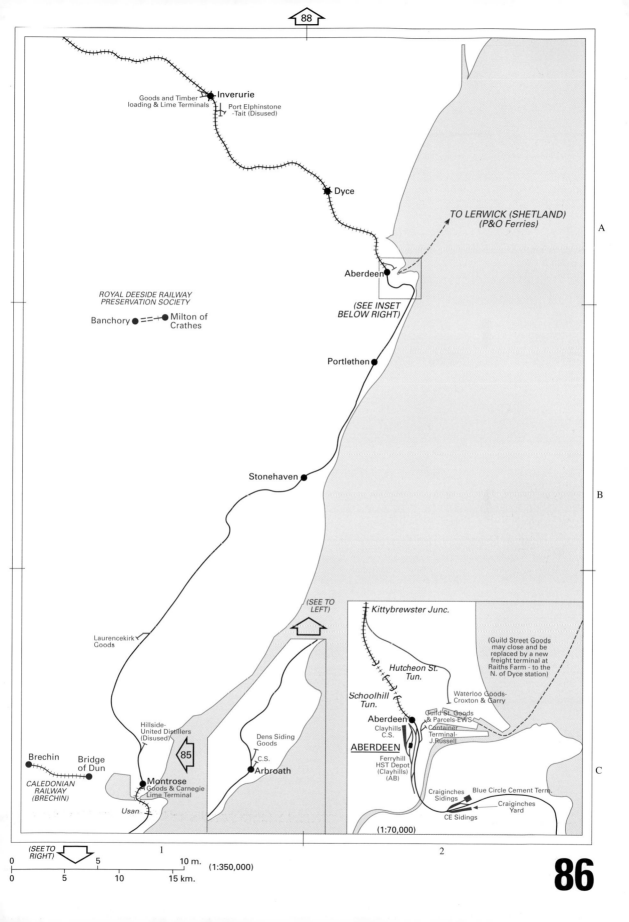

Inverurie

Goods and Timber
loading & Lime Terminals
Port Elphinstone
-Tait (Disused)

Dyce

TO LERWICK (SHETLAND)
(P&O Ferries)

A

Aberdeen

*(SEE INSET
BELOW RIGHT)*

*ROYAL DEESIDE RAILWAY
PRESERVATION SOCIETY*

Banchory ●==●●= Milton of
Crathes

Portlethen

Stonehaven

B

*(SEE TO
LEFT)*

Kittybrewster Junc.

(Guild Street Goods
may close and be
replaced by a new
freight terminal at
Raiths Farm - to the
N. of Dyce station)

Laurencekirk
Goods

*Hutcheon St.
Tun.*

Waterloo Goods-
Croxton & Garry

*Schoolhill
Tun.*

Aberdeen

Guild St. Goods
& Parcels-EWS

Hillside-
United Distillers
(Disused)

Dens Siding
Goods

Clayhills
C.S.

Container
Terminal-
J. Russell

85

C.S.

ABERDEEN

Brechin

Bridge
of Dun

Ferryhill
HST Depot
(Clayhills)
(AB)

Blue Circle Cement Term.

*CALEDONIAN
RAILWAY
(BRECHIN)*

Arbroath

Craiginches
Sidings

Craiginches
Yard

Montrose
Goods & Carnegie
Lime Terminal

CE Sidings

Usan

(1:70,000)

C

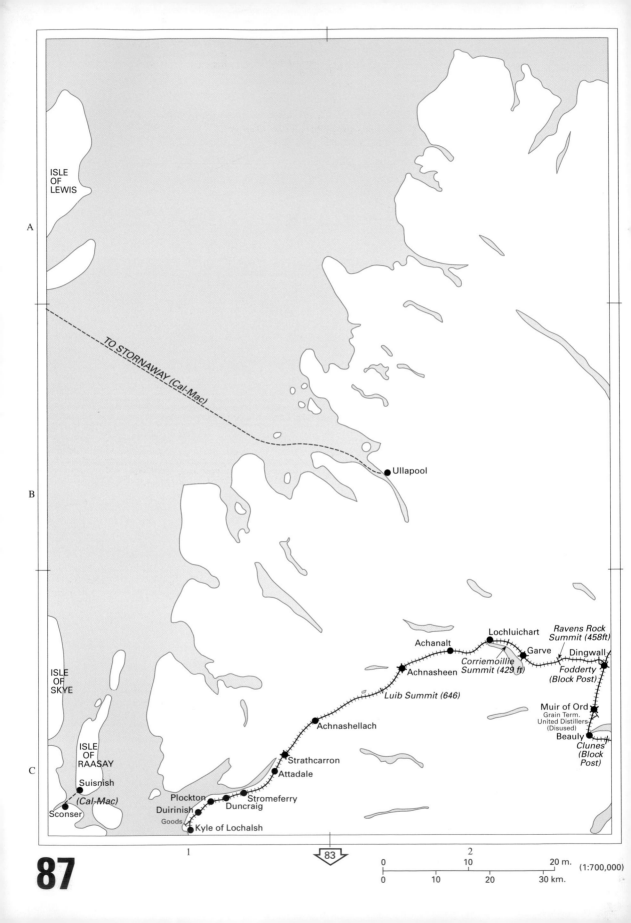

ISLE
OF
LEWIS

A

TO STORNAWAY (Cal-Mac)

Ullapool

B

ISLE
OF
SKYE

ISLE
OF
RAASAY

Lochluichart
Achanalt
Ravens Rock Summit (458ft)
Garve
Dingwall
Corriemoillie Summit (429 ft)
Achnasheen
Fodderty (Block Post)
Luib Summit (646)
Muir of Ord
Grain Term.
United Distillers
(Disused)
Achnashellach
Beauly
Clunes (Block Post)

C

Strathcarron
Attadale
Suisnish
(Cal-Mac)
Plockton
Stromeferry
Sconser
Duirinish
Duncraig
Goods
Kyle of Lochalsh

1

83

2
10
20 m.

0
0   10   20   30 km.

(1:700,000)

87

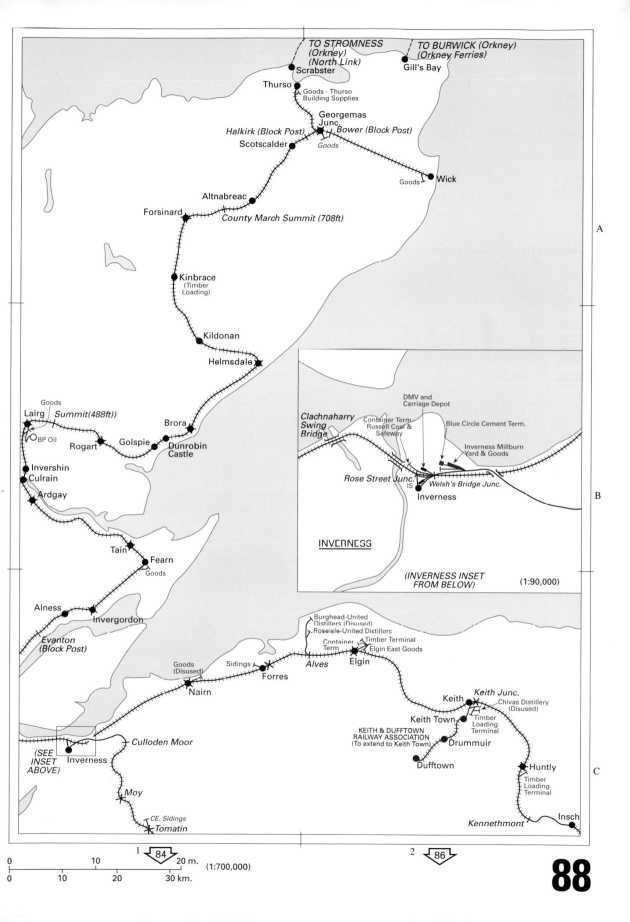

TO STROMNESS
(Orkney)
(North Link)

TO BURWICK (Orkney)
(Orkney Ferries)

Scrabster

Gill's Bay

Thurso

Goods - Thurso
Building Supplies

Georgemas
Junc.

Halkirk (Block Post)

Bower (Block Post)

Scotscalder

Goods

Wick

Goods

Altnabreac

Forsinard

County March Summit (708ft)

Kinbrace
(Timber
Loading)

Kildonan

Helmsdale

Goods

Lairg

Summit(488ft))

BP Oil

Brora

Rogart

Golspie

Dunrobin
Castle

Invershin

Culrain

Ardgay

Tain

Fearn

Goods

Alness

Invergordon

Evanton
(Block Post)

DMV and
Carriage Depot

Clachnaharry
Swing
Bridge

Container Term.
Russell Coal &
Safeway

Blue Circle Cement Term.

Inverness Millburn
Yard & Goods

Rose Street Junc.

IS

Welsh's Bridge Junc.

Inverness

INVERNESS

(INVERNESS INSET
FROM BELOW)

(1:90,000)

Burghead-United
Distillers (Disused)
Roseisle-United Distillers

Container
Term.

Timber Terminal
Elgin East Goods

Goods
(Disused)

Sidings

Alves

Elgin

Nairn

Forres

Keith Junc.

Keith

Chivas Distillery
(Disused)

Keith Town

Timber
Loading
Terminal

KEITH & DUFFTOWN
RAILWAY ASSOCIATION
(To extend to Keith Town)

Drummuir

(SEE
INSET
ABOVE)

Inverness

Culloden Moor

Dufftown

Huntly

Timber
Loading
Terminal

Moy

CE. Sidings
Tomatin

Kennethmont

Insch

0   10   20 m.
1 ⏌84⏌
2 ⏌86⏌

0   10   20   30 km.   (1:700,000)

88

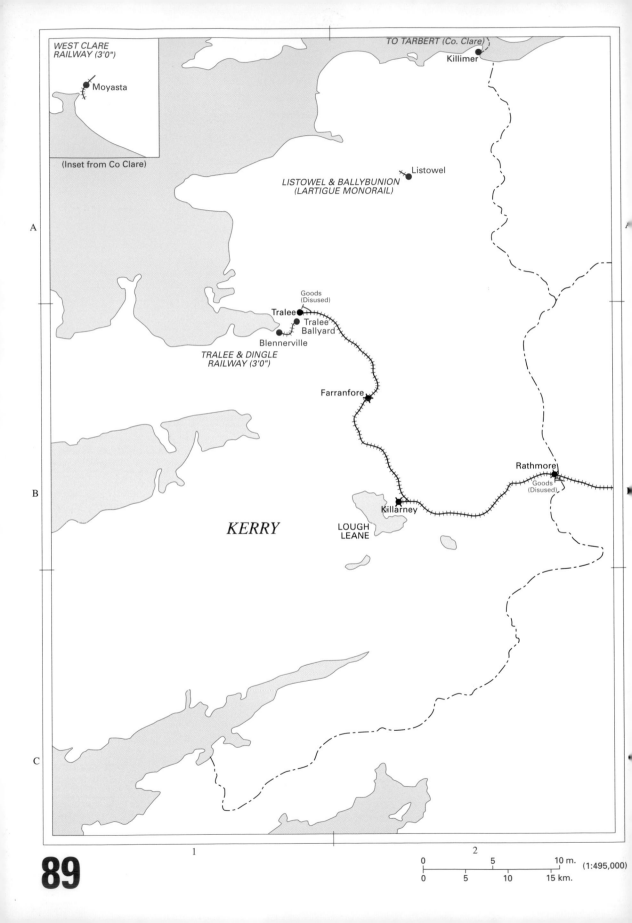

WEST CLARE
RAILWAY (3'0")

● Moyasta

(Inset from Co Clare)

TO TARBERT (Co. Clare)

● Killimer

× Listowel

LISTOWEL & BALLYBUNION
(LARTIGUE MONORAIL)

A

Goods
(Disused)

Tralee ●
● Tralee
Ballyard

● Blennerville

TRALEE & DINGLE
RAILWAY (3'0")

Farranfore

Rathmore ●
Goods
(Disused)

B

KERRY

Killarney

LOUGH
LEANE

C

1

2

0   5   10 m.

0   5   10   15 km.

(1:495,000)

89

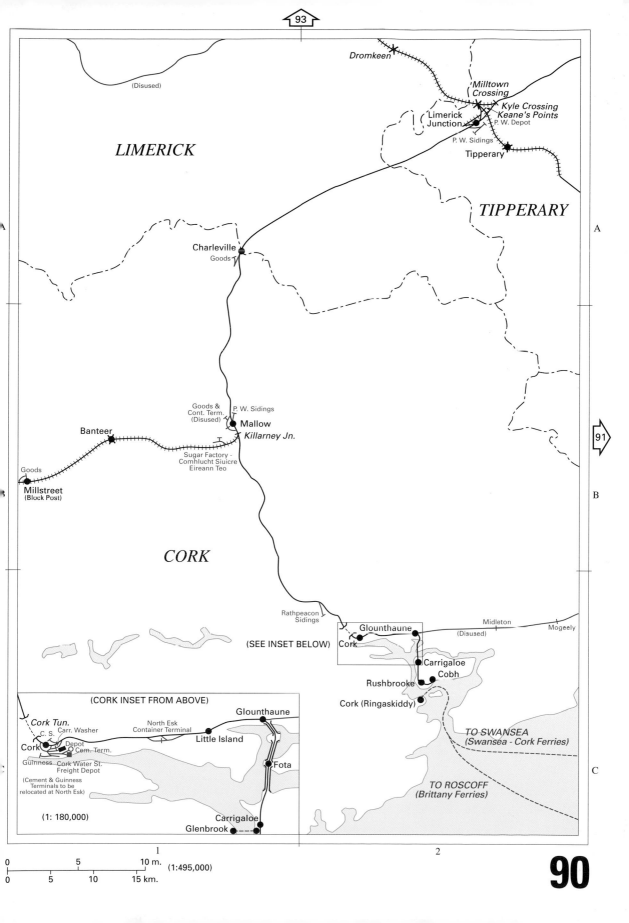

Dromkeen

Milltown Crossing

Kyle Crossing
Keane's Points
Limerick
Junction
P. W. Depot
P. W. Sidings
Tipperary

LIMERICK

TIPPERARY

Charleville
Goods

CORK

Goods &
Cont. Term.
(Disused)
P. W. Sidings
Mallow
Killarney Jn.

Banteer

Sugar Factory -
Comhlucht Siuicre
Eireann Teo

Goods
Millstreet
(Block Post)

91

Rathpeacon
Sidings

Glounthaune
Cork

(SEE INSET BELOW)

Midleton
(Disused)
Mogeely

Carrigaloe
Cobh
Rushbrooke

Cork (Ringaskiddy)

TO SWANSEA
(Swansea - Cork Ferries)

TO ROSCOFF
(Brittany Ferries)

(CORK INSET FROM ABOVE)

Cork Tun.
C. S.
Carr. Washer
Cork
Depot
Cem. Term.
North Esk
Container Terminal
Glounthaune

Little Island

Guinness
Cork Water St.
Freight Depot
(Cement & Guinness
Terminals to be
relocated at North Esk)

Fota

(1: 180,000)

Carrigaloe
Glenbrook

0   5   10 m.
(1:495,000)
0   5   10   15 km.

90

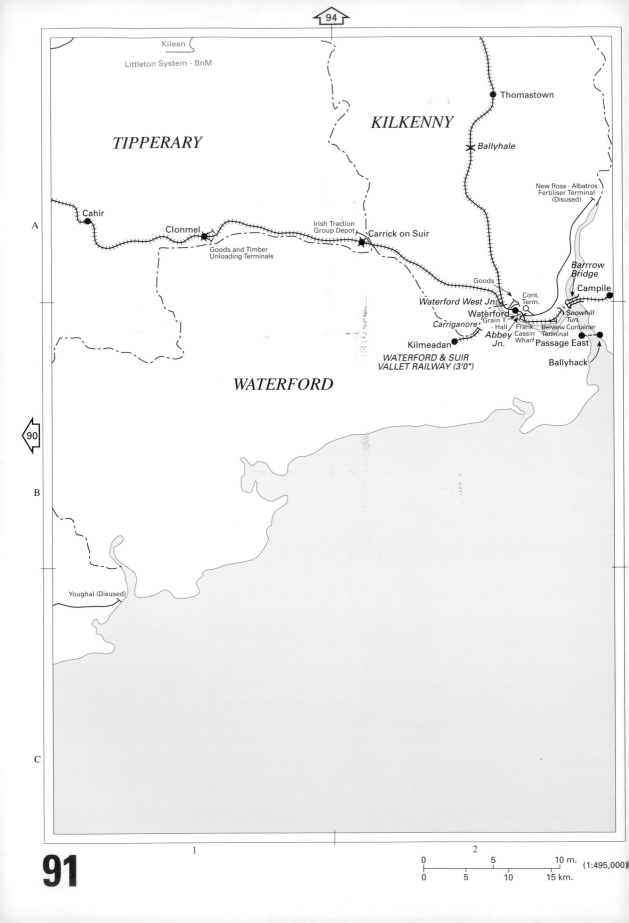

Kileen

Littleton System - BnM

● Thomastown

KILKENNY

TIPPERARY

✕ *Ballyhale*

New Ross - Albatros
Fertiliser Terminal
(Disused)

● Cahir

A

Clonmel ★
Goods and Timber
Unloading Terminals

Irish Traction
Group Depot

★ Carrick on Suir

*Barrrow
Bridge*

● Campile

Goods

Cont.
Term.

Waterford West Jn.

Waterford

*Snowhill
Tun.*

Carriganore

Grain T.
- Hall

Frank
Cassin
Wharf

Belview Container
Terminal

● Passage East

*Abbey
Jn.*

Kilmeadan ●

● Ballyhack

*WATERFORD & SUIR
VALLET RAILWAY (3'0")*

WATERFORD

B

Youghal (Disused)

C

1

2

0   5   10 m.

0   5   10   15 km.

(1:495,000)

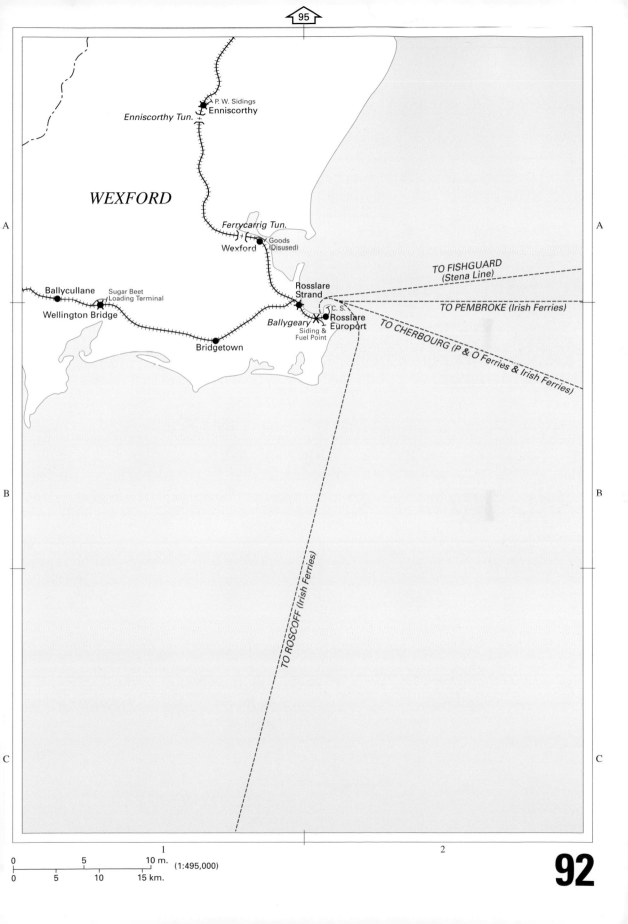

WEXFORD

Enniscorthy Tun.

P. W. Sidings
Enniscorthy

Ferrycarrig Tun.

Wexford
Goods
(Disused)

Rosslare
Strand

TO FISHGUARD
(Stena Line)

Ballycullane

Sugar Beet
Loading Terminal

Wellington Bridge

Bridgetown

Ballygeary
Siding &
Fuel Point

C. S.
Rosslare
Europort

TO PEMBROKE (Irish Ferries)

TO CHERBOURG (P & O Ferries & Irish Ferries)

TO ROSCOFF (Irish Ferries)

A   A

B   B

C   C

1   2
10 m.   (1:495,000)
0   5   10
0   5   10   15 km.

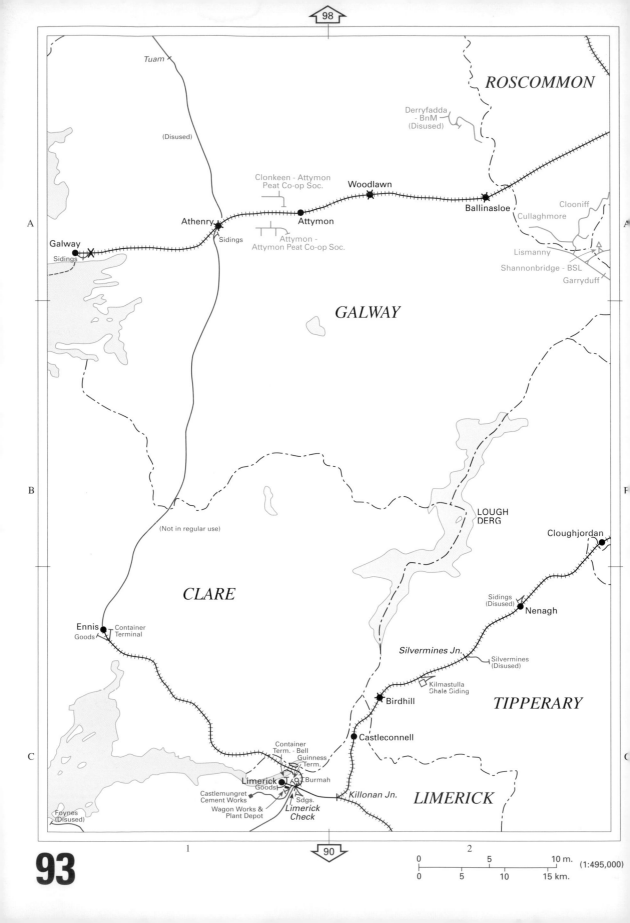

ROSCOMMON

Tuam

(Disused)

Derryfadda
- BnM
(Disused)

Clonkeen - Attymon
Peat Co-op Soc.

Woodlawn

Clooniff

Cullaghmore

A   Athenry   Attymon   Ballinasloe

Sidings

Attymon -
Attymon Peat Co-op Soc.

Lismanny

Shannonbridge - BSL

Galway

Garryduff

Sidings

GALWAY

LOUGH
DERG

Cloughjordan

B

(Not in regular use)

Sidings
(Disused)

Nenagh

CLARE

Silvermines Jn.

Silvermines
(Disused)

Ennis

Container
Terminal

Kilmastulla
Shale Siding

TIPPERARY

Goods

Birdhill

Castleconnell

Container
Term. - Bell
Guinness
Term.

C   Limerick   Burmah

Limerick

Goods

Castlemungret
Cement Works

Killonan Jn.

LIMERICK

Wagon Works &
Plant Depot

Sdgs.

Limerick
Check

Foynes
(Disused)

0   5   10 m.   (1:495,000)

0   5   10   15 km.

1

2

93

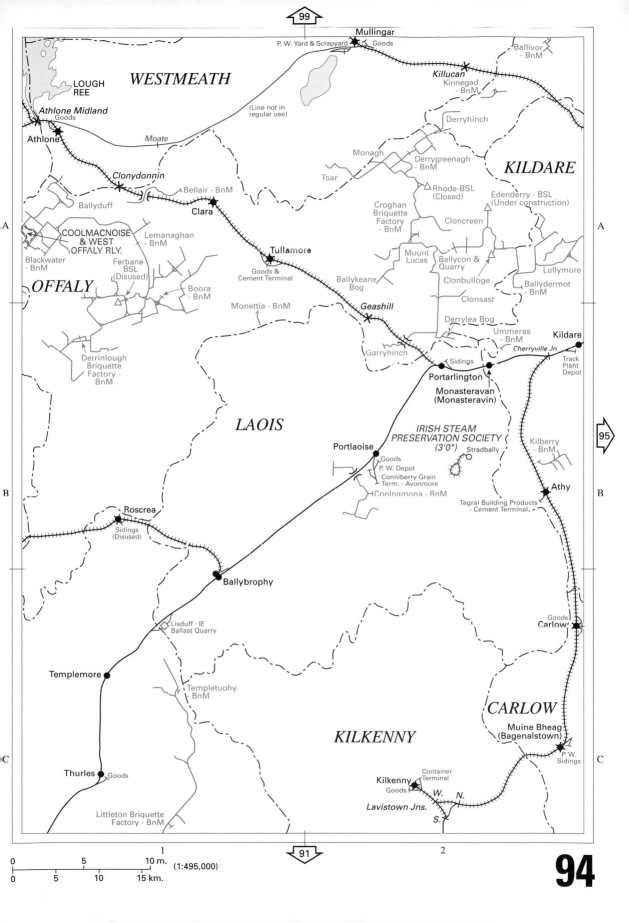

Mullingar
P. W. Yard & Scrapyard — Goods

Ballivor - BnM

WESTMEATH

Killucan
Kinnegad - BnM

Derryhinch

LOUGH REE

Athlone Midland — Goods

Athlone

Moate

Monagh

Toar

Derrygreenagh - BnM

Rhode-BSL (Closed)

KILDARE

Edenderry - BSL (Under construction)

Clonydonnin

Bellair - BnM

Ballyduff

Clara

Croghan Briquette Factory - BnM

Cloncreen

A — A

COOLMACNOISE & WEST OFFALY RLY.

Lemanaghan - BnM

Tullamore
Goods & Cement Terminal

Mount Lucas

Ballycon & Quarry

Clonbulloge

Lullymore

Blackwater - BnM

Ferbane BSL (Disused)

Boora - BnM

Ballykeane Bog

Clonsast

Ballydermot - BnM

OFFALY

Monettia - BnM

Geashill

Derrylea Bog

Ummeras - BnM

Cherryville Jn.

Kildare

Track Plant Depot

Derrinlough Briquette Factory - BnM

Garryhinch

Sidings

Portarlington

Monasteravan (Monasteravin)

LAOIS

IRISH STEAM PRESERVATION SOCIETY (3'0")

Stradbally

Kilberry - BnM

Portlaoise
Goods
P. W. Depot
Conniberry Grain Term. - Avonmore
Coolnamona - BnM

Tegral Building Products - Cement Terminal

Athy

B — B

Roscrea
Sidings (Disused)

Ballybrophy

Lisduff - IE Ballast Quarry

Goods
Carlow

Templemore

Templetuohy - BnM

CARLOW

Muine Bheag (Bagenalstown)

P. W. Sidings

C — C

Thurles — Goods

Container Terminal

KILKENNY

Kilkenny
Goods

W. N.

Lavistown Jns.

S.

Littleton Briquette Factory - BnM

0 5 10 m.
0 5 10 15 km.
(1:495,000)

1   2

94

(Line not in regular use)

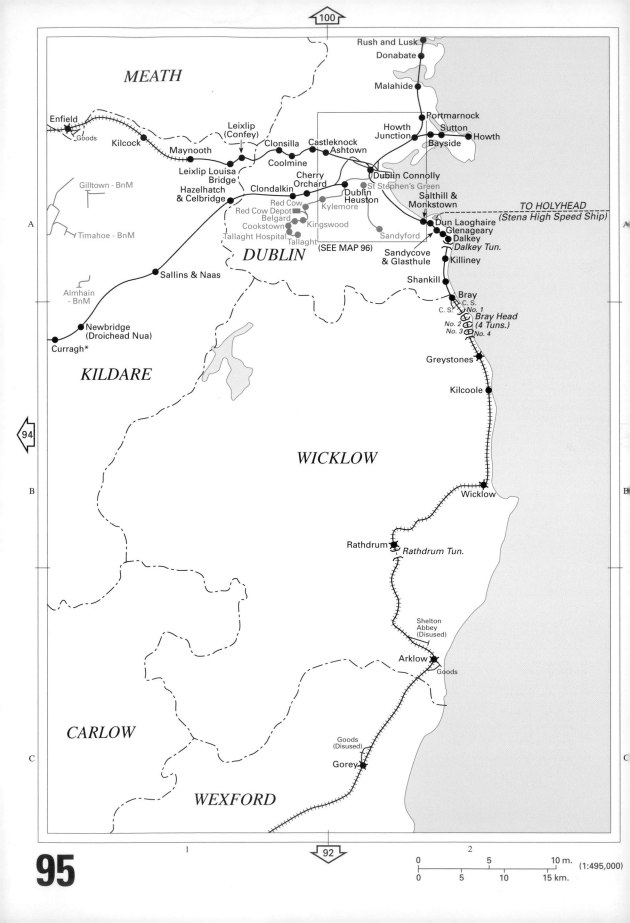

MEATH

Rush and Lusk

Donabate

Malahide

Enfield
Goods
Kilcock

Leixlip
(Confey)

Clonsilla
Castleknock
Ashtown

Portmarnock
Sutton
Howth

Maynooth

Coolmine

Howth
Junction
Bayside

Leixlip Louisa
Bridge

Cherry
Orchard

Dublin Connolly

Hazelhatch
& Celbridge

Clondalkin

Dublin
Heuston

St Stephen's Green

Salthill &
Monkstown

Gilltown - BnM

Red Cow
Red Cow Depot
Belgard
Kylemore
Kingswood

TO HOLYHEAD
(Stena High Speed Ship)

A

Timahoe - BnM

Cookstown
Tallaght Hospital
Tallaght

Sandyford

(SEE MAP 96)

Dun Laoghaire
Glenageary
Dalkey
Dalkey Tun.

A

DUBLIN

Sandycove
& Glasthule

Killiney

Almhain
- BnM

Sallins & Naas

Shankill

Bray
C. S.
No. 1

Newbridge
(Droichead Nua)

C. S.
No. 2
No. 3

*Bray Head
(4 Tuns.)*
No. 4

Curragh*

Greystones

KILDARE

Kilcoole

94

WICKLOW

B

Wicklow

B

Rathdrum

Rathdrum Tun.

Shelton
Abbey
(Disused)

Arklow

Goods

CARLOW

Goods
(Disused)

C

Gorey

C

WEXFORD

1

2

0   5   10 m.

0   5   10   15 km.

(1:495,000)

95

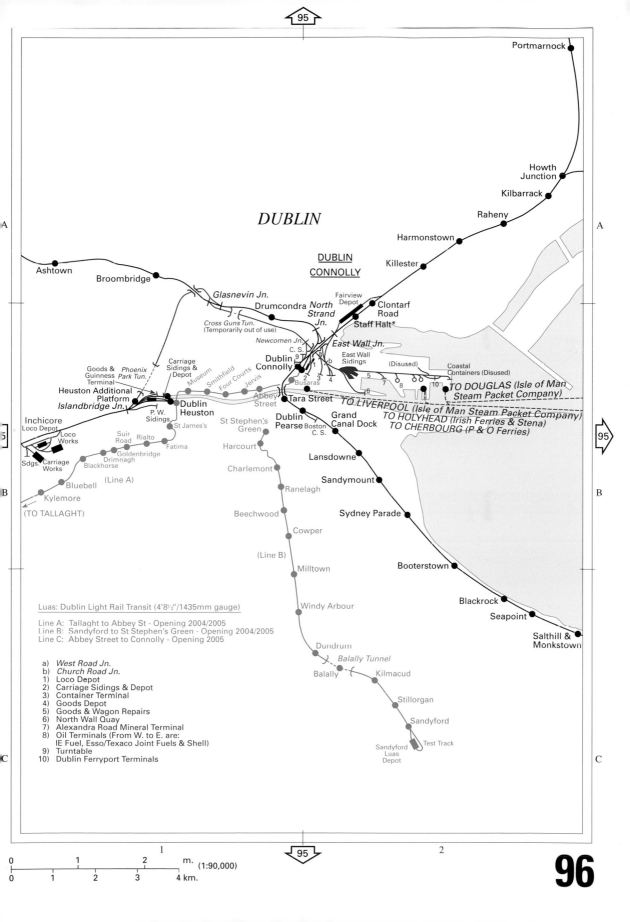

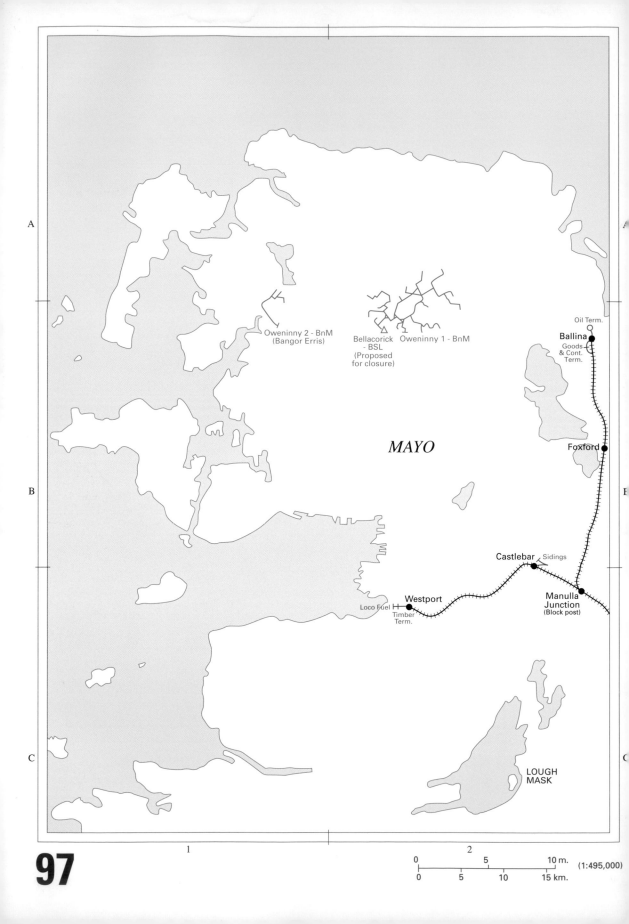

Oil Term.

Ballina

Goods
& Cont.
Term.

Oweninny 2 - BnM
(Bangor Erris)

Bellacorick   Oweninny 1 - BnM
- BSL
(Proposed
for closure)

MAYO

Foxford

Castlebar Sidings

Westport

Loco Fuel
Timber
Term.

**Manulla
Junction**
(Block post)

**LOUGH
MASK**

A   A

B   B

C   C

1   2

97

0   5   10 m.   (1:495,000)
0   5   10   15 km.

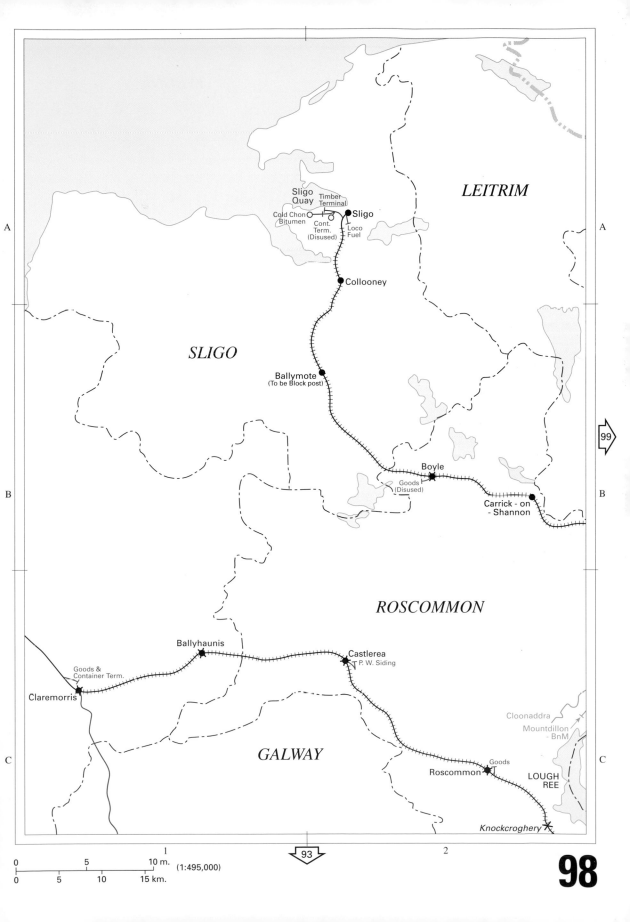

LEITRIM

SLIGO

Sligo
Quay
Timber
Terminal
Cold Chon
Bitumen
Cont.
Term.
(Disused)
Sligo
Loco
Fuel

Collooney

Ballymote
(To be Block post)

Boyle
Goods
(Disused)
Carrick - on
- Shannon

ROSCOMMON

99

Ballyhaunis
Castlerea
P. W. Siding

Goods &
Container Term.
Claremorris

GALWAY

Cloonaddra
Mountdillon
- BnM

Roscommon
Goods
LOUGH
REE

Knockcroghery

0   5   10 m.
1
(1:495,000)

0   5   10   15 km.

98

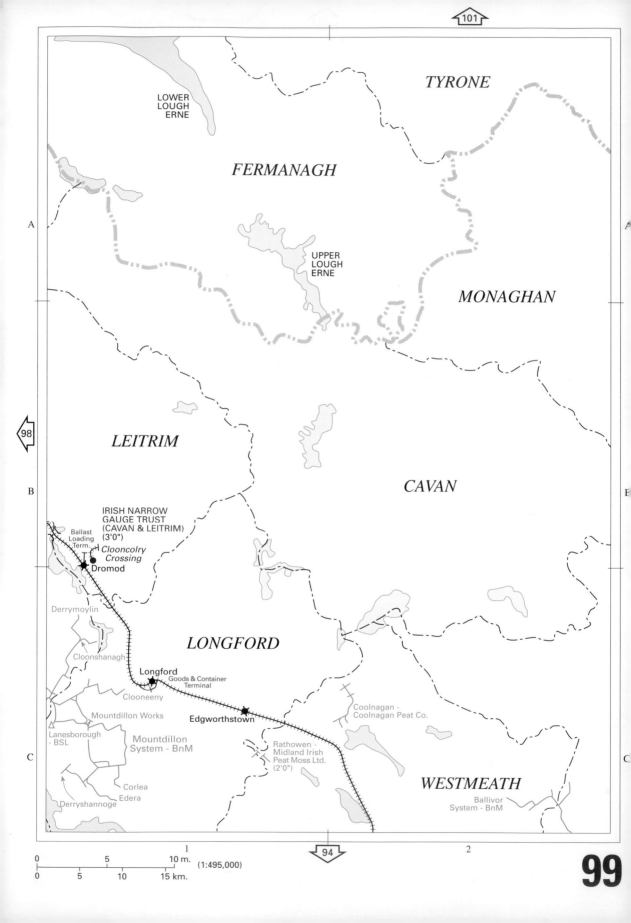

TYRONE

LOWER
LOUGH
ERNE

FERMANAGH

UPPER
LOUGH
ERNE

MONAGHAN

LEITRIM

CAVAN

IRISH NARROW
GAUGE TRUST
(CAVAN & LEITRIM)
(3'0")

Ballast
Loading
Term.

*Clooncolry
Crossing*

Dromod

Derrymoylin

LONGFORD

Cloonshanagh

Longford
Goods & Container
Terminal

Clooneeny

Mountdillon Works

Edgworthstown

Coolnagan -
Coolnagan Peat Co.

Lanesborough
- BSL

Mountdillon
System - BnM

Rathowen -
Midland Irish
Peat Moss Ltd.
(2'0")

Corlea

Edera

WESTMEATH

Derryshannoge

Ballivor
System - BnM

1

2

0   5   10 m.
(1:495,000)

0   5   10   15 km.

99

P.W. Sidings

Portadown

PORTADOWN

Sidings

Scarva

P. W. Siding

Poyntzpass

*DOWNPATRICK
STEAM RAILWAY
(5'3")*

Inch Abbey

Downpatrick

Ballydugan

King Magnus's
Halt

DOWN

A

ARMAGH

Newry

TRANSLINK
(5'3")

IARNROD
EIREANN
(5'3")

C.S.

Dundalk

Ardee Road
Goods &
Container
Terminal

MONAGHAN

LOUTH

B

Kingscourt
(Gypsum
Loading)

Dunleer*

(Disused)

*Boyne
Bridge*

Sidings &
Fuel Point

Goods

DMU Depot

Platin Cement
Works

Gypsum

Oil

Cement

Drogheda

Laytown

Mosney

Gormanston

Tara Mines
(Lead &
Zinc Ores)
-Outokumpu

*Tara
Mines
Jn.*

P. W.
Sidings

Navan*

MEATH

Balbriggan

C

Skerries

DUBLIN

1

10 m.

(1:495,000)

0   5

0   5   10   15 km.

100

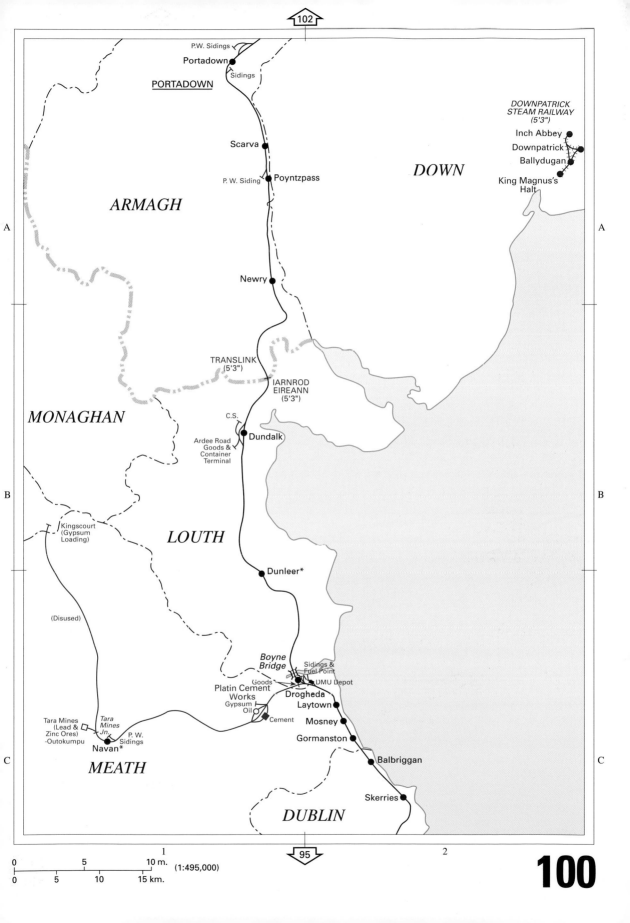

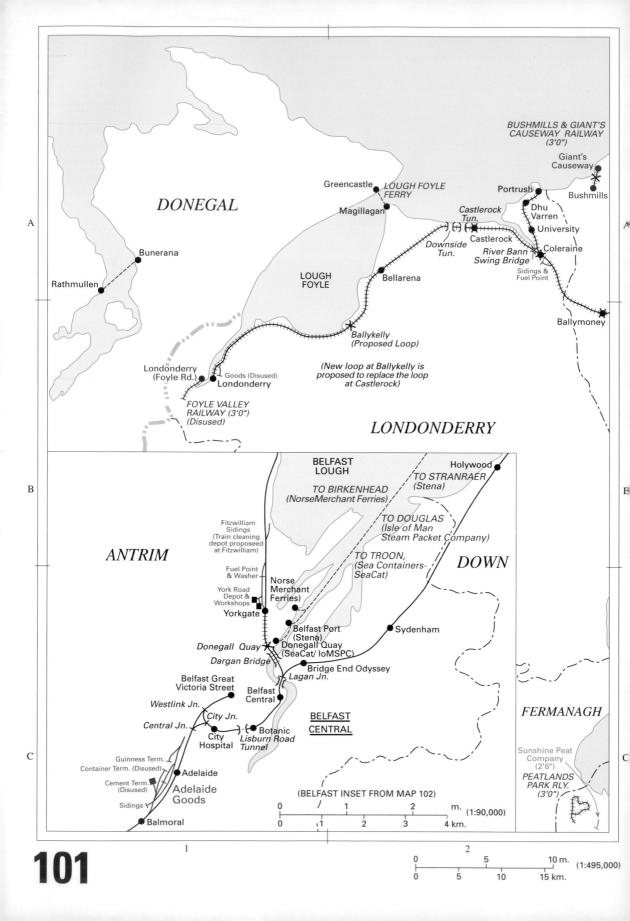

BUSHMILLS & GIANT'S
CAUSEWAY RAILWAY
(3'0")

Giant's
Causeway

Bushmills

DONEGAL

Greencastle   *LOUGH FOYLE*
               FERRY

Magillagan

Castlerock
Tun.

Portrush

Dhu
Varren

University

Coleraine

Bunerana

Downside
Tun.

Castlerock

River Bann
Swing Bridge

Sidings &
Fuel Point

Rathmullen

LOUGH
FOYLE

Bellarena

Ballymoney

Ballykelly
(Proposed Loop)

(New loop at Ballykelly is
proposed to replace the loop
at Castlerock)

Londonderry
(Foyle Rd.)   Goods (Disused)
               Londonderry

FOYLE VALLEY
RAILWAY (3'0")
(Disused)

LONDONDERRY

A   A'

B   B'

BELFAST
LOUGH   Holywood

TO BIRKENHEAD   *TO STRANRAER*
(NorseMerchant Ferries)   *(Stena)*

ANTRIM

Fitzwilliam
Sidings
(Train cleaning
depot proposeed
at Fitzwilliam)

TO DOUGLAS
(Isle of Man
Steam Packet Company)

TO TROON,
(Sea Containers-
SeaCat)

DOWN

Fuel Point
& Washer   Norse
                Merchant
York Road   Ferries)
Depot &
Workshops
Yorkgate

Belfast Port
(Stena)

Sydenham

Donegall Quay   Donegall Quay
                        (SeaCat/ IoMSPC)
Dargan Bridge

FERMANAGH

Belfast Great
Victoria Street

Bridge End Odyssey

Lagan Jn.

Westlink Jn.   Belfast
                   Central
City Jn.

Central Jn.   City
                   Hospital

Botanic
Lisburn Road
Tunnel

BELFAST
CENTRAL

Sunshine Peat
Company
(2'6")

PEATLANDS
PARK RLY.
(3'0")

Guinness Term.
Container Term. (Disused)   Adelaide
Cement Term.
(Disused)   Adelaide
                  Goods
Sidings
Balmoral

(BELFAST INSET FROM MAP 102)

| 0 | | 1 | | 2 | m. | (1:90,000) |

| 0 | 1 | 2 | 3 | 4 km. |

101

1   2

| 0 | | 5 | | 10 m. | (1:495,000) |

| 0 | 5 | 10 | 15 km. |

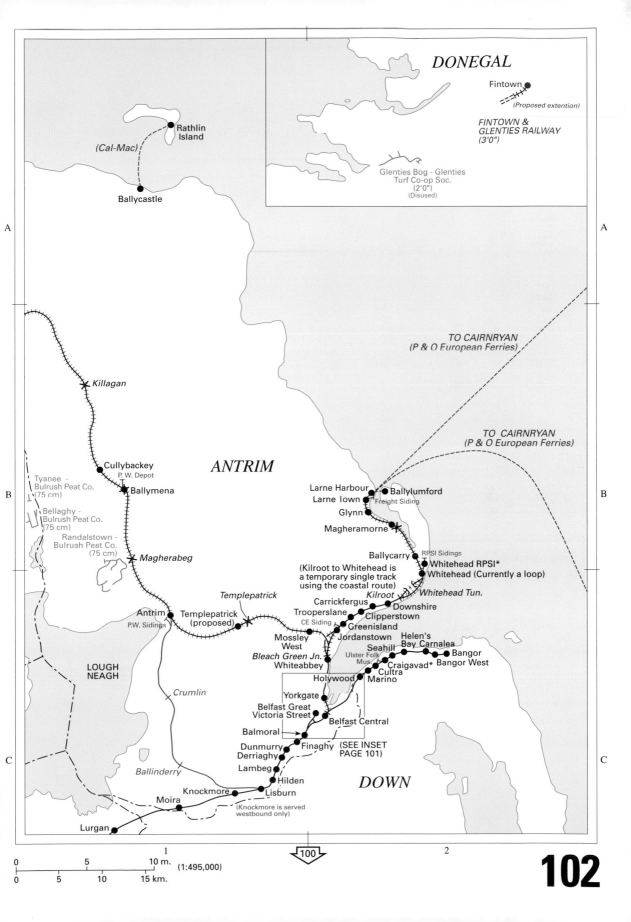

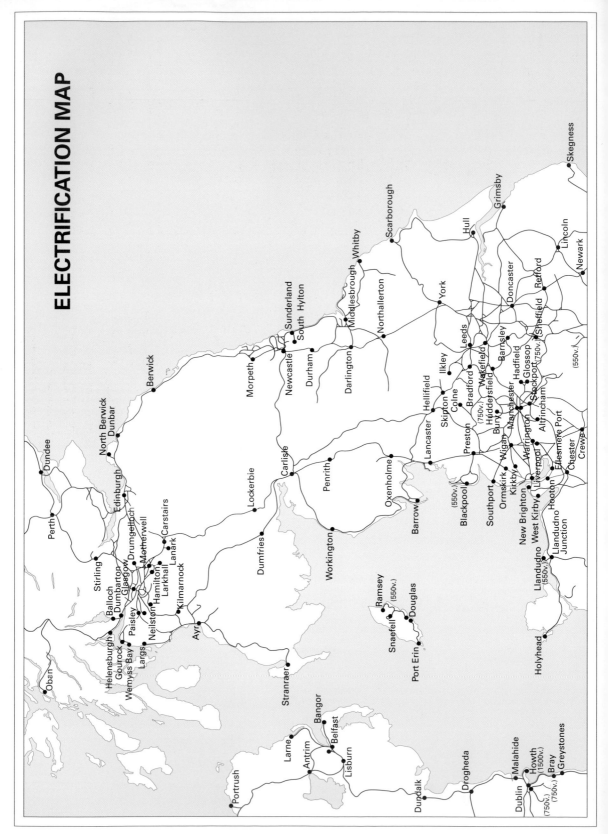

ELECTRIFICATION MAP

103

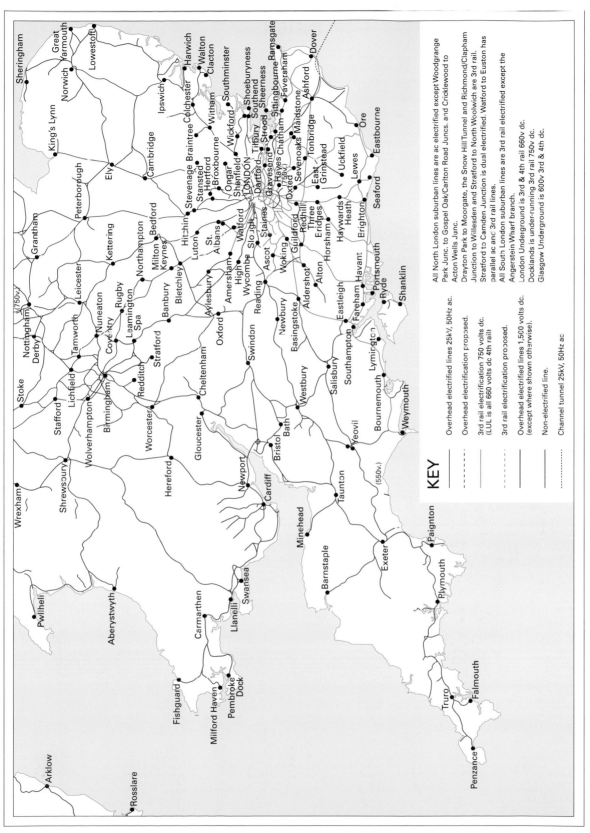

KEY

— Overhead electrified lines 25kV, 50Hz ac.

------ Overhead electrification proposed.

······· 3rd rail electrification 750 volts dc.
(LUL is all 660 volts dc 4th rail)

······· 3rd rail electrification proposed.

—— Overhead electrified lines 1,500 volts dc.
(except where shown otherwise).

—— Non-electrified line.

········· Channel tunnel 25kV, 50Hz ac.

All North London suburban lines are ac electrified except Woodgrange
Park Junc. to Gospel Oak/Carlton Road Juncs. and Cricklewood to
Acton Wells Junc.

Drayton Park to Moorgate, the Snow Hill Tunnel and Richmond/Clapham
Junction to Willesden and Stratford to North Woolwich are 3rd rail.
Stratford to Camden Junction is dual electrified. Watford to Euston has
parallel ac and 3rd rail lines.

All South London suburban lines are 3rd rail electrified except the
Angerstein Wharf branch.

London Underground is 3rd & 4th rail 660v dc.
Docklands is under-running 3rd rail 750v dc.
Glasgow Underground is 600v 3rd & 4th dc.

INDEX

All passenger stations are included in this index. Freight terminals, junction names, tunnels and other significant locations are indexed where their names or map references differ from a passenger station.

* denotes an unadvertised or excursion station. (eg Curragh*)

Location	Page No.	Page Ref.	Location	Page No.	Page Ref.	Location	Page No.	Page Ref.
Ballycarry	102	B2	Bathgate	78	A2	Berry Brow	61	C2
Ballycon	94	A2	Batley	62	B1	Berrylands	16	B2
Ballycullane	92	B1	Battersby	68	B2	Berwick (Sussex)	12	C2
Ballydermot	94	A2	Battersea Bridge	21	C1	Berwick-upon-Tweed	80	C2
Ballyduff	94	A1	Battersea Park	21	C1	Berwyn	51	C1
Ballydugan	100	A2	Battersea Pier Junction	21	C1	Bescar Lane	60	C2
Ballygeary	92	B2	Battle	13	C1	Bescot	47	A2
Ballyhale	91	A2	Battlesbridge	37	C1	Bescot Stadium	47	A2
Ballyhaunis	98	C1	Bayford	36	B1	Bessacarr Junction	64	B2
Ballykeans	94	A2	Bayside	95	A2	Besses-o'-th'-Barn	57	A2
Ballkelly (Proposed)	101	B2	Bayston Hill	40	A2	Bestwood Park Junction	53	C2
Ballymena	102	B1	Bayswater	21	B1	Betchworth	11	A2
Ballymoney	101	B2	Beachland	11	C1	Bethnal Green	22	B1
Ballymote	98	B2	Beacon Hill Tunnel	61	B2	Betws-y-Coed	50	B1
Balm Road	63	B1	Beaconsfield	35	C1	Beverley	63	B2
Balmoral	101	C1	Beaconsfield Street	55	A1	Bewdley	41	B1
Balmossie	85	B2	Beam Mill Junction	69	A2	Bexhill	13	C1
Bamber Bridge	60	B2	Bearley	42	C1	Bexley	36	C2
Bamford	53	A1	Bearsden	81	A2	Bexleyheath	36	C2
Bamfurlong Junction	60	C2	Bearsted	13	A1	Bibbington Summit	52	A2
Bamforth Street	53	A1	Beasdale	83	A2	Bicester North	34	A2
Banavie	84	B1	Beattock	71	A2	Bicester Town	34	B2
Banbury	34	A2	Beauly	87	C2	Bickley	18	B2
Banbury Road	34	B2	Beaulieu Road	10	C1	Bicton	3	A2
Banchory (Proposed)	86	B1	Beaverpool Tunnel	50	B1	Bidston	51	A1
Bangor (Co. Down)	102	C2	Bebington	59	C1	Bidston East Junction	59	B1
Bangor (Gwynedd)	49	A2	Beccles	46	B1	Biggleswade	35	A2
Bangor West	102	C2	Beckenham Hill	18	A1	Bilbrook	41	A1
Bank	21	B2	Beckenham Junction	18	A1	Billericay	36	C2
Bank Foot	75	A1	Beckenham Road	18	B1	Billingham	69	A1
Bank Hall	59	B1	Beckfoot	66	B1	Billingshurst	11	B2
Bank House Tunnel	61	B2	Beckton	22	B2	Bilston Central	47	A1
Bank Junction	71	A1	Beckton Park	22	B2	Bincombe Tunnel	5	A1
Banstead	17	C1	Becontree	36	C1	Bingham	54	C1
Banteer	90	B1	Bedale	68	C1	Bingley	61	B2
Barassie	77	C2	Beddgellert (proposed)	49	C2	Birchgrove	27	A2
Barbican	21	B2	Beddington Lane	17	B2	Birchington-on-Sea	14	A1
Bardon Hill	42	A2	Bede	76	B1	Birchwood	52	A1
Bardon Mill	73	C1	Bedford	43	C2	Birdhill	93	C2
Bare Lane	60	A2	Bedford Park Junction	20	C2	Birkbeck	18	B1
Bargeddie	82	B2	Bedford St. Johns	43	C2	Birkdale	60	C1
Bargoed	32	B1	Bedhampton	11	C1	Birkenhead Central	59	C1
Barham	45	C2	Bedlam Tunnel	9	A1	Birkenhead Hamilton Square	59	B1
Barking	22	B2	Bedlington North	74	B1	Birkenhead North	59	B1
Barkingside	22	A2	Bedminster	28	C2	Birkenhead Park	59	B1
Barkston Junctions	54	C1	Bedworth	42	B1	Birkett Tunnel	67	B1
Barlaston	52	C1	Bedwyn	10	A1	Birkhill	78	A2
Barleith	77	C2	Beechgrove	9	B1	Birley Lane	56	C1
Barming	13	A1	Beechwood (Dublin)	96	B1	Birley Moor Road	56	C2
Barmoor Clough Tunnel	52	A2	Beechwood Tunnel	42	B1	Birmingham Curve Junction	53	C1
Barmouth	38	A2	Beeston	53	C2	Birmingham International	42	B1
Barnby Dun	64	A2	Beighton	56	B2	Birmingham Moor Street	48	C1
Barncluith Tunnel	78	B1	Bekesbourne	13	A2	Birmingham New Street	48	C1
Barnehurst	36	C2	Delasis Lane	69	A1	Birmingham Snow Hill	48	C1
Barnes	20	C2	Belfast Central	101	C1	Bishop Auckland	68	A1
Barnes Bridge	20	C2	Belfast City Hospital	101	C1	Bishopbriggs	82	A1
Barnet Tunnels	25	C1	Belfast Great Victoria Street	101	C1	Bishops Lydeard	8	B1
Barnetby	63	C2	Belfast Yorkgate	101	C1	Bishops Stortford	36	B2
Barnham	11	C2	Belgard	95	A1	Bishopsgate Tunnel	21	B2
Barnhill (Glasgow)	82	B1	Belgrave Walk	17	B1	Bishopstone	12	C2
Barnhill (Perth)	85	B1	Bellacorrick	97	B2	Bishopton	77	A2
Barnsley	62	C1	Bellair	94	A1	Bispham	60	B1
Barnstaple	6	B2	Bellarona	101	A2	Bitterne	9	C2
Barnt Green	41	B2	Belle Vue (Isle of Man)	65	B2	Bitton	9	A1
Barnwell	44	C1	Belle Vue (Manchester)	58	B1	Black Bridge	66	B1
Barnwood Junction	33	B2	Bellgrove	82	B1	Black Carr Junction	64	B2
Baron Wood Tunnels	66	A2	Bellingham	18	A1	Black Fell Incline	75	C2
Barons Court	21	C1	Bellshill	78	B1	Black Lake	47	B2
Barrhead	81	C1	Belmont	17	C1	Blackboy Tunnel	3	A1
Barrhill	70	B1	Belmont Tunnel	49	A2	Blackburn	61	B1
Barrington	44	C1	Belmont Yard	64	B1	Blackfriars	21	B2
Barrow Bridge	91	B2	Belper	53	C1	Blackfriars Junction		
Barrow Haven	63	B2	Belsize Park	21	A1	(Portsmouth)	10	C2
Barrow Hill	53	A1	Belsize Tunnels	21	A1	Blackhams Hill	75	C2
Barrow Road	28	C2	Beltring	12	A2	Blackheath	22	C1
Barrow-In-Furness	60	A1	Belvedere	36	C2	Blackheath Tunnel	22	C2
Barrow-upon-Soar	42	A2	Belview	91	B2	Blackhorse	96	B1
Barry	27	C1	Bempton	69	C2	Blackhorse Lane	17	B2
Barry Docks	27	C1	Ben Rhydding	61	A2	Blackhorse Road	22	A1
Barry Island	27	C1	Benfleet for Canvey Island	37	C1	Blackpool North	60	B1
Barry Links	85	B2	Bennerley	53	C2	Blackpool Pleasure Beach	60	B1
Bartholomley Junction	52	B1	Benny Halt	1	B2	Blackpool South	60	B1
Barton Hill	28	C2	Bensham Tunnel	75	B2	Blackrock	96	C2
Barton Junctions	42	A1	Bentham	61	A1	Blackrod	60	C2
Barton Mill	10	A2	Bentinck	53	B2	Blackwall	22	B1
Barton-on-Humber	63	B2	Bentley (Hants.)	11	B1	Blackwater (Co. Offaly)	94	A1
Basford	55	A1	Bentley (south Yorks.)	64	A1	Blackwater (Surrey)	11	A1
Basford Hall	52	C1	Benton	75	A2	Blackwell Summit	41	C2
Basildon	36	C2	Bere Alston	2	B2	Blackwell South Junction	53	B1
Basingstoke	10	A2	Bere Ferrers	2	B2	Blaenau Ffestiniog	50	C1
Bat & Ball	12	A2	Berkeley	33	B1	Blaenavon	32	B1
Bates Staithes	74	B1	Berkhamsted	35	B2	Blair Atholl	84	B2
Bath Row Tunnel	48	C1	Berkswell	42	B1	Blairhill	78	C1
Bath Spa	9	A1	Bermondsey	21	C2	Blake Street	48	A2
Bathampton Junction	9	A1	Berney Arms	46	A1	Blakedown	41	B1

Location	Page No.	Page Ref.	Location	Page No.	Page Ref.	Location	Page No.	Page Ref.
Headcorn	13	B1	Highbury Vale	55	A1	Hounslow East	20	C1
Headingley	63	A1	Highgate	21	A1	Hounslow Junction	15	A2
Headland	65	C2	Highley	41	B1	Hounslow West	19	C2
Headstone Lane	24	C1	Hightown	60	C1	Hove	12	C1
Heald Green	52	A1	Highworth Junction	33	C2	Hoveton & Wroxham	46	A1
Healey Mills	62	C1	Hilden	102	C1	How Wood	24	A1
Healing	64	C1	Hildenborough	12	A2	Howden	63	B1
Heath High Level	27	A2	Hill Top Tunnel	47	B2	Howdon	76	B1
Heath Low Level	27	A2	Hillfield Tunnels	32	A2	Howstrake	65	C2
Heath Town Junction	47	A1	Hillfoot	81	A2	Howth	95	A2
Heathfield	3	A1	Hillhead	81	B2	Howth Junction	96	A2
Heathrow Airport Junction	19	C2	Hillhead Summit	71	A2	Howwood	77	B2
Heathrow Terminals 1,2 & 3	19	C1	Hillhouse	60	B1	Hoxton (Proposed)	21	B2
Heathrow Terminal 4	19	C1	Hillingdon	19	A1	Hoylake	51	A1
Heathrow Terminal 5			Hillington East	81	B2	Hubbert's Bridge	55	C1
(Proposed)	19	C1	Hillington West	81	B2	Hucknall	53	B2
Heathrow Tunnel	19	C1	Hillsborough	53	A1	Huddersfield	61	C2
Heaton	75	B2	Hillsborough Park	53	A1	Hull	63	B2
Heaton Chapel	58	C1	Hillside (Merseyside)	60	C1	Humber	64	C2
Heaton Lodge Junction	62	C1	Hillside (Tayside)	86	C1	Humber International Terminal	64	C2
Heaton Norris Junction	58	C1	Hilsea	10	C2	Humber Road Junction	64	C2
Heaton Park	57	A2	Hilton Junction	85	B1	Humbly Grove	11	B1
Hebburn	76	B1	Hinchley Wood	16	B1	Humphrey Park	57	B2
Hebden Bridge	61	B2	Hinckley	42	B2	Huncoat	61	B1
Hebron	49	B2	Hinderton Field Tunnel	59	C1	Hungerford	10	A1
Heck	62	C2	Hindley	60	C2	Hungerford Bridge	21	B2
Heckington	54	C2	Hindlow	52	B2	Hunmanby	69	C2
Hedge End	10	C2	Hinksey Yard	34	B2	Hunsbury Hill Tunnel	43	C1
Hednesford	41	A2	Hinton Admiral	6	A1	Hunslet	63	B1
Heighington	68	A1	Hipperholme Tunnel	61	B2	Hunslet East	63	B1
Helen's Bay	102	C2	Hitchin	35	A2	Hunt's Cross	51	A2
Helensburgh Central	77	A1	Hither Green	18	A1	Hunt's Cross West Junction	59	C2
Helensburgh Upper	77	A1	Hockley	37	C1	Hunterston	77	B1
Hellifield	61	A1	Hockley Tunnels	48	C1	Huntingdon	44	C1
Helm Tunnel	67	B1	Holbeck	63	A1	Huntly	88	C2
Helmsdale	88	B1	Holbeck Junction	63	A1	Hurst Green	12	A1
Helpston	43	A2	Holborn	21	B2	Hutcheon Street Tunnel	86	C2
Helsby	51	A2	Holderness Limeworks	52	A2	Hutton Cranswick	63	A2
Hemel Hempstead	35	B2	Holesmouth Junction	28	B1	Huyton	51	A2
Hemingfield	62	C1	Holgate Junction & Sidings	62	A1	Hyde Central	58	B2
Hendon	20	A2	Holland Park	21	B1	Hyde North	58	B2
Hendon Central	20	A2	Holliday Street Tunnel	48	C1	Hyde Park	56	B1
Hendy Junction	30	B2	Hollingbourne	13	A1	Hyde Park Corner	21	B1
Hengoed	32	C1	Hollinsend	56	B1	Hykeham	54	B2
Heniarth	39	A2	Hollinwood	58	A1	Hyndland	81	B2
Henley-in-Arden	41	C2	Holloway Road	21	A2	Hyson Green Market	55	A1
Henley-on-Thames	35	C1	Holm Junction	77	C1	Hythe (Essex)	37	A2
Henllan	30	A2	Holme Tunnel	61	B1	Hythe (Hants)	10	C1
Hensall	62	B2	Holmes Chapel	52	B1	Hythe (Kent)	13	B2
Henwick	41	C1	Holmes Junction	56	A2			
Hepscott Junction	74	B1	Holmwood	11	B2	IBM Halt	77	A1
Herbrandston Junction	29	B2	Holt	56	C1	Ibrox	81	B2
Herdings	56	C1	Holt Lane Tunnel	53	B1	Ickenham	19	A1
Herdings Park	56	C1	Holton Heath	5	A2	Ifield	12	B1
Hereford	32	A2	Holybourne	11	B1	Ilford	22	A2
Hermitage	3	A2	Holyhead	49	A1	Illford Road	75	B2
Herne Bay	13	A2	Holytown	78	B1	Ilkley	61	A2
Herne Hill	17	A2	Holywell Halt	61	A2	Immingham	64	C2
Heron Quays	22	B1	Holywood	101	B2	Imperial Wharf Chelsea		
Hersham	15	B2	Homerton	22	A1	(Proposed)	21	C1
Herston Halt	5	A2	Honeybourne	33	B2	Ince & Elton	51	A2
Hertford East	36	B1	Honiton	8	C1	Ince (Greater Manchester)	60	C2
Hertford North	36	B1	Honley	61	C2	Ince Marshes	51	A2
Hessay	62	A2	Honor Oak Park	18	A1	Ince Moss	60	C2
Hessle	63	B2	Hoo Junction	36	C2	Inch Abbey	100	A2
Hessle Road Junction	63	B2	Hoo Staff Halt*	36	C2	Inchicore	96	B1
Hest Bank	60	A2	Hook	11	A1	Infirmary Road	56	B1
Heswall	51	A1	Hooton	51	A1	Ingatestone	36	B2
Heuston (Dublin)	96	B1	Hope (Clwyd)	51	B1	Ingrave Summit	36	C2
Hever	12	B1	Hope (Derbyshire)	53	A1	Ingrow West	61	B2
Hewish Summit	8	C2	Hope Street	57	B2	Insch	88	C2
Heworth	75	B2	Hopton Heath	40	B1	Inver Tunnel	84	B2
Hexham	73	C2	Horbury	62	C1	Invergordon	88	C1
Hexthorpe	64	B1	Horley	12	B1	Invergowrie	85	B2
Heyford	34	A2	Hornbeam Park	62	A1	Inverkeithing	79	A1
Heysham Port	60	A1	Hornby Halt	11	C1	Inverkip	77	A1
Heywood	61	C1	Hornchurch	36	C2	Inverness	88	C1
Heywood Road Junction	9	A1	Hornsey	21	A2	Invershin	88	B1
Hibel Road Tunnel	52	A2	Hornsey Up Sidings	25	C2	Inveraire	86	A1
Hicks Lodge	42	A1	Horrocksford	61	B1	Ipswich	37	C2
High Barnet	25	B1	Horsefall Tunnel	61	B2	Irlam	57	C1
High Brooms	12	B2	Horsehay & Dawley	41	A1	Ironbridge	41	A1
High Level Bridge	75	B2	Horsforth	62	B1	Ironville	53	B2
High Marnham	54	B1	Horsham	11	B2	Irton Road	66	B1
High Meads Junction	22	A1	Horsley	11	A2	Irvine	77	C2
High Rocks Halt	12	B2	Horsted Keynes	12	B1	Irwell Vale	61	C1
High School (Nottingham)	55	A1	Horton Road Junction	33	B2	Isfield	12	C1
High Street (Glasgow)	82	B1	Horton-in-Ribblesdale	67	C1	Island Gardens	22	C1
High Street, Kensington	21	C1	Horwich Parkway	60	C2	Islandbridge Junction	96	B1
High Tor Tunnel	53	B1	Hoscar	60	C2	Isleworth	20	C1
High Wycombe	35	C1	Hotchley Hill	53	C2	Islip	34	B2
Higham	36	C2	Hothfield	13	B1	Iver	19	B1
Highams Park	26	C1	Hough Green	51	A2	Ivybridge	3	B1
Highbridge & Burnham	8	B1	Hounslow	20	C1			
Highbury & Islington	21	A2	Hounslow Central	19	C2	James Watt Dock	77	A1

Location	Page No.	Page Ref.
Levisham	69	C1
Lewaigue	65	B2
Lewes	12	C1
Lewisham	22	C1
Leyburn	67	C2
Leyland	60	B2
Leyton	22	A1
Leyton Midland Road	22	A1
Leytonstone	22	A1
Leytonstone High Road	22	A1
Lhen Coan	65	C2
Lichfield City	41	A2
Lichfield Trent Valley	41	A2
Lidlington	35	A2
Lifford Junctions	41	B2
Lillie Bridge	21	C1
Limbury Road	35	A2
Lime Kiln Halt	65	C2
Limehouse	22	B1
Limerick	93	C1
Limerick Junction	90	A2
Limpsfield Tunnel	12	A1
Lincoln Central	54	B2
Lindal Tunnel	66	C1
Lindsey	64	C2
Linford Street Junction	21	C1
Lingfield	12	B1
Lingwood	46	A1
Linkswood	85	B2
Linlithgow	78	A2
Linslade Tunnels	35	A1
Liphook	11	B1
Lipson Junction	21	A2
Lisburn	102	C1
Lisburn Road Tunnel	101	C1
Lisduff	94	C1
Liskeard	2	B1
Lismanny	93	A2
Liss	11	B1
Listowel	89	A2
Lisvane & Thornhill	27	A2
Litchfield Tunnel	10	B2
Little Bispham	60	B1
Little Eaton Junction	53	C1
Little Hautbois	45	A2
Little Island	90	C1
Little Kimble	35	B1
Little Sutton	51	A1
Littleborough	61	C2
Littlebury Tunnel	36	A2
Littlehampton	11	C2
Littlehaven	11	B2
Littlemore	34	B2
Littleport	44	B2
Littleton	94	C1
Liverpool Central	59	B1
Liverpool James Street	59	B1
Liverpool Lime Street	59	B1
Liverpool Moorfields	59	B1
Liverpool Street (London)	21	B2
Livingston North	78	B2
Livingston South	78	B2
Llanaber	38	A2
Llanbadarn	38	B2
Llanbedr	49	C2
Llanberis	49	B2
Llanbister Road	40	C1
Llanbradach	32	C1
Llandaf	27	A1
Llandanwg	49	C2
Llandarcy	31	A2
Llandecwyn	50	C1
Llandegai Tunnel	49	B2
Llandeilo	31	A1
Llandeilo Junction	30	B2
Llandovery	31	A1
Llandrindod	39	C2
Llandudno	50	A1
Llandudno Junction	50	A1
Llandudno Victoria	50	A1
Llandybie	31	B1
Llandyfriog	30	A1
Llanelli	30	B2
Llanfair Caereinion	39	A2
Llanfairfechan	50	A1
Llanfairpwll	49	A2
Llangadog	31	A1
Llangammarch	31	A2
Llangennech	30	B2
Llangollen	51	C1
Llangyfelach Tunnel	31	B1
Llangynllo	40	B1
Llangywair	50	C2
Llanishen	27	A2
Llanrwst	50	B1
Llansamlet	31	A2
Llantrisant	31	C2
Llantwit Major (Proposed)	7	A2
Llanuwchllyn	50	C2
Llanwern	32	C2
Llanwrda	31	A1
Llanwrtyd	31	A2
Lloyd Park	17	C2
Llwfan Cerrig	30	A2
Llwyngwril	38	A2
Llwynypia	31	C2
Llynfi Junction	31	C2
Loch Awe	84	C1
Loch Eil Outward Bound	84	A1
Lochaber	84	B1
Lochailort	83	A2
Locheilside	83	A2
Lochgelly	85	C1
Lochluichart	87	C2
Lochwinnoch	77	B2
Lockerbie	72	B1
Lockwood	61	C2
Lodge Road West Bromwich Town Hall	47	B2
London Bridge	21	B2
London City Airport (Proposed)	22	B2
London Fields	22	B1
London Road (Brighton)	12	C1
London Road (Guildford)	11	A2
London Road (Worcester)	41	C1
London Road Depot (Lambeth)	21	C2
Londonderry (Foyle Road)	101	B1
Londonderry	101	B1
Long Buckby	42	C2
Long Dyke Junction	27	B2
Long Eaton	53	C2
Long Marston	33	A2
Long Preston	61	A1
Long Rock	1	A1
Longannet	78	A2
Longbeck	68	A2
Longbenton	75	A2
Longbridge	41	B2
Longcross	11	A2
Longfield	12	A2
Longford	99	C1
Longhedge Junction	21	C1
Longlands Junction	68	C1
Longniddry	79	A2
Longport	52	B1
Longsight Staff Halt*	58	B1
Longton	52	C2
Longtown	72	C2
Longueville Junction	43	C2
Lonlas Tunnel	31	A2
Looe	2	B1
Lord's Tunnel	21	B1
Lostock	61	C1
Lostock (ICI)	52	A1
Lostock Gralam	52	A1
Lostock Hall	60	B2
Lostock Junction	61	C1
Lostwithiel	2	B1
Loughborough	42	A2
Loughborough Central	42	A2
Loughborough Junction	21	C2
Loughor Viaduct	30	B2
Loughton	26	B2
Lounge	42	A1
Low Fell	75	C2
Lowdham	53	C2
Lower Crianlarich	84	C1
Lower Sydenham	18	A1
Lowestoft	46	B2
Lowton Junction	51	A2
Loxdale	47	A1
Ludgershall*	10	A1
Ludlow	40	B2
Lugton	77	B2
Luib Summit	87	C2
Lullymore	94	A2
Lurgan	102	C1
Luton	35	B2
Luton Airport Parkway	35	B2
Luxulyan	1	B2
Lydden Tunnel	14	B1
Lydney	32	B2
Lydney Lakeside	32	B2
Lye	47	C1
Lymington Junction	10	C1
Lymington Pier	6	A1
Lymington Town	6	A1
Lympstone Commando	3	A1
Lympstone Village	3	A1
Lynemouth	74	B1
Lynmouth	7	A1
Lynton	7	A1
Lytham	60	B1
Macclesfield	52	A2
Machen	32	C1
Machynlleth	38	A2
Madeley Junction (Salop.)	41	A1
Madeley Junctions (Staffs.)	52	C1
Maesglas	32	A2
Maespoeth	39	A1
Maesteg	31	C1
Maesteg Ewenny Road	31	C1
Magherabeg	102	B1
Magheramorne	102	B2
Maghull	60	C1
Maida Vale	21	B1
Maiden Newton	4	A2
Maidenhead	35	C1
Maidstone Barracks	13	A1
Maidstone East	13	A1
Maidstone West	13	A1
Maindee Junctions	32	A2
Malahide	95	A2
Malden Manor	16	B2
Malin Bridge	53	A1
Maliphant	31	A2
Mallaig	83	A2
Mallow	90	B1
Maltby	53	A2
Malton	69	C1
Malvern Link	41	C1
Malvern Wells	33	A1
Manchester Airport	52	A1
Manchester Oxford Road	58	B1
Manchester Piccadilly	58	B1
Manchester Square	60	B1
Manchester United Football Ground*	57	B2
Manchester Victoria	58	B1
Manea	44	B2
Mann Island Junction	59	B1
Mannez Quarry	5	C1
Manningtree	37	A2
Manor House	21	A2
Manor Park	22	A2
Manor Road	51	A1
Manor Top	56	B1
Manorbier	29	B2
Manors	75	B2
Mansfield	53	B2
Mansfield Woodhouse	53	B2
Mansfield Junction	55	B1
Mansion House	21	B2
Mantle Lane	42	A1
Mantles Wood	35	B2
Manton Junction & Tunnel	43	A1
Manulla Junction	97	C2
Marble Arch	21	B1
March	44	B1
Marchey's House Junction	74	B1
Marchwood	9	C2
Marden	13	B1
Margam	31	C1
Margate	14	A1
Marino	102	C2
Mark Beech Tunnel	12	B2
Market Bosworth	42	A1
Market Harborough	43	B1
Market Rasen	54	A2
Market Street	58	B1
Markinch	85	C1
Marks Tey	37	A1
Marley Hill	75	C1
Marley Tunnels	3	B1
Marlow	35	C1
Marple	58	C2
Marple Wharf Junction	58	C2
Marsden	61	C2
Marsh Barton	3	B1
Marsh Junction	28	C2
Marsh Lane	63	A1
Marsh Mills	2	C2
Marsh West Junction	64	C1
Marshgate	64	B1
Marske	68	A2
Marston Green	42	B1
Martello Tunnel	13	B2
Martin Mill	14	B1
Martin's Heron	11	A1
Marton	68	B2
Maryhill	81	A2
Maryland	22	A1
Marylebone	21	B1
Maryport	65	A2

117

INDEX TO LOCOMOTIVE and MULTIPLE UNIT STABLING POINTS, CARRIAGE DEPOTS and RAILWAY WORKS